AF694991

# Human Capital Management Research

## Influencing Practice and Process

A Volume in
Contemporary Perspectives in Human Capital and Development

*Series Editors:*
Bing Ran, *Penn State Harrisburg*
Stephen T. T. Teo, *RMIT University, Australia*

**Contemporary Perspectives in Human Capital and Development**

**Bing Ran and Stephen T. T. Teo, Series Editors**

*Human Capital Management Research: Influencing Practice and Process* (2016)
Edited by Deborah Blackman, Michael O'Donnell, and Stephen T. T. Teo

# Human Capital Management Research

## Influencing Practice and Process

**Edited by**

**Deborah Blackman**
***University of New South Wales***

**Michael O'Donnell**
***University of New South Wales***

**and**

**Stephen T. T. Teo**
***RMIT University, Australia***

**Information Age Publishing, Inc.**
Charlotte, North Carolina • www.infoagepub.com

**Library of Congress Cataloging-in-Publication Data**

CIP data for this book can be found on the Library of Congress website:
http://www.loc.gov/index.html

**Paperback:** 978-1-68123-464-9
**Hardcover:** 978-1-68123-465-6
**E-Book:** 978-1-68123-466-3

Copyright © 2016 IAP–Information Age Publishing, Inc.

All rights reserved. No part of this publication may be reproduced, stored in a retrieval system, or transmitted in any form or by any electronic or mechanical means, or by photocopying, microfilming, recording or otherwise without written permission from the publisher.

Printed and bound by CPI Group (UK) Ltd, Croydon, CR0 4YY

# CONTENTS

# PREFACE TO THE SERIES

**Bing Ran and Stephen T. T. Teo**

As a central concept of modern managerial and organizational theories and practices, *human capital* has its long history rooted in the exploration of the question: what is the role of human beings in the organized activities in human society? From classical theories of bureaucracy and scientific management, to human relation and human resources movements, from open system theories and cybernetics, to more modern contingency theories and postmodernism, numerous theories have been proposed to explain the role of human beings in achieving values for organizations, with the hope to shed some lights to the managerial practices. However, the answer to this very core question of all organized activities of human society is yet clear and definite.

This book series will continue our exploration in this key question from a more contemporary perspective. The volumes in this book series will be the milestones of researchers' and practitioners' understanding, theorizing, analysis, and application of how employees of modern organizations are inspired to achieve their full potential in the process of contributing to the larger good of the collectivity in which they are part of. The intended audience of this book series includes but not limited to academic researchers, university professors and graduate students, management scientists, industry economists, government officials, public policy developers and analysts, research and laboratory managers, marketing, human resources and operations managers, and anyone who is interested at understanding the current progress of human resources management and human capital development.

*Human Capital Management Research: Influencing Practice and Process*
pp. vii–viii
Copyright © 2016 by Information Age Publishing
All rights of reproduction in any form reserved.

As the editors of this book series, *Contemporary Perspectives in Human Capital and Development*, we are glad to see the publication of the first volume of the series. The first volume is entitled *Human Capital Management Research: Influencing Practice and Process*, and edited by Deborah Blackman, Michael O'Donnell, and Stephen Teo. This volume started our journey from a more traditional perspective of managing humans as organizational resources, the so-called "human resource management" perspective, and makes a wonderful effort in bridging our understanding of the role of humans in organized society as a capital versus as a resource. Written by academics teamed with practitioners, each of the 11 chapters in this volume provides an overview of the most current research in human resource management, links to current human capital management practices, and identifies potential implications for future implementation. With its theoretical rigorousness and practical applicability, we are sure this volume will move our understanding on human capital management and development a step further. Let the journey start here.

# INTRODUCTION

## Setting the Scene—Applied Human Resources Into the 21st Century

**Deborah Blackman, Michael O'Donnell, and Stephen T. T. Teo**

Welcome to this edited collection: *Human Capital Management Research: Influencing Practice and Process*. The objective of the book is to not only outline some new ideas and research in the human capital management area, but to focus on what these ideas will mean for practice. Human capital is a way to describe the critical people element when determining value within an organization. It is often seen as intangible and hard to define, but is also recognized as making the difference between the success or failure of an innovation, change or even the entity itself. Managing human capital, therefore, is about getting the best from people and being successful in this endeavor will depend on understanding: what motivates employees to perform, how the organizational systems may act as performance barriers and how leadership and human resources management processes are likely to affect outcomes and outputs. This book is designed to offer some ideas and advice as to how to undertake effective human capital management.

The novelty of this book is that it is designed to act as a bridge between theory and practice, containing contributions from both academics and practitioners—a core theme is that almost every chapter reflects ideas from both worldviews. Moreover, the examples come from both the

*Human Capital Management Research: Influencing Practice and Process*
pp. ix–xv
Copyright © 2016 by Information Age Publishing
All rights of reproduction in any form reserved.

private and the public sector—highlighting the importance of human capital management across all sectors. Discussions with those who span the academic/practice worlds show that they are regularly struck by the disconnects between the journals that report current academic research and ideas, textbooks that often fail to reflect new ideas or research for several years, and the practitioner literature which may be current but is sometimes oversimplified. The argument is made that one of the reasons for the divide is that, although some of the journal articles carry some implications for practice, many do not. They are often vague as to the real value of the research and only outline potential interventions in a very rudimentary way.

An example is the concept of "organizational commitment." When entered into Google Scholar there are more than 1,600,000 hits, yet commitment still has limited coverage in most texts and, where it is included, it is usually a very simplistic approach. Current work on continuance commitment and commitment profiles implies that organizations need to be much more careful about the forms of commitment within their organizations, yet many current students confirm that their organizations only seek to know if there is commitment and assume that, if so, this is a good thing. Commitment to the organization could, in fact, be because there are few alternatives for employees who stay but are not necessarily motivated to deliver discretionary effort or to demonstrate organizational citizenship behaviors to the level that the organization may desire. The issue of commitment is, therefore, more complex than sometimes thought. The implications for practice will include the need to potentially rethink recruitment processes, as assumptions of employees arriving with affective commitment might be completely wrong.

So why is there such a divide? Much has been written on the research–practice gap which emerges when either research findings are not translated appropriately into practice, or research is not seen as relevant to the context it is designed for. The need to find ways for researchers, policymakers and practitioners to work together effectively is widely recognized and yet, for the most part academics suggest that the challenges inherent in working together are largely insurmountable.[1] The literature relating to the research–practice gap focuses on the potential disconnect between rigor and relevance (Antonacopoulou, 2010; Cepiku, 2011). Concerns with rigor focus on the construction, or refinement, of theories or new knowledge underpinned by rigorous investigation, data collection and advanced analysis methods, often in the quest for establishing general principles, while relevance concerns practitioners' need for context and problem-specific research which aligns with real-life problems (Armstrong & Alsop, 2010). Rasche and Behnam (2009) argue that the quest for relevance is problematic in itself due to the false assumption that knowledge can be transferred from research to practice in a linear fashion; they suggest the effectiveness of transfer depends instead on practitioners' capacity to interpret the knowledge and recognize it is relevant. Others suggest the gap exists because either researchers lack practical experience and skills in the business environment (Ellson, 2009), or they present their findings as descriptive rather than explanatory accounts of real-life phenomena without explaining its potential impact (Hales, 1999).

Despite the apparent difficulties there are gains to be made from bridging the gap, primarily that knowledge uptake, adoption, and utilization are essential for optimizing the impact of new ideas and that it is increased dialogue and partnerships between researchers and practitioners which can lead to more opportunities for innovation and change (Cepiku, 2011; Tranfield, Denyer, Marcos, & Burr, 2004). It is into this arena that we present this book which specifically called for researchers to apply their work to practice in a more thorough and concrete manner by working with practitioners. Each chapter provides an overview of the research which is then applied to current human resource management practices, identifying what this means for a set of current practices and how they should be changed. The key objective is to extend the range of concepts being discussed by both academics and practitioners. The importance of this academic/practice debate is highlighted in Chapters 1 and 3. In Chapter 1, David Schmidtchen (a self-confessed scientist–practitioner) discusses the academic/practitioner divide in terms of why new research is largely ignored by organizations. He suggests that practitioners and academics both point to the chasm between their respective worlds and express a genuine desire to cross it. However, despite much debate and discussion, at present this is not occurring; in his view it may be because each wants the other to move into their world. What is needed, he suggests, is increased collaboration between the two.

In Chapter 2, Tony Cotton, Alastair Warren, and Deborah Blackman demonstrate the possibilities of using secondary data to work together and develop mutually beneficial outcomes. They highlight a concern raised by David Scmidtchen in Chapter 1 that many organizational surveys (often developed and/or administered by consultants) lack academic rigor, longitudinal relevance or statistical usefulness. They argue that by rethinking the way the surveys are developed, administered, and analyzed, the data can be more useful for all stakeholders, including academics. Case examples are given demonstrating the potential of this approach and giving some advice as to how organizations should proceed in the future.

Chapter 3 sees the first of several chapters outlining new research. Natalie Jones and Sally Sambrook consider the importance of employee engagement in the public sector. The chapter offers practical suggestions based on new research which incorporates different methods from those usually employed when researching employee engagement. They suggest that although there is considerable practitioner interest and advice available regarding employee engagement, recent academic research can help human resources (HR) professionals practice engagement development more effectively, affordably, thereby benefitting employees with whom they work. They found that the public sector is a tough environment in which to create effective engagement and that, as a consequence, human capital management practices to encourage it need to be more holistic, more realistic and more aware of the constraints imposed by the institutional contexts and conditions. They stress the importance of research being able to provide evidence in contexts where there is continual scrutiny regarding expenditure. They suggest human capital management practices need to be reoriented toward an approach which provides a much-needed rebalancing of the employee engagement research agenda toward meeting employee as well as organizational needs. They outline an autoethnographic approach whereby an individual working in the organization (usually as a member of an HR team) diagnoses their own levels and types of engagement, then diagnoses the organization's culture and its wider context and impact on your engagement levels, and then blends these diagnoses to generate plans relevant to an individual, an HR team and the organization.

In Chapter 4, Damian West (pracademic) explains his research related to organizational commitment. He argues that the current paradigm of employee commitment, as discussed in the HR literature, is built on the concept that it is the relationship between the employee and the organization that forms the basis of employee commitment. His research provides considerable new insight and knowledge on how commitment works by providing empirical evidence on how the concept of side bets operates from the perspective of the employee. This research has demonstrated that the structure of the organizational and people management policies used by the organization can create the situation where the idea of a relationship or link between the employee and the organization has been brought into question. He shows that current HR practices need to have a much more nuanced approach to measuring, developing and managing employee commitment, particularly in large organizations.

In Chapter 5 the focus is on the important aspect of employee turnover—in particular Gerry Treuren (academic) and Julie Goods (practitioner) are looking at ways to diagnose and reduce voluntary turnover. Three areas of recent research in the turnover literature—the unfolding theory of turnover, job embeddedness theory, and proximal withdrawal state theory are combined to develop a three-stage approach to identifying and dealing with an organization's turnover and retention problems. Each recent research development is explained and then they are brought together in a way that enables the concept of employee embeddedness to be considered as a critical element in the reduction of voluntary turnover. This approach permits an organization to identify the reasons for current turnover and the early signs of potential turnover, and provides guidance in devising appropriate interventions to improve employee retention. The novelty is in the combination of approaches which permits a more thoughtful approach to turnover.

The theme of nuancing accepted research is continued in Chapter 6 where Samantha Johnson (pracademic) considers some alternative perspectives on organizational commitment. She argues that understanding current research into the complex state of organizational commitment and commitment profiles is valuable, especially in terms of how other practices affect the development of commitment in potentially unexpected ways. Her chapter leads us to wonder whether if a human capital management practice such as large-scale recruitment is inadvertently perpetuating a commitment profile that is reducing performance and inhibiting a performance culture, then is there an added dimension to performance management that may not be clearly understood. The chapter demonstrates how much practitioner literature is overly simplistic and stresses the need to keep up to date with academic research in order to develop more multifaceted HR practices.

Chapters 7 and 8 are both related to effective staff development in different ways; Chapter 7 sees a move to looking at the role of technology in helping support effective employee learning, while Chapter 8 looks at how to develop the effective provision of ethics-related training and development. In Chapter 7 Adam Kanar (academic), Matisha Montgomery (practitioner), Rebecca Fraser (practitioner), and Tara Behrend (academic) review the theory and practice of a technology-based training case example and they present an example from a government agency based in the United States. They show that despite careful reflection on theory when designing the new training, there were still problems with the completion rates. The lessons learnt are presented and it is of note that they suggest that a full move to e-learning may not be appropriate for effective development. The criticality of matching the need, the content, the learners and the delivery is stressed, with recommendations to consider whether the support systems within an organization are really maximizing completion. There are some similar themes in Chapter 8 where Sheldene Simola (pracademic) provides first, an overview of recent themes from behavioral business ethics, many of which challenge conventional and commonly held beliefs about workplace ethical decision making and action; and second, contextual guidance for HR professionals on the provision of ethics-related training and development. Reflecting some of the learning in Chapter 7, she stresses the need for an organization to be ready and to actively embrace the desired training and development outcomes if it is to succeed. Moreover, the actual training needs to be contextually appropriate despite the need for specific outcomes. Her key message is the need to develop behaviorally based ethics training and development programs creating appropriate values as well as rules, and the difference in program design and implementation that this necessitates.

The last two chapters in the book are both concerned with employee performance management. In Chapter 9 Alan Colquitt (pracademic) recognizes the breadth of interest, research, and practitioner advice available for those wishing to undertake performance management, and yet so often it fails to achieve its espoused goals. As a response to this, "Next Generation Performance Management" is presented based on principles grounded in sound theory and research as well as practical experience that should guide the tactical design of a company's performance management process. The argument is that while the details can vary by company, the design and implementation should be consistent with these principles which include being about enabling employee achievement and performance (rather than measuring performance), offering support to get work done and being seen as a regular part of routine work. This positive approach to performance management is reinforced in Chapter 10 where Deborah Blackman (academic), Fiona Buick (academic), Michael O'Donnell (academic), Janine O'Flynn (academic), and Damian West (pracademic) present a framework designed not to replace a performance management system but to enable an organization to improve the effectiveness of their current process. They suggest that instead of seeing performance management as a standalone, often hated, human capital management process, it can be seen as a framework for change, as it can provide an integrating mechanism for effectively implementing the human capital management processes necessary to support the development of new organizational initiatives. In the chapter they explain why there should be a focus on high performance workplaces and why the framework supports the achievement of such practices. Their advice to practitioners is clear: performance management needs to have a purpose (such as change initiative), it needs to be developed to support organizational outcomes and it needs to be supported by managers at all levels.

Finally, the editors present a conclusion reflecting on the key themes of the book which suggests there are several areas where differences between scholars and practitioners affect the potential for either developing effective human capital management or creating potential schisms between research and practice. These include: the types of data used, where the research is presented, the level of complexity presented around a topic, the context/prediction divide, and who are the researchers.

## NOTE

1. A discussion on this can be found in Buick, Blackman, O'Flynn, O'Donnell, and West (2016)

## REFERENCES


Antonacopoulou, E. P. (2010). Beyond co-production: practice-relevant scholarship as a foundation for delivering impact through powerful ideas. *Public Money & Management, 30*(4), 219–226.

Armstrong, F., & Alsop, A. (2010). Debate: Co-production can contribute to research impact in the social sciences. *Public Money & Management, 30*(4), 208–210.

Buick, F., Blackman, D., O'Flynn, J., O'Donnell, M., & West, D. (2016). Effective practitioner–scholar relationships: Lessons from a coproduction partnership. *Public Administration Review, 76*(1), 35–47.

Cepiku, D. (2011). Two ships passing in the night? Practice and academia in public management. *Public Money & Management, 31*(2), 131–138.

Ellson, T. (2009). Assessing contribution of research in business to practice. *Journal of Business Research*, *62*(11), 1160–1164.

Hales, C. (1999). Why do managers do what they do? Reconciling evidence and theory in accounts of managerial work. *British Journal of Management, 10*(4), 335–350.

Rasche, A., & Behnam, M. (2009). As if it were relevant: A systems theoretical perspective on the relation between science and practice. *Journal of Management Inquiry, 18*(3), 243–255.

Tranfield, D., Denyer, D., Marcos, J., & Burr, M. 2004. Co-producing management knowledge. *Management Decision, 42*(3/4), 375–386.

CHAPTER 1

# IS THERE A NEW PATH TO ADVANCING THE ART AND SCIENCE OF MANAGEMENT?

**David Schmidtchen**

After scanning the management literature, an interplanetary visitor to Earth might reasonably ask: how much of what is written on management has contributed positively to the sum of human knowledge? Whether it is the formal academic literature or the practitioner literature, our curious guest might read the literature with the not unreasonable hope that he or she might learn something new, insightful, or even helpful. Unfortunately, they are likely to be disappointed.

Our caller might observe that many people are engaged in management and that it is a substantial and important part of the daily lives of the planet's inhabitants. Indeed, work and organization might be described as one of the more important endeavors in modern society. However, there seems to be little convincing evidence that the understanding or practice of management has advanced. Certainly, it has not advanced in relation to the considerable investment that is put into thinking, researching and communicating on every conceivable aspect of work, the workplace, the workforce or how it is organized. There needs to be a new path to advancing the art and science of management.

*Human Capital Management Research: Influencing Practice and Process*
pp. 1–12
Copyright © 2016 by Information Age Publishing
All rights of reproduction in any form reserved.

This chapter will raise more questions than it answers, maybe because it is not a piece by a management academic. It makes assertions, draws selectively from the literature, is philosophical and historical, and it asks the reader to compare and contrast what is raised here with their own experience. Most of all it asks the reader to reflect, expand, and question. The intention is to set an intellectual and philosophical background for what follows in the remainder of this book. It is hoped the observations made here, and the questions raised, might be carried by the reader not only through the contents of this book but also back to the workplace.

This approach means the perspective of the author is important and should be stated up front. I have been raised in the scientist–practitioner model, which after years of practice means I am no longer sure I am either. Daily I am required to provide managers with evidence to support decision making but also for injecting new ways of thinking about work and organization into a large public-sector organization. I am also a leader and manager looking to constantly improve my own practice.

I feel torn and conflicted about whether leaders and managers make any difference at all in the workplace, reflecting daily on the question: are leaders as important as we make them out to be? I am an avid reader of the academic and practitioner literature but have come to feel that both are stale and directionless. I work with managers every day, from the experienced to the new, wondering why the experienced have chosen to stop learning. I really worry about the new leaders and managers questioning whether they are learning the "right things" in the "right ways." When I was a management consultant I was deeply concerned about the immediacy of the environment and the provision of shallow advice on issues that were in reality deep, embedded, complicated and philosophical. So, this chapter has a cathartic quality to it. It is reflective, seeking to offer the chance to surface shared concerns.

We might take as our first issue the considerable effort that is devoted to describing how things are but which does not seem to help with the question of how to do things better. By way of example, in 2008, Wayne Casico and Herman Aguinis reviewed 45 years of literature on industrial and organizational (I-O) psychology concluding that:

> On the basis of our review, if we extrapolate past emphases in published research to the next 10 years, we are confronted with one compelling conclusion, namely, that I–O psychology will not be out front in influencing the debate on issues that are (or will be) of broad organizational and societal appeal. It will not produce a substantial body of research that will inform HR practitioners, senior managers, or outside stakeholders, such as funding agencies, public policymakers (including elected officials), or university administrators who control budgets (2008, p. 1074).

More recently, in a review of the literature on employee engagement, a sceptical David Guest concludes his review with the observation that:

> it is puzzling and disappointing that this strong evidence is largely ignored by organizations. Possible explanations include the failure of the academic voice to be heard above the voices of consultants, the lack of interest in individual issues, the absence of any attempt to link work engagement to financial outcomes and a disinterest in evidence. Whatever the reasons, a central argument of this paper has been that employee engagement lives in two very different worlds, with different discourses, and these separate existences are a loss to both engagement communities but more particularly for those who would wish to promote organizational employee engagement (2014, p. 151).

In a variety of ways exasperated and distressed academics express concern to each other that only a modest portion of the intellectual and practical effort undertaken by them ever captures the imagination of practicing managers. Or maybe, the subterranean concern is that it does not get read at all. This sentiment from academics is often followed by quietly envious statements about the grip consultants seem to have over managers, and is accompanied by passive disdain for the research the organizations conduct.

There is also considerable evidence for concern about the lack of theoretical rigor, openness to critical review and the relevance of the conclusions drawn from consultant-driven research. David Guest makes this point clearly in relation to the widely marketed and used Gallup 12 survey:

> Although the survey items may point to the antecedents of job satisfaction, there is no theoretical basis comparable to the job demand—resources model to help explain and justify the potential policy levers. However, this has not stopped organizations from enthusiastically using the Gallup 12 measure and as engagement attracted more attention several other consultancies developed their own proprietary measures of engagement and marketed them on the same basis as Gallup, namely the association between higher scores on the measure and higher organizational performance, and the need to address the "engagement deficit." (2014, pp.147–148).

There are real concerns about the quality of the "research" marketed and sold by some consultants, but that is not the core of the issue. The issue for academics is more profound and difficult. Most practicing managers are not even aware the academic community is concerned and distressed. While the majority of managers would recognize the Gallup Company and the findings of the Gallup survey, far fewer managers would be able to name a prominent management academic and associate that person with an insight that has helped managers to improve their performance.

At best, a lot of what is done in academic management research contributes obscure and abstract additions to the body of management knowledge. At worst, it is all the same knowledge (ever more finely diced) reflected in an academic hall of mirrors. It is barely comprehensible to managers and as such deemed to be of no practical value.

Unfortunately, the practitioner literature is in a more parlous state. Here, those working as managers—who should be the focal point for applying the accumulated wisdom of academics, consultants and other practitioners—are treated to morsels of insight that are packaged for quick digestion. They are provided with a list-based, in-flight magazine approach to knowledge—an imagined sample of titles might include "10 tips on active leadership" or "5 steps to effective change management" or "8 ways to motivate Gen X." The crumb of knowledge passes undigested through the manager's system leaving no trace of its existence. Indeed, it briefly distracts the valuable digestive attention of the manager from more productive tasks.

The management fads embodied in such "headlines" are an interesting phenomenon—the way they arise, the way they are embraced and the impact they can have on the thinking of a generation of managers (Miller, Hartwick, & Le Breton-Miller, 2004). By way of example, think on the lasting impact of management fads such as "excellence" (Peters & Waterman, 1982), "knowledge management" (Nonaka, 1991), "just-in-time" (Ohno, 1988), "business process reengineering" (Hammer & Champy, 1993), "the learning organization" (Senge, 1990), or "management by objectives" (Odiorne, 1965). Interestingly, at the core of these fads is good quality academic research. It is what they evolve into that makes them a fad.

Broadly, a management fad can be recognized by the way it offers a simple but comprehensive theory to explain a complex workplace experience such as strategy, change, performance or learning. However, the simplicity of the central idea is cloaked in a special language that hints at a privileged knowledge of *the* solution to a problem that has long plagued *all* managers. For example, my own experience of the trajectory of the learning organization through my own career as a manager may illustrate the key points. The learning organization was popularized by Peter Senge (1990). It sought to deal with the fragmentation of knowledge within modern organizations, which was (and remains) a problem for all managers.

The learning organization concept was accompanied by its own language, including "personal mastery," "mental models," and "shared vision." The literature underpinning the concept was sound at its core.

Senge (1990) was drawing on the work of Chris Argyris and Donald Schön (1978). However, as it grew into a fad more consultants and self-proclaimed experts took on the advocacy of the central ideas. Concurrently, the supporting evidence seemed to become increasingly anecdotal. In particular, there was an increased reliance on story-based case studies to illustrate key points. Indeed, as an aside, many fads might be seen as "just-so" stories or narrative explanations of manager experiences that are unverifiable or not falsifiable. Implementing learning organization concepts that were largely intangible proved a significant barrier for day-to-day managers (Finger & Brand, 1999). Today, the learning organization is rarely a topic of conversation among managers, but the problem of "organizational learning" and its corollary "knowledge management" (which followed the same evolutionary trajectory as a fad at about the same time) persists. As an area of research interest for academics, interest in the idea remains. For managers, the learning organization has been supplanted by new fads many times over in the last 25 years.

This is not to say management fads are of no value. Within each fad there is a body of high quality research into previously unasked questions. The learning organization is a good example of this. Fads also alert managers to new ways of thinking about the practice of management. Again, the learning organization drew attention to the impact on performance of fragmented knowledge and provided some useful ways of understanding the issues. However, when good ideas and good research become fads they also tend to become thin, derivative, repetitive and banal. The meaning and practical application is quickly lost.

The persistent obsession with influential management fads (or maybe more correctly "management fashions") that subsequently prove to be incorrect, or in need of qualification, is difficult to kill off in the minds of managers. The ideas seem to become fossilized in the mind of managers and evolve into touchstones to be used in times of uncertainty. Yet, the speed with which fads are embraced is testament to the voracious thirst for knowledge among managers about work and organizations. And, the issues they address should be matters for wider engagement, debate and conversation. Fads do, at their core, tap into the deep concerns of managers. Importantly, they often provide managers with "checklists" to guide managerial practice. It is easy to ridicule the simplicity of checklists, but in other professions, for example aviation and medicine, checklists are central to expert practice.

Recently, Atul Gawande (2014) argued that where simple checklists were introduced into the practice of eight hospitals from London and Toronto to Delhi and Tanzania, the reduction in patient complications reduced on average by 35% and average reductions in deaths was 47%. While these reductions could not be attributed only to the use of checklists, it is likely that checklists are a tangible and regular expression of the important practice standards of the prevailing organizational system, and ultimately, key to a professional culture of expert practice. Management would benefit from more recognized and widely used standards and it may be that some fads satisfy the manager's desire for a simple management checklist. So, fads may be meeting a practical demand that is not satisfied by the academic community.

Management is a deeply pragmatic activity. It is predominately learned through practice rather than education. Indeed, for many managers the specifics of management education come well after they have been practicing. This differs from the professions where education is a requirement prior to practice. Consequently, for most managers the "truth" of management is that they must make do with the information that is available to practice management. Interestingly, as a philosophy, pragmatism has its roots in a reaction to the abstract, technical and absolutist philosophies of the late 19th century. This is also an adequate description of the view practicing managers have of many management academics.

At its core, pragmatism is the perspective of the participant as opposed to the perspective of the observer. The truth of management practice is arrived through some combination of: (a) the common understanding that we arrive at collectively through practice; (b) the truth that can be asserted from the available evidence (usually a combination of prior experience and what is readily to hand); and (c) what works to solve the problem. It is a philosophy and approach that is heavily embedded in the moment.

However, there are also some inconvenient truths in the workplace that exist independently of pragmatic efforts of managers; issues and problems that keep recurring are managed around rather than addressed and resolved. Human behavior contains some immovable facts that cannot be solved through a pragmatic approach alone. For example, people are heterogeneous which confounds the need for stability and consistency in organizational systems. People make mistakes (the curse of human fallibility), which introduces destabilizing errors into operations. People are prone to an extraordinary range of decision biases that lead to faulty judgments. So, whilst there remains a need to pursue the deeper truths of people, work and organization, managers may not best placed to lead these investigations.

Management practitioners can take the anti-intellectual streak of pragmatism to new levels. There are too many examples of extravagant managerial interpretation. An "I know boats" mindset that leads managers to ignore facts in favor of "doing something" occurs too frequently for us not to be concerned about the dangers of anti-intellectualism in the practice of management. The continuing struggle to gain traction with the idea and practice of evidence-based policy in management would seem to support this view (Rousseau, 2006).

Pervasive information technology has ensured that a broader management group has access to real-time information about business, the workforce, market, competitors and business trends. The sense of speed and the need for responsiveness has moved from upper echelons to be a feature of all management. This is accompanied by the expectation that the answer to any questions is only a mouse click and a small number of keyboard strokes away. The increase in speed, the compression of time and the volume of information all conspire to reinforce the pragmatic nature of management activity. However, questions remain as to whether an individual manager knows more or less about the detail of the organization and its business as a consequence of these advances.

The manager's knowledge seems to become quickly out of date and the manager's dependence on the specialist knowledge of others inside and outside the organization grows. Yet, the need to demonstrate that you are in control through your grasp of the details remains a stubborn expectation of the position. Is it any wonder the art of management, work and organization has been colonized by the simplistic and superficial? Why are we surprised at the speed with which evidence-free fads and half-truths take hold in the practice of management? Managers are drowning in the sea of facts, expert opinions and personal experiences until they can find through their own efforts some driftwood on which to clamber and gasp for air. Fads are driftwood.

The practice of management seems to be firmly grounded in the endless present of doing. The image of the manager is that of Sisyphus endlessly rolling the boulder up the mountain:

> The gods had condemned Sisyphus to ceaselessly rolling a rock to the top of a mountain, whence the stone would fall back of its own weight. They had thought with some reason that there is no more dreadful punishment than futile and hopeless labor. (Camus, 1955, p. 116)

The work of managers can appear as futile, hopeless and repetitive as that of Sisyphus. There is no time or room for imagination and reflection, and little reward for innovation. So, if our managers are trapped in the present, what risks are accruing for future organizational capability around those distinct and seemingly independent decisions that are being made in the moment by an individual under pressure? Is it any wonder that research is distant from practice when, for managers, speed and responsiveness are paramount. There is much gnashing of teeth from academics that managers are not reading or applying their research. The main reasons are that it is not timely, it is abstract from practice and it is communicated in a form that is indigestible.

In the management realm, decisions are taken at a macro level on the understanding that management is not static and routine, but rather a constant web of change, interaction, and development. There are no comfortable formulas that can be relied on to guide managers through a known process toward achieving a clear outcome. In discussing the way organizations learn, James March notes that:

> The underlying process is one in which an organization is conditioned through trial and error to repeat behavior that has been successful in the past and to avoid behavior that has been unsuccessful. (1981, p. 565)

The same is true for individual managers. So, maybe what distinguishes the manager from the academic is the need to generalize. The daily concern of managers is the relationship between the unique and the general. A manager cannot separate the unique from the general, or give precedence to one over the other. They cannot separate fact from interpretation from action. Managers work with the dynamic whole, not the parts. They are interested in the unique observation only insofar as it can tell them about the general condition. They are principally reasoning through induction. For managers, the sun has always risen in the East and so it will rise in the East tomorrow morning. There is no need (or time) to fuss the detail on the passage of the sun. If the sun does not show up tomorrow, well, that is a new problem that can be tackled when it happens.

This causes at least two problems for the academic community. First, management is always operating in the moment and academic inquiry seeks to place itself outside the moment. The objectivity of the observer that is central to scientific inquiry puts distance between the researcher, the manager and the subject. This is a distance that the consulting community does not share. It seeks to work with the manager to solve practical problems. The outcome of this distance is that managers talk to consultants and other managers, and academics talk to academics. This is not a healthy outcome for either group. Finding new ways to bridge this gap from both sides is central to improving the practice of management.

Second, research looks to isolate, deconstruct and narrow in order to understand. Consequently, the subject is made frozen and static—it is pinned and placed under glass. Atomizing the management subject matter through ever finer academic studies distances managers from researchers. The findings of studies where the focus is on whether "factor x" is a mediating or moderating variable for "factor y" do not lend themselves to generalization or practical application in the dynamic world of the manager.

Indeed, in most cases the investment of effort does not seem warranted, given the modicum of knowledge discovered. So, does the study of management require more methodological creativity and innovation from the academic community? Should it be a methodology that has pragmatism at its core, but one that is accompanied by the discipline and differentiation that comes with science? The closest managers have to this approach at the moment seems to be in the practice of evaluation. Evaluation has a tested set of methodologies and tools that can be applied to provide managers with valid and reliable information about a practical activity. At its best, evaluation is a practice that couples a pragmatic focus and scientific method. The issue is, therefore, what other areas might this pragmatic and creative method be applied to and how would it advance theory and/or practice?

Ultimately, management is about applying method and practice such that the combination of people, processes, systems and culture are all brought together to deliver collective performance. The difficult part, the bit where uncertainty arises, comes from the interaction between these components, but also the poorly understood, and yet surprisingly resilient, human at the center of the system. Organizations and workplaces, even with the introduction of automation, remain heavily under the influence of humans, and consequently, subject to strengths and frailties of human behavior. Peter Drucker captures the essence of the manager's world:

> No institution can possibly survive if it needs geniuses or supermen to manage it. It must be organized in such a way as to be able to get along under the leadership composed of average human beings. (1946, p. 135)

Managers deal daily with the complicated and complex problems that arise from the interaction people, processes, systems and culture. Alone, any one of these is difficult enough. But they also work with average people doing their best. It is the effort of these people that needs to be coordinated to achieve an outcome. It is these people that need to cooperate to share the knowledge and experience that enables good collective performance.

So, the vital questions for managers and researchers alike, in the past and in the future, is how much, or how little, this human element has changed in response to what seems to be a more complicated and complex workplace? How can our explorations of people and systems improve management practice, and thereby organizational performance?

## WHAT MIGHT WE DO TOGETHER TO IMPROVE THE SITUATION?

Idealistically, we need an age where academics and practitioners challenge, test and advance their understanding of work and organization with a focus on the core questions of humans and the organization, and the way they interact to impact performance. We need a time when we are concerned with the facts not fads. A time when the lessons of the classics of management and history are widely read and understood in relation to the modern practice of management. Where the subjects of people, work and organization are topics for wide-ranging conversation. It would be a time when consultant research would be opened up for critical reflection and testing, and academic output would be similarly tested for practical relevance. There is a need for managers to free their imaginations from the chains of the endless present in order to think progressively about the future. There is a need for academics to acknowledge and work with the pragmatism of managers.

This is an unashamedly idealistic position. However, early management researchers were often managers with "academic tendencies." The research was conducted on the factory floor and was firmly embedded in understanding the nature and character of work. There were real attempts to understand and solve real world management problems. This practice was evident immediately after World War I and World War II. Luther Gulick in his *Administrative Reflections From World War II* outlines the importance of this practical approach:

> Things happen fast in war. Men act along new lines boldly, decision jostling decision. Mistakes are many, and new approaches are sudden and frequent. This environment creates a situation which is extraordinarily fertile in institutional experimentation. If it is equally productive in demonstrating what will and will not work in peace time administration, careful attention to our war experience may prove extremely rewarding for those whose prime consideration is found in challenging the problems of peace. (1948, pp. xi–xii)

In becoming more distant from the topic of management, academics seem to have moved away from the evaluation that necessarily informs practice and closer to recording the innumerable facts of management. Managers, in eschewing academic research and insight in favor of the immediate and practical, have become lost in the immediate and are increasingly vulnerable to management "fashionistas."

The manager and the academic are necessary to one another. The academic is distant and irrelevant without the manager. The manager without the academic is rootless and ineffective. The way forward is to understand that management knowledge is best built through the process of interaction between the manager and the academic. This is a continuous dialogue between the endless present (manager) and the unknowable future (academic).

This chapter has not told an original story, indeed much of what has been said here has been said by many others many times over. It is a story that is recycled repeatedly by both academics and managers. However, if managers and academics collectively point to the chasm between their respective worlds and express a genuine desire to cross it, then there is a need to stop admiring the problem and do something more productive toward achieving it. Alternatively, turn your back on the chasm and get on with your lives.

Management, in its attempts to establish itself as a coherent body of doctrine, has attempted to differentiate itself from other disciplines but it does not seem to have got very far. The remaining chapters in this book provide examples of the ways that this might be achieved. However, as managers and academics move to cross the gap between them each must also work to maintain the distinctiveness of their identity and contribution. An overly pragmatic academic is as useless to crossing the divide as an overly academic manager. Progress will be made not through merger, but rather through collaboration.

## REFERENCES

Argyris, C., & Schön, D. A. (1978). *Organizational learning: A theory of action perspective*. Reading MA: Addison-Wesley.

Camus, A. (1955). *The myth of Sisyphus and other essays* (J. O'Brien, Trans.). New York, NY: Vintage Books.

Casico, W., & Aguinis, H. (2008). Research in industrial and organizational psychology from 1963 to 2007: Changes, choices, and trends. *Journal of Applied Psychology, 93*(5), 1062–1081.

Drucker, P. (1946). *Concept of the corporation*. New York, NY: The John Day Company.

Guest, D. (2014). Employee engagement: A sceptical analysis. *Journal of Organizational Effectiveness: People and Performance, 1*(2), 141–156.

Gulick, L. (1948). *Administrative reflections from World War II*. Tuscaloosa, AL: University of Alabama Press.

Gawande, A. (2014). *The future of medicine, Lecture 2, The Reith Lectures 2014*. Retrieved May 29, 2015, from http://downloads.bbc.co.uk/radio4/open-book/2014_reith_lecture2_wellcome.pdf

Finger, M., & Brand, S. (1999). The concept of the 'learning organization' applied to the transformation of the public sector: Conceptual contributions for theory development. In M. Easterby-Smith, L. Araujo, & J. Burgoyne (Eds.), *Organizational learning and the learning organization: Developments in theory and practice* (pp.130–157). London, England: SAGE.

Hammer, M., & Champy, J. A. (1993). *Reengineering the corporation: A manifesto for business revolution*. New York, NY: Harper Business Books.

March, J. G. (1981). Footnotes to organizational change. *Administrative Science Quarterly, 26*, 563–577.

Miller, D., Hartwick, J., & Le Breton-Miller, I. (2004). How to detect a management fad and distinguish it from a classic. *Business Horizons, 47*(4), 7–16.

Nonaka, I. (1991). The knowledge creating company. *Harvard Business Review, 69*(6), 96–104.

Odiorne, G. S. (1965). *Management by objectives: A system of managerial leadership*. New York, NY: Pitman.

Ohno, T. (1988). *Toyota production system: Beyond large-scale production*. Tokyo, Japan: Productivity Press.

Peters, T. J., & Waterman, R. H. (1982). *In search of excellence: Lessons from America's best-run companies*. New York, NY: Warner Books.

Rousseau, D. M. (2006). Is there such a thing as evidence-based management? *Academy of Management Review, 31*(2), 256–269.

Senge, P. (1990). *The fifth discipline: The art and practice of the learning organization*. New York, NY: Doubleday.

CHAPTER 2

# NOT SO "SECONDARY" DATA

## The Use of Staff Surveys in Human Capital Management Research

**Tony Cotton, Alastair Warren, and Deborah Blackman**

Work is one of the most researched of human activities. The academic enquiry into work is a major subdiscipline in both psychology and sociology, while the management discipline is devoted entirely to the scientific study of people at work. In addition to the plethora of academic inquiry into work, there is a substantial body of work reported in the practitioner literature; however, the gap between research and practice in management is substantial, despite efforts to establish "evidence-based management" (Rynes, Giluk, & Brown, 2007). While both groups study work (and workers), the immediate aims of the two are different. Academics seek to understand the relationship between work and human capital at a fundamental level and to build theories to advance our understanding of how human capital contributes to the performance of work organizations. Practitioners, on the other hand, seek immediate and direct understanding of how to influence the human capital at their disposal in order to improve the productivity of the workplace. Put another way—the practitioner wants to know *what* happened and how (s)he can address the issue, whereas the academic wants to know *why* it happened.

*Human Capital Management Research: Influencing Practice and Process*
pp. 13–29
Copyright © 2016 by Information Age Publishing
All rights of reproduction in any form reserved.

Yet the two are interdependent—we must understand human capital to act on it—but there are different demands placed on both academics and practitioners. To meet their epistemological needs, academics need a high degree of methodological *rigor* in their work, whereas the practitioner needs a high degree of *relevance* in the work that they do in order to meet business needs of their organization. The two concepts of rigor and relevance are not, however, inconsistent; King, Keohane, and Verba (1994) state that research should "ideally" address a question that is at the same time important in the real world and contributes to our ability to make verifiable scientific claims about the world. Rigor and relevance are two characteristics of good research, just as they are characteristics of good organizational practice—which must be relevant to the business need but must also be based on sound scientific theory to be sustainable and the effects predictable and replicable. Without a solid base in theory management, intervention runs the risk of becoming a fad rather than an enduring management practice (Miller, Hartwick, & Le Breton-Miller, 2004).

Academics and practitioners use similar tools; most commonly, surveys of people who work. However in their pursuit of rigor and relevance, the two groups use this tool in slightly different ways—management academics routinely conduct *surveys of staff* to study different aspects of human capital that can then be used to contribute to the scientific claims made about the world. Practitioners routinely use *staff surveys* to help them understand human capital issues in a specific organizational setting. Both types of survey do the same thing; their emphasis is different but not irreconcilable and the purpose of this chapter is to demonstrate how these two approaches can be combined to better meet the needs of management academics and practitioners alike.

## SURVEYS OF STAFF

Academics build theories; fundamental to this is the need to ensure that the theories are a *valid* representation of the phenomena they are considering. Validity comes in one of two forms: internal or external (Shadish, Cook, & Campbell, 2002). Internal validity refers to the ability of the researcher to make statements about the causal relationship between two phenomena, while external validity refers to the ability to generalize these statements beyond the particular research setting. If the purpose of research is to contribute to enhanced understandings of the world around us, both are equally important, and internal and external validity are fundamental to the use of surveys in the workplace.

Explaining the causal relationships among a set of variables, whether in the workplace or otherwise, requires the use of formal deductive logic (Popper, 2002). There are a number of criteria for establishing causality and Wright, Gardner, Moynihan, and Allen (2004) suggest the key criteria are:

- the cause and effect covary, that is, they occur together,
- the cause occurs before the effect, and
- there are no other alternative explanations.

In attempting to build a theory, management academics will use measures of constructs they have designed for that purpose or that have been validated in previous scientific work; this is known as "primary data" (see for example, Slavec & Drnovsek, 2012). To determine whether or not two constructs covary, the common practice is to develop measures of the cause and effect constructs based on a theoretical understanding of the characteristics of each, and then use these measures to make inferential links between them in an appropriate sample (Binning & Barrett, 1989). There are widely accepted steps to be taken in the development of such measures that lead to valid and reliable measures of the construct and allow the management academic to make legitimate statements about the theory they are building (see for example, Worthington & Whittaker, 2006).

In a workplace, this translates into either developing a specific set of survey questions to measure the cause and effect variables or using existing questionnaires, and then administering the survey in the workplace. By doing so, researchers obtain measures of both cause and effect variables in the same sample and are, therefore, able to clearly identify whether or not the two constructs do covary.[1]

One of the limitations with surveys of staff is that they are typically a single point in time measure, and there is rarely an opportunity to revisit a workplace for the purposes of examining the chronological nature of the cause and effect variables, unless the academic has been engaged to do longitudinal research. As a result, determining whether the cause occurs before the effect requires asking respondents to recall detail from some period prior to when they are actually responding to the survey, which can introduce an extra source of error into survey responses. Wright et al. (2004), for example, were able to demonstrate a clear relationship between organizational human resource (HR) practices and a range of workforce and organizational outcomes, but when the temporal relationships between these were considered, they found it was impossible to determine whether HR practices influenced performance, performance influenced HR practices, or whether there was an alternative explanation for the relationship. Determining the temporal relationship between constructs is often difficult.

The final component in determining causality is to rule out as many alternative explanations as possible. In practical terms this means that the management academic will seek to measure as many likely constructs as possible. However, a critical concern of management academics is the continuing decrease in survey response rates which is attributed to, among other things, survey fatigue caused by overly long surveys (Porter, Whitcomb, & Weitzer, 2004). One of the strategies for dealing with survey fatigue is to reduce the "survey burden" on respondents by making them as short as possible, which creates an obvious tension with the desire to measure as many plausible alternative constructs in order to remove them as possible alternate explanations for the causal relationship. The ability of the management academic to balance these two concerns—comprehensiveness of coverage of alternative constructs and reducing survey burden in order to support higher response rates—is a unique challenge.

The issue of response rates is also critical to the external validity of surveys of staff used in the work of the management academic. A low response rate and the consequent nonresponse bias occurring as a result of an unrepresentative sample undermines the ability of the research to make verifiable scientific claims about the world. It can also undermine the ability of the research to answer any real world questions specific to the workplace where the survey has been conducted. The causes of low response rates are many and varied, and one of the most common approaches to improving response rates is the use of individual incentives for respondents (Edwards et al., 2009). For the management academic seeking to conduct surveys of staff in a workplace the incentives for individuals are important, but the incentives for an organization to participate are also critical.

Typically, organizations that support academic research being undertaken in their workplace will expect some feedback from the research that can contribute to understanding their workforce or can directly impact their business planning. A critical activity for the management academic, therefore, is to consider the nature of the feedback provided to the organization—by understanding the business needs of the workplace, the academic can provide better feedback which in turn leads to greater organizational support for the research activity, and hence increases the probability of participation. In this way the *relevance* of the research activity directly contributes to the *rigor* of the research.

Another related factor is the relationship between the management academic and the organization where the research is occurring. Workplaces are nothing if not practical places and the sense that the academic is to some degree removed from the organization can contribute a sense (in the workplace) that the relationship between the management academic and the workplace is unidirectional, and that the work is not focused on practical outcomes for the workplace. While the perceived independence of the researcher can contribute to the honesty of the responses, if the academic is seen to be "using" the organization for their own academic or generalist purposes without having the interests of the organization or its staff at heart, this can result in varying levels of support for the survey of staff with concomitant reduced response rates or unobservable reduction in the validity of responses.

Surveys of staff conducted by management academics are a critical tool for the causal relationships among workplace and workforce variables, and they tend to be strong in the development of measures of these variables. They are good at identifying whether these variables covary, that is, whether there is a relationship between the variables, however, they are limited in their ability to identify the temporal nature of this relationship. They are often required to compromise on the range of variables considered, and hence their ability to rule out alternative explanations for any relationships found, because of considerations of the length of the survey in order to reduce any anticipated effect this might have on response rates. Finally, there are some very practical considerations for the management academic in terms of their relationship with the workplace and how their motives are perceived by survey respondents and the organization as a whole.

## STAFF SURVEYS

The staff survey is almost ubiquitous in modern organizational practice. The most common form is conducted regularly, perhaps annually, it tends to focus on staff attitudes towards a broad range of specific workplace practices, and it often includes measures of more general constructs such as job satisfaction or employee engagement. The most common driver for conducting a staff survey is the organization's management, or HR area, seeking input to business decisions or to inform the development and implementation of workplace strategies. As a result, the *relevance* of the information collected in a staff survey is the paramount consideration and has two components—how well it addresses the specific immediate business decision needs, and how timely is the provision of this information to the business decision makers.

However, while the relevance of a staff survey is important, the validity of the instrument (or the *rigor* with which it is developed) is no less important, and some would argue that it is more important for the management practitioner. Any business decision is based on a causal inference—when a senior HR executive decides to implement a new performance management framework, (s)he is making a critical inferential link, implicit or otherwise, that implementing the framework will lead to better performance among employees and hence better organizational performance. This is no different to those links made in the course of the theory building of the management academic (Binning & Barrett, 1989). As a result the evidence base for this decision needs to meet the same requirements as that of the management academic described above, that is:

- the cause and effect covary,
- the cause occurs before the effect, and
- there are no other alternative explanations.

How well staff surveys address these needs, depends on the *rigor* with which they are developed. However, because they are developed to address specific business needs rather than theory-building needs, they are considered "secondary" data and, typically, are not considered as useful for explaining causal relationships and, consequently, theory building (Slavec & Drnovsek, 2012).

Perhaps the weakest element of a staff survey in explaining causal relationships is their ability to demonstrate that two factors covary, largely because the measurement of the constructs in the cause and effect relationship under consideration is often poor. Fundamental to this is the fact that because the staff survey is primarily designed to address direct business questions, the content of staff surveys is often designed around questions that have high *face* validity rather than necessarily high *construct* validity (Shadish et al., 2002). For example, questions that ask about general satisfaction with work might have high face validity, but they have been shown to be driven as much by the personality of the respondent as by their actual working conditions and not clearly linked to the underlying motivation of work performance (Muchinsky, 2012).

Compounding this, managers, because of their need to respond quickly to their immediate business needs, seek to reduce complexity in their environment and will often seek to simplify workplace or workforce issues beyond reasonable bounds. But work and the workforce are complex and while the need to respond to immediate business decisions requires some degree of clarity, it does not mean that the complexity of the workplace can be ignored. Rather, it needs to be interpreted or aggregated in such a way that managers can usefully accommodate it into their decision making. Theory building can contribute to this, but it is the ability of the academic to operationalize their theory that is crucial to explain the need for theory building and hence the role of the staff survey in this.

According to Kurt Lewin "there is nothing more practical than a good theory" (1952, p. 169), but organizations need to understand this to be prepared to invest in developing their staff surveys to support theory building.

While staff surveys may be weak in their measurement of cause and effect constructs, and hence the likelihood that they covary, the routine nature of staff surveys provides two valuable features. First, staff surveys are able to measure the temporal nature of the relationship between the variables of interest, although this can only be done at the organizational level as employee surveys are usually anonymous. However, the ability to track variables over a period of time, even at the organizational level, allows for far greater explanatory power than a point in time measure. Second, because they are routinely administered, the staff survey allows refinement of its measures based on data collected in a previous administration of the survey. By balancing this refinement (or evolution) process with the need to retain comparability over administration for temporal comparisons, it is possible to use the staff survey to develop psychometrically robust measures that provide good comparisons across time.

Staff surveys are typically omnibus instruments, that is, they often include questions about a broad range of workplace issues that might be indicators of alternative explanations of the cause and effect relationship of interest. Staff surveys might include questions about the efficacy of communications in an organization, satisfaction with workplace initiatives, leader behaviors, or the impact of workplace policies. While there is typically pressure to keep a staff survey short and because a staff survey is "owned" by the organization, completing the survey is a bona fide task for employees (some organizations have been known to roster time for shift workers to complete staff surveys), there can be more latitude in a staff survey to canvas a broader range of issues and, therefore, alternate causal explanations, than in a survey of staff conducted by an external academic. Staff surveys also have the ability to legitimately canvas issues that the organization might not be prepared to allow an academic; Wright et al. (2004), for example, describe how they were unable to address certain aspects of high-performing work systems in their in depth work with an organization.

Staff surveys are a very common tool for management practitioners that can provide highly relevant and timely information for management to contribute to business decision making. However, the rigor with which they are developed is, at times, compromised by the need to meet the immediate business requirements of the organization. Nonetheless, the repeated, regular administration of staff surveys and the potentially greater breadth of issues that can be addressed in a staff survey make them a potentially useful vehicle for the development of causal models in organizational settings.

## PRIMARY OR SECONDARY DATA—OR SOMETHING ALTOGETHER DIFFERENT?

For the management academic the collection of primary data is the "gold standard" for examining causal relationships, and primary data largely requires the development of specific measures of the constructs under consideration, or the use of measures previously published in the academic literature. There is clear guidance about how to develop adequate construct measures, but adherence to these is often variable, which threatens the internal validity of the research process. Similarly, inadequacies in sampling, for example conducting research in undergraduate students (for example, Neff, 2003) or using convenience samples (see for example, Rich, Lepine, & Crawford, 2010) limit the external validity of primary data collection efforts conducted by management academics. Finally, as point in time measures, primary data collection through surveys of staff are limited in their ability to contribute to understanding causality.

Staff surveys, on the other hand, are "secondary data"; they are developed for other than theory-building purposes and the measures used are often considered inadequate from a measurement point of view, but they do meet the organization's need for direct answers and timely feedback. However, staff surveys have some very positive potential attributes for studying causal relationships in organizations, among other things, because they are repeatedly collected over time, they provide the opportunity to study temporal relationships among constructs which provides a stronger evidence base for causality as suggested by Wright et al. (2004). They also provide an opportunity for continuously testing and refining measures of constructs of the workplace and workforce that is not possible with point in time measures.

It has been argued that both surveys of staff and staff surveys have demands for relevance and rigor, both can be used for building practical theories, as well as providing valid defensible answers to business needs. Our analysis would also suggest that the strengths and weaknesses of these two approaches are complementary; surveys of staff have strength in the quality of the measures they use, staff surveys have strength in their repeated regular administration. Based on this, we would propose that a closer collaboration between management academics and practitioners on the design and delivery of staff surveys could, in fact, lead to staff surveys more closely resembling primary data, while retaining the strengths of the traditional staff survey. This would provide organizations with a stronger basis for the causal inferences that underpin business decisions, while providing management academics with a potentially much richer source of data than is usually available through the application of cross-sectional surveys of staff.

Building a more collaborative approach to developing staff surveys requires compromise and some concessions on the part of both the management academics and practitioners. Academics must be efficient in the development of potential measures and be prepared to include questions that address specific, current, organizationally critical concerns, and to provide this information in a timely and accessible fashion. The practitioner, for their part, must be prepared to challenge the desire to simplify the complexities of the workplace in order to realize a more comprehensive and fundamental understanding of the workplace and, in particular, the nature of the causal inferences underpinning business decisions.

In order to demonstrate how this more collaborative approach might be achieved, two case studies will be given from recent work conducted around the ongoing development of the Australian Public Service (APS) Employee Census, these are:

- Fitting existing staff survey data to a theoretical model. Noting that "essentially, all models are wrong, but some are useful" (Box & Draper, 1987, p. 424), this case study will show how a set of existing staff survey data was able to fit an existing theoretical model of employee engagement.
- Adapting an existing theoretical model to a staff survey. This will describe how a model of organizational culture developed largely in the private sector was used to develop a measure of organizational culture in a staff survey.

## THE AUSTRALIAN PUBLIC SERVICE CENSUS

The APS is one of Australia's largest employers, with over 150,000 employees representing over two thirds of the Commonwealth public sector or 1% of the entire Australian workforce. The APS has been using a staff survey to inform the writing of the annual State of the Service Report (SoSR) for over 10 years (Australian Public Service Commission, 2014). Previously based on a stratified random sample of approximately 5% of the total APS workforce, in 2012 a census sampling methodology was adopted, where every employee in the APS was invited to participate in the survey, known as the APS Employee Census (the Census).

The Census is administered as an online survey over a period of 4 weeks in May–June of each year and overall it has been successful, receiving a 55% response rate ($n$ = 86,214) in 2012, increasing to a 68% response rate in 2014 ($n$ = 99,392). The survey instrument is large and comprehensive, containing over 200 distinct questions, some of which are multipart, yielding over 250 variables for each case. Originally based predominantly on single-issue questions, the Census is evolving to become more focused on the use of validated measurement scales (e.g., the HSE First Pass Tool; Cousin et al., 2004) or as a vehicle to develop and validate construct measures using sound psychometric principles.

## CASE STUDY—THE DEVELOPMENT OF THE APS EMPLOYEE ENGAGEMENT MODEL

The management of APS employees to improve organizational performance is a key activity of APS managers and HR practitioners—one of the key concepts used in this is employee engagement.

The APS has been measuring employee engagement since 2006. The approach used was largely data driven using the annual staff survey to provide responses to a range of questions about the APS workplace. These questions were grouped under a set of broad headings and each year an exploratory factor analysis was conducted on "a broad range of the 2006 State of the Service Employee Survey questions, and the questions selected based on their relevance to employee engagement" (Australian Public Service Commission, 2006, p. 290). This approach meant that the "factor structure" of the employee engagement items changed from year to year (for example, there was a 10 factor structure in 2006 but a 12 factor structure in 2007), which is inconsistent with the academic literature which views engagement as, among other things, a relatively stable construct (Macey & Schneider, 2008).

In 2011 the APS determined that a more theoretically based approach to measuring employee engagement was preferable, and began investigating the academic and practitioner literature for models of engagement that might be appropriate in the APS context. There are two broad schools of thought in the academic literature on employee engagement: one came from the work on employee burnout (Maslach, Schaufeli, & Leiter, 2001; Schaufeli, Leiter, & Maslach, 2009), and the other is based on the work of Kahn (1990, 1992). The former has seen the development of the most commonly used instrument for measuring engagement, the multidimensional Utrecht Work Engagement Scale (Schaufeli, Salanova, Gonzalez-Roma, & Bakker, 2002), however, this instrument is not without its criticisms (Wefald, Mills, Smith, & Downey, 2012; Saks & Gruman 2014). Research using Kahn's model has seen the development of instruments for research purposes but none have been used beyond very limited research studies (see for example, May, Gilson, & Harter, 2004; Rich et al., 2010; Saks, 2006).

The practitioner literature, on the other hand, has a plethora of "models" of employee engagement, most of which appear to have been developed in a data-driven way with limited theoretical underpinning, and many of which are proprietary. Another concern with many of the practitioner models was that they reduced what is a complex process into a single index, typically the proportion of "engaged" employees in the workforce. However, the model developed by the Corporate Leadership Council (Corporate Executive Board, 2006) stood out, as it is based on a multidimensional conceptualization of employee engagement and draws on the ideas of Kahn (1990, 1992) in terms of employees' ability to engage with their work. A central feature of the Corporate Leadership Council model is that employees can engage with four dimensions of their work: their job, the team they work in, their immediate supervisor and the organization where they work.

This provided the APS with a structure for a measure of employee engagement that was found to map to the content of the 2010 State of the Service Employee Survey. To develop and test a potential measure, the data set from the 2010 APS Employee Survey ($n$ = 5,594) was split into an experimental ($n$ = 3,422) and a validation data set ($n$ = 2,172). Although the employee survey contained over 200 separate and distinct questions, not all were considered to be likely to provide a measure of how well employees might engage with their work (for example, demographic items, questions about the efficiency of recruitment processes), so a preliminary screening of the questions in the survey identified a total of 85 from the full set of questions in the 2010 Survey to be included in the analysis. A combination of exploratory factor analyses and reliability analyses were conducted which identified 10 distinct univariate constructs that could be mapped into the hypothesized structure. A confirmatory factor analysis was then conducted using the validation data set, which showed an acceptable fit of the data to the model. The final measures have been shown to be related to a range of organizationally relevant measures, including self-report work performance, hours worked, sickness absence and employee's intention to leave their job (Australian Public Service Commission, 2011).

The APS had used its annual staff survey to measure employee engagement for some time prior to the development of the APS Employee Engagement model, but this had been very much a secondary task to providing organizational information. As a result of a simplistic, data-driven approach the "model" developed was counterintuitive and not usable—if the "structure" of engagement changes each year, it is not possible to implement strategies to influence engagement from one year to the next.

However, by adopting a more theory-driven approach to the existing staff survey data to the model, the APS has developed a more stable and useful measure of this important management construct. The resultant data can provide both a greater understanding of the theoretical construct for academics, while still providing managers with useful practical information.

## CASE STUDY: MEASURING APS CULTURE

A more recent innovation has been the integration of a formal model of organizational culture into the annual APS Employee Census. A complex phenomenon which has featured in the literature for decades, organizational culture is frequently defined as:

> a pattern of shared basic assumptions that was learned by a group as it solved its problems of external adaptation and internal integration, that has worked well enough to be considered valid and, therefore, to be taught to new members as the correct way to perceive, think, and feel in relation to those problems. (Schein, 2010, p. 17)

In part, this interest has been driven by the direct and indirect links organizational culture has been shown to have with organizational effectiveness (Sackmann, 2011). Public sector reform has also played a role, particularly the New Public Management movement, by attempting to move organizations away from the traditional values of bureaucracy and administration (Box, Marshall, Reed, & Reed, 2000; Lynn, 2001). While the APS Employee Surveys have historically covered issues such as work-life balance, staff consultation and ethical leadership; organizational culture has not been dealt with in a cohesive way, instead considering different issues in isolation. Studying APS culture required a new approach. However, in this case rather than adapting existing items into a new product, a new way of generating insight into APS agencies was required.

While there is a strong tradition of using qualitative methods, such as observation and interviews, to study an organizations' culture (Bellot, 2011; Cai, 2008; Yammarino & Dansereau, 2011), this is not a viable way to measure culture in an organization as large and complex as the APS. Exploring organizational culture in this context requires a quantitative measure of culture. As a first step, the APS engaged with the existing literature to find a useful lens through which to view organizational culture.

From a range of extant models of organizational culture, the Competing Values Framework (the Framework) (Cameron & Quinn, 2011) was identified as a possible model for the APS because it is widely used and uses language familiar to the APS. A scale based on the Framework was selected because of the robustness it had demonstrated in earlier studies.

However, this scale did not perform well in the APS context. It failed to show construct validity, and as such the data collected could not be interpreted clearly. This was possibly because either the questions were not suited to the APS context or because of modifications required to include it in the APS annual survey. Although this attempt was not successful, the very fact that the questions and analysis could not work automatically demonstrated the importance of using a more academic approach rather than just "borrowing" questions on an ad hoc basis.

It was decided to persevere and to develop a new scale specific to the APS that would have a theoretical model for its foundation. While a model unique to the APS could have been developed looking at APS-centric values and beliefs, this path was not taken. If it had been, the APS would have lost the ability to look at itself in relation to other organizations. Despite the initial failure, the Competing Values Framework was retained because, by using it as theoretical foundation, the APS results would be comparable to wide a range of other public and private sector organizations.

Rather than drawing on items that were already in the employee survey, new questions were created specifically to create the APS Performance Culture Scales. As well as allowing stronger links to the Scales' theoretical foundation by tailoring the items to them, this also allowed more rigor in developing the scales. Items were developed and reviewed by subject-matter experts from the APS, the University of Canberra and the University of New South Wales, Canberra. Draft versions of the Scales were then tested in focus groups to ensure that employees understood the language and the questions, and were able to characterize their agency in these terms. After the scales had been refined, they were pilot tested in an APS agency to investigate whether they showed construct validity and reliability. Using the positive results from the pilot testing, the APS Performance Culture Scales were refined and included in the 2014 APS Employee Census. Initially the performance of the Scales was examined in six agencies of varying sizes and functions to ensure they were robust in a wide range of organizational contexts. After demonstrating construct validity and high reliability in all agencies, the evidence suggests that the APS Performance Culture Scales are a robust, theoretically grounded measure of organizational culture.

The development of the APS Performance Culture Scales, while still in the early stages, demonstrates the value of staff surveys in the development of theory, particularly how the ongoing nature of staff surveys allows for the testing and refinement of the measures needed to develop theory. The engagement with theory at the earliest stages of measure development, combined with the unique ability of a staff survey to test and refine the measure over time, demonstrates that applied management research can generate measures that are theoretically sound and robust, meeting the epistemological needs of the management academic. Moreover, this robustness means that these scales themselves can be used as a source of secondary data, providing other researchers with the opportunity to study organizational culture in the APS.

## CONCLUSION

Management practitioners and academics alike seek to understand causality in the workplace; the academic does this explicitly in the form of theory building, while the practitioner does so implicitly, as any business decision they make has an implicitly causal basis. So, the search for causality and the methods required to achieve this are critical to both groups. Management academics and practitioners use a common data collection method—the survey of employees—but place different emphases on the rigor and relevance of the development and use of surveys, which we have characterized in this chapter by using the terms "surveys of staff" and "staff surveys." However, we have also shown that the two approaches are complementary, with strengths for academics and practitioners alike that may encourage increased collaboration between both groups. Surveys of staff by academics allow more rigorous scale development, in terms of the constructs measured and the method of measuring these, than is often the case in the staff survey, which has the ability to cover a wide range of topics and take measures repeatedly. By applying more rigor to the theoretical development of measures for staff surveys while taking into consideration the immediate information needs of a staff survey, both rigor and relevance can be improved.

However, a more collaborative approach will require some degree of compromise between academics and practitioners. The academic will have to be more conscious of the efficiency with which they design their measuring instruments and will have to include considerations of the immediate relevance of the data collected to the organization, including providing immediate feedback. The practitioner will have to work with more complex measurements that may lack immediate face validity but which have the potential to provide them with more robust measures on which to base business decisions (that is, causal decisions). While both groups might argue that compromise between the two approaches is difficult or impossible, the real life cases studies described in this chapter demonstrate their complementarity and how they can be applied. We suggest that academic research and practitioner outcomes will both benefit by rethinking what constitutes secondary data in the future.

## NOTE

1. There are some methodological problems with including measures of both cause and effect in the same survey that, some have argued, causes inflation in the measures of association between the two that are due to the common method of data collection rather than a "real" relationship between the two variables (Podsakoff & Organ, 1986). However it has been shown that the scale of these problems is minor (Meade, Watson, & Kroustalis, 2007) and that any effect is not automatically an inflation of observed correlations (Spector, 2006).

## REFERENCES

Australian Public Service Commission. (2006). *State of the service report 2005–2006*. Canberra, Australia: Commonwealth of Australia.

Australian Public Service Commission. (2011). *State of the service report 2010–2011*. Canberra, Australia: Commonwealth of Australia.

Australian Public Service Commission. (2014). *State of the service report 2013–2014*. Canberra, Australia: Commonwealth of Australia.

Bellot, J. (2011). Defining and assessing organizational culture. *Nursing Forum 46*(1), 29–37.

Binning, J. F., & Barrett, G. V. (1989). Validity of personnel decisions: A conceptual analysis of the inferential and evidential bases. *Journal of Applied Psychology, 74*(3), 478–494.

Box, G. E. P., & Draper, N. R. (1987). *Empirical model building and response surfaces*. New York, NY: John Wiley & Sons,

Box, R. C., Marshall, G. S., Reed, B. J., & Reed, C. M. (2000). New public management and substantive democracy introduction: the challenge. *Public Administration Review, 61*(5), 608–619.

Cai, Y. (2008). Quantitative assessment of organizational cultures in post-merger universities. *Cultural Perspectives on Higher Education* (pp. 213–226). Retrieved from http://link.springer.com/chapter/10.1007/978-1-4020-6604-7_14

Cameron, K., & Quinn, R. (2011). *Diagnosing and changing organizational culture* (3rd ed.). San Francisco, CA: Jossey-Bass.

Corporate Executive Board. (2006). The Employment Value Proposition—A Key to Attraction and Commitment. *Corporate Leadership Council Research*. Retrieved May 29, 2015, from C:/Users/z3497979/Downloads/Attracting_and_Retaining_Critical_Talent_Segments_Exec_Summ.pdf

Cousins, R., Mackay, C. J., Clarke, S. D., Kelly, C., Kelly, P. J., & McCaig, R. H. (2004). 'Management standards' and work-related stress in the UK: Practical development. *Work & Stress, 18*(2), 113–136.

Edwards P. J., Roberts I., Clarke M. J., DiGuiseppi, C., Wentz, R., Kwan, I., … Pratap, S. (2009). Methods to increase response to postal and electronic questionnaires (Review). *The Cochrane Library*, Issue 3. Retrieved May 29, 2015, from http://onlinelibrary.wiley.com/doi/10.1002/14651858.MR000008.pub4/pdf

Kahn, W. A. (1990). Psychological conditions of personal engagement and disengagement at work. *The Academy of Management Journal, 33*(4), 692–724.

Kahn, W. A. (1992). To be fully there: psychological presence at work. *Human Relations, 45*(4), 321–349.

King, G., Keohane, R. O., & Verba, S. (1994). *Designing social enquiry: Scientific inference in qualitative research.* Princeton, NJ: Princeton University Press.

Lewin, K. (1952). *Field theory in social science: Selected theoretical papers by Kurt Lewin.* London, England: Tavistock.

Lynn, L. (2001). The myth of the bureaucratic paradigm: What traditional public administration really stood for. *Public Administration Review, 61*(2). Retrieved from http://onlinelibrary.wiley.com/doi/10.1111/0033-3352.00016/full

Macey, W. H., & Schneider, B. (2008). The meaning of employee engagement. *Industrial and Organizational Psychology: Perspectives on Science and Practice, 1*(1), 3–30.

Maslach, C., Schaufeli, W. B., & Leiter, M. P. (2001). Job burnout. *Annual Review of Psychology 52,* 397–422.

May, D. R., Gilson, R. L., & Harter, L. M. (2004). The psychological conditions of meaningfulness, safety and availability and the engagement of the human spirit at work. *Journal of Occupational and Organizational Psychology 77,* 11–37.

Meade, A. W., Watson, A. M., & Kroustalis, C. M. (2007, April). *Assessing common methods bias in organizational research.* Paper presented at the 22nd annual meeting of the Society for Industrial and Organizational Psychology, New York. Retrieved May 29, 2015, from http://www4.ncsu.edu/~awmeade/Links/Papers/Methods_Bias(SIOP07).pdf

Miller, D., Hartwick, J., & Le Breton-Miller, I. (2004). How to detect a management fad – and distinguish it from a classic. *Business Horizons, 47*(July–August), 7–16.

Muchinsky, P. (2012). *Psychology applied to work: An introduction to industrial and organizational psychology.* Summerfield, NC: Hypergraphic Press.

Neff, K. D. (2003). The development and validation of a scale to measure self-compassion. *Self and Identity 2,* 223–250.

Podsakoff, P. M., & Organ, D. W. (1986). Self-reports in organizational research: Problems and prospects. *Journal of Management, 12*(4), 531–544.

Popper, K. (2002). *The logic of scientific discovery.* London, England: Routledge Classics.

Porter, S. R., Whitcomb, M. E., & Weitzer, W. H. (2004). Multiple surveys of students and survey fatigue. *New Directions for Institutional Research, 2004*(121), 63–73.

Rich, B. L., Lepine, J. A., & Crawford, E. R. (2010). Job engagement: Antecedents and effects on job performance. *Academy of Management Journal, 53*(3), 617–635.

Rynes, S., Giluk, T., & Brown, K. (2007). The very separate worlds of academic and practitioner periodicals in human resource management: Implication for evidence-based management. *Academy of Management Journal, 50*(5), 987–1008.

Sackmann, S. (2011). Culture and performance. In N. Askanasy, C. Wilderom, & M. Peterson (Eds.), *The handbook of organizational culture and climate* (2nd ed., pp. 188–225). Thousand Oaks, CA: SAGE.

Saks, A. M. (2006). Antecedents and consequences of employee engagement. *Journal of Managerial Psychology, 21*(7), 600–619.

Saks, A. M., & Gruman, J. A. (2014). What do we really know about employee engagement? *Human Resource Development Quarterly, 25*(2), 155–182.

Shadish, W. R., Cook, T. D., & Campbell, D. T. (2002). *Experimental and quasi-experimental designs for generalized causal inference.* Belmont, CA: Wadsworth Cengage Learning.

Schaufeli, W. B., Leiter, M. P., & Maslach, C. (2009). Burnout: 35 years of research and practice. *Career Development International 14*(3), 204–220.

Schaufeli, W.B., Salanova, M., Gonzalez-Roma, V., & Bakker, A.B. (2002). The Measurement of Engagement and burnout: a two sample confirmatory factor analytic approach. *Journal of Happiness Studies, 3,* 71–92.

Schein, E. (2010). *Organizational culture and leadership* (4th ed.). San Francisco, CA: Jossey-Bass.

Slavec, A., & Drnovesek, M. (2012). A perspective on scale development in entrepreneurship research. *Economic and Business Review, 14*(1), 39–62.

Spector, P. E. (2006). Method variance in organizational research truth or urban legend? *Organizational Research Methods, 9*(2), 221–232.

Yammarino, F., & Dansereau, F. (2011). Multilevel issues in organizational culture and climate research. In N. Ashkanasy, C. Wilderom, & M. Peterson (Eds.) *The handbook of organizational culture and climate* (2nd ed., pp. 50–75). Thousand Oaks, CA: SAGE.

Wefald, A. J., Mills, M. J., Smith, M. R., & Downey, R. G. (2012). A comparison of three job engagement measures: Examining their factorial and criterion-related validity. *Applied Psychology: Health and Wellbeing, 4*(1), 67–90.

Worthington, R., & Whittaker, T. (2006). Scale development research: A content analysis and recommendations for best practice. *The Counseling Psychologist, 34*(6), 806–838.

Wright, P. M., Gardner, T. M., Moynihan, L. M., & Allen, M. R. (2004). *The relationship between HR practices and firm performance: Examining casual order* (CAHRS Working Paper #04-06). Ithaca, NY: Cornell University, School of Industrial and Labor Relations, Center for Advanced Human Resource Studies.

CHAPTER 3

# EMPLOYEE ENGAGEMENT IN THE PUBLIC SECTOR

## What Needs to Change

**Natalie Jones and Sally Sambrook**

Many human resource (HR) professionals will be familiar with the hugely popular concept of employee engagement (EE), generally perceived as individual enthusiasm for, and high performance in, work. Advice for HR professionals on how to encourage more engagement at work is already available (Australian Public Service Commission, 2015; Chartered Institute of Personnel and Development, 2012; MacLeod & Clarke, 2009; Vance, 2006). What can academic research really add? We think it can help HR professionals practice EE more effectively, affordably and most importantly, benefit employees with whom they work.

We begin with a summary of the findings of EE research including autoethnographic (AE) work we undertook in the public services in the United Kingdom (UK) (Jones, 2012; Sambrook, Jones, & Doloriert, 2014). In the light of this research, we offer three ways in which practice needs to change in order for HR professionals working in the EE field to make more of a difference. But first, we consider the public sector context in which HR professionals are attempting to improve the EE of workers.

*Human Capital Management Research: Influencing Practice and Process*
pp. 31–45
Copyright © 2016 by Information Age Publishing
All rights of reproduction in any form reserved.

## THE PUBLIC SECTOR

The provision of services for the public good funded through the tax base is a feature of many developed societies. In the UK, the state traditionally has employed workers directly to deliver a range of health, education, social and economic wellbeing, welfare and justice services although, in England especially, this is giving way to a mixed economy model of public, private and voluntary sector providers (Gregory, Dixon & Ham, 2012). Despite recent cuts in budgets and jobs (Wales Audit Office, 2011), the public services remain a substantial area of public expenditure and a significant employer. It is much more highly unionized than the private sector, with more than half the UK workforce in 2013 being a member of a trade union (Department of Business, Innovation and Skills, 2014). Women dominate the public services workforce in the UK, contrary to the balance found in the private sector workforce (Millard & Machin, 2007).

The public services have been characterized as model employers (Bach, 2011) due to relatively transparent recruitment and employment practices, security of employment, the presence of employee voice mechanisms and flexible working arrangements. This is being challenged by the introduction of workforce cuts, pay freezes and changes to pension arrangements as a result of the UK coalition government's 2010 policy of austerity and long-standing calls for public services reform. This is not exclusive to the UK, as governments across the world have argued that their public services need to change (Australian Public Service Commission, 2015). Organizations and their workforces have been restructured and incentivized to make better use of resources, cut running costs, involve citizens more closely in the design and delivery of services, and operate in more businesslike ways (Cameron, 2011). It has been suggested that more and better EE can help public sector workers not only cope in these difficult conditions but also to perform better and enjoy their work (Welsh Government, 2012). It is to the topic of EE that we turn to next.

## ACADEMIC RESEARCH ON EMPLOYEE ENGAGEMENT

For an accessible overview of EE, we suggest the work of Albrecht (2010, Chapter 1) and Bakker and Leiter (2010, Chapter 2, *Defining and Measuring Work Engagement* and Chapter 12, *Building Engagement: The Design and Evaluation of Interventions*). The work by Macey, Schneider, Barbera, and Young (2009) is especially useful for practitioners who want to gain support for and design EE programs within organizations. To understand the job and organizational factors associated with higher levels of EE, we recommend Kahn (1990) for a discussion of the individual and the social factors that support engagement within individuals and Albrecht (2010, Part IV) for commentaries on organizational strategies.

## Definitions

Definitions of EE are numerous. While this diversity may seem frustrating for HR professionals, we think that a variety of meanings is useful, as it offers HR professionals different ways of approaching the topic in practice. For us, as noted by Shuck and Rocco (2011), it is something experienced by individuals within the context of their own personalities and the organizations, labor markets and societies they occupy.

Employee engagement is normally viewed by academic researchers in two ways. First, EE comprises positive thoughts, feelings and behaviors that individuals experience, which we call "state" engagement. Two studies have reviewed the academic literature on state engagement: Simpson (2009) and Shuck and Wollard (2011). William Kahn, cited by a number of scholarly authors as a key contributor to the understanding of state engagement, developed the concept of personal engagement at work from ethnographic research in two small private sector organizations in the United States. In a personally engaged state, an individual is able to bring all of their self that they wish into their work role. Engaged individuals "are described as being psychologically present, fully there, attentive, feeling, connected, integrated and focused in their role performances. They are open to themselves and to others, connected to work and others, and bring their complete selves to perform" (Kahn, 1990, p. 701).

Whereas state engagement is concerned with the thoughts, feelings and behaviors of *an individual employee*, EE is also viewed by a minority of researchers as an approach performed in organizations to increase staff commitment to their jobs and their organization's goals *at the level of the whole workforce*. We call this "device" engagement. This type of definition was used in a UK government-sponsored review of EE which described it as "a workplace approach designed to ensure that employees are committed to their organization's goals and values, motivated to contribute to organizational success, and are able at the same time to enhance their own sense of well being" (MacLeod & Clarke, 2009, p. 9). For many organizations, we contend this is what EE really means—corporate action to increase organizational commitment by groups of workers. While many HR professionals will recognize device engagement from their work and will be very familiar with trying to build engagement across a workforce, few academic researchers have examined this form of EE. Even fewer have researched the interplay between the individual (state) and organizational (device) forms of EE. This was an explicit goal in our research, which we describe more fully later.

## How We Know About Employee Engagement

Other than in Kahn's (1990) influential study, which asked individuals to describe moments of personal engagement and disengagement at work, the dominant means of knowing about EE is through surveys administered by employers to their workforces. Almost all we know about EE as state and device comes from the private sector whose workforce shares few of the characteristics found in the public services. Surveys and quantitative methods can be useful in the study of EE. HR professionals, managers and employees can become informed about levels of reported EE across the workforce, compare groups of employees and assess levels of EE at different time points. They can help employers identify the job and organizational factors associated with higher levels of engagement to inform interventions that are intended to strengthen EE. However, as mainstream EE surveys are normally designed, they are not effective in providing feedback to individual staff on their own levels of engagement and that of their line manager, an important factor in an employee's sense of engagement at work (Truss et al., 2006). Most EE surveys ask respondents—employees, but seldom HR professionals or line managers—to report on their own degree of engagement with work and rarely include more objective performance information or feedback from colleagues. Overreliance on data produced using this method has been cautioned with surveys needing to "be effective and well designed with the confidence of the employees as well as the senior managers" (Purcell, 2010, p. 6). While we did administer a small survey in our research, the majority of the methods we used were qualitative, which we felt responded appropriately to the call from Kahn for methods able to "get at the depth" (Kahn, 1992, p. 340) of EE in ways that survey-based research is not so well equipped to achieve.

## What Do We Know About Employment Engagement in the Public Sector?

As in the private sector, we know about EE in the public sector through employer-administered surveys. As the public services are not a single employer, instruments vary, which means that a comparison across employers is difficult. In addition, many employers do not repeat their workforce surveys. The UK Civil Service People Survey (CSPS) is a notable exception of a commitment to measuring EE in the UK public sector comparatively and over the longer term. The Civil Service People Survey is "based on understanding the levels of employee engagement within the Civil Service and the experiences of work which influence engagement" (Civil Service, 2013, p.1). Since the inception of the Civil Service People Survey in 2009, overall engagement[1] in the civil service workforce has remained steady and it compared advantageously with the private sector in 2012, when it was found that in relation to "staff's interest in their work, the quality of line managers and innovation, the UK civil service performs well" (Civil Service, 2013, p. 19). Despite the relatively positive news about workforce-level EE at the organizations that took part in the Civil Service People Survey, it is claimed that an "engagement deficit" (MacLeod & Clarke, 2009, p. 14) persists. In response to this, many public and private sector organizations have been swift to create programs to increase engagement among their employees, with similarities in approaches being observed across sectors (Alfes, Truss, Soane, Rees, & Gatenby, 2010). As part of our research, we wanted to examine how EE was being pursued in the public sector at a time of considerable financial pressure.

## Our Research on the Practice of Employee Engagement in the Public Sector

It has been asserted that "there are no consistent or distinctive differences between public and private sector strategies around employee engagement ... the details and underlying initiatives are very similar" (Alfes et al., 2010, p. 12). While similarity in approach has been observed across sectors, at the same time it is argued that organizations 'should' develop initiatives that reflect their own circumstances, needs and characteristics (Alfes et al., 2010; MacLeod & Clarke 2009). To address this, we wanted to investigate how EE was conceived, managed and experienced by different groups who worked in the public sector in Wales: HR professionals, managers and nonmanagerial employees. We undertook research between 2009 and 2012. We chose to conduct AE research, which we felt was particularly well suited to understanding both state and device EE.

AE is a research approach that enables the researcher to draw on themselves as a source of data (auto) in order to understand a social phenomenon or wider culture (ethno) through analytical writing (graphy) (Wall, 2006). The researcher not only collects data from others but also turns to, and uses, their own personal experiences to inform the research. Our research blended a study of our own state EE through an analysis of engagement with work (auto) with a study of device EE, principally by way of a case study of an EE program taking place in a public sector organization in Wales (ethno). We analyzed these two levels of data—personal and organizational—within the context of official statistics, a survey of HR professionals in Wales and policy documents, to understand the broader environment.

Confirming evidence from other research we reviewed (Civil Service 2013), we found relatively high reported levels of EE at the case organization compared with other public sector organizations. Despite this, and like the wider public services in Wales, higher levels of EE were considered necessary by the HR team at the case organization. As discussed earlier, the focus among the research participants and one of the research team was on EE as a device. The in-house HR team wanted to identify lots of new initiatives. HR professionals in Wales that we surveyed also shared this preference for novelty and large numbers of activities, which we categorized into nine sets of practices (Jones, 2012), presented in Figure 3.1.

These included staff surveys, consultative committees, electronic knowledge-sharing systems, job secondments, off and on the job training,

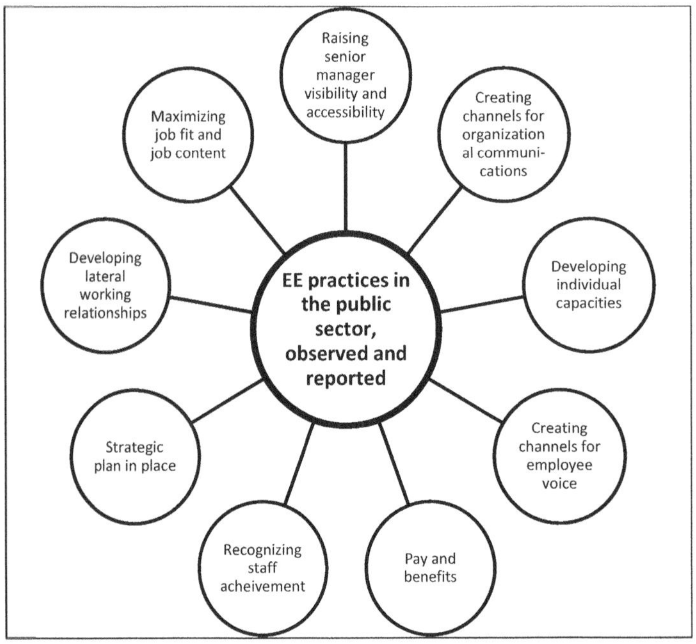


*Source:* Based on a survey of 18 HR professionals plus results of observations at a public sector organization between 2010 and 2011 (Jones, 2012).

Figure 3.1. EE practices in the public sector: Observed and reported, 2010-2011

social and leisure events, and opportunities for nonmanagerial staff to meet with senior executives (Jones, 2012). More than half of the sets of practices were aimed at creating organizational climates that are associated with higher levels of workforce-level EE (Albrecht, 2010). Far fewer were designed to encourage staff to discover, understand and manage their own state engagement with work.

Managers can face considerable challenges in implementing EE initiatives and improvements can be difficult to realize (Jenkins & Delbridge, 2013; Luisis-Lynd & Myers, 2011). The organization whose EE program we researched adopted a linear, transactional approach to managing EE, where "employee engagement is essentially a set of activities ... reflects a degree of compartmentalized thinking.... There is little about any of the component parts that can be criticized ... nonetheless ... employee engagement is still an 'add-on.' It is not integral to the overall business approach" (MacLeod & Clarke, 2009, p. 72). In our view, the organization struggled, as many do (Kinnie, Hutchinson, Purcell, Rayton, & Swart, 2005), to bridge the gap between intended and actual implementation of EE practices.

We observed that many of the actions developed by the HR team and employees were not completed by the time the staff survey was repeated, which did not surprise us. Actions were not prioritized and staff were expected to carry out these actions without additional resources, such as time or managerial support or other duties being reallocated. The HR team regularly expressed frustration at the lack of perceived commitment from line managers and employees to implement activities arising from their corporate EE plan. Staff, on the other hand, saw these activities as extra work at a time when work intensity was increasing as vacant posts were left unfilled due to budget cuts. They did not view the corporate plan as an opportunity to increase their personal EE.

The auto data we contributed (drawing on recollections from 5 years of work experience and longer term career trajectories) helped us to learn about EE in new ways. We created timelines of our careers and discussed recollections of our work to verify how our own EE felt to us at different times in our careers. We used Kahn's (1990) three psychological conditions of meaningfulness, safety and availability to structure our sense making about our personal engagement—and disengagement—at work. We identified changes in job content, workload increase, different life stages and organizational change to be important factors in explaining why our EE fluctuated, and revealed our attempts to sustain—and regain—engagement (Jones, 2012; Sambrook et al., 2014). Our auto data contributed knowledge on the ebbs and flows in individuals' sense of engagement at work which failed to be captured by workforce wide surveys, the sense of grief that accompanied the loss of a strong sense of engagement with work and the lack of tools available to managers (e.g., lack of skills in job redesign, little flexibility over pay or opportunities to progress to new areas of work) to address fluctuations in engagement.

This meant that in the public sector there were very real constraints both on the maintenance of state EE and on the likely impact of device engagement. Using AE helped us find that state EE is personal and dynamic. What we found through the "ethno" element of our study was that device engagement did not engage staff in the management of their own state EE. From our "auto" data we found we had our own devices that we used to try and maintain and improve our state EE which were not related to our employers' device EE. Conventional academic research can tell HR professionals about the reported engagement levels of "them": other employees. Our AE-based research showed us the value of learning about "us" (auto) and our state EE for the design and management of device EE aimed at them (ethno), and the importance of connecting state and device EE to one another.

In conclusion, we found that EE in the public services in Wales was mainly concerned with trying to increase compliance by employees with organizational objectives and policy frameworks that encouraged them to place others before themselves, in the spirit of being modern public servants (Welsh Assembly Government, 2004). We found that the device EE practices being pursued by HR professionals did not connect with individual needs or with initiatives being pursued by staff to improve their own sense of state engagement. There was no consideration in device EE that staff working in the public services could, or should, realize that state EE was possible, let alone capable of being managed. This extended as far as the HR professionals and the senior managers who participated in our research. Very few of the respondents related EE to themselves and their own personal experience. EE was a set of attitudes and visible behaviors to be witnessed and developed in others, designed to benefit primarily the organization and wider stakeholders. Our AE approach to studying EE contributed a greater depth of understanding than conventional survey-based approaches and confirmed the importance of connecting state and device engagement in both theory and practice. AE also showed us how the practices of HR professionals, normally focused on delivering device engagement, needed to place an understanding of state engagement at the heart of their programs for them to be more effective. We explore how HR professionals can do this more fully in the next section

## WHAT NEEDS TO CHANGE ABOUT EMPLOYEE ENGAGEMENT IN PRACTICE?

We do not intend to add to the several reports aimed at practitioners who want guidance on undertaking organizationwide EE programs (Macey et al., 2009; MacLeod & Clarke, 2009). We encourage HR professionals who wish to adopt the mainstream practices set out in these publications to collaborate with academic researchers to evaluate the effectiveness of EE interventions, and also to work closely with employees to design interventions that are sensitive to the resources available within organizations.

Our AE-based investigation of EE research offers HR professionals a different way of thinking about effective EE practice. We think the practices of EE by HR professionals need to change in (at least) three particular ways.

- *Change in HR Practice 1: Awareness of Our Own State Engagement:* From conventional academic research we know very little about the state EE of HR professionals and line managers, the very people tasked with implementing device EE. If HR professionals and line managers are unaware of—or not asked to consider—their own levels of engagement, this suggests they may lack sensitivity to understand just what they are demanding of employees. They may fail to appreciate the deeply personal and dynamic characteristics of EE, fluctuating in response to changes to perceptions of meaningfulness, safety and resource availability in jobs (Kahn, 1990). We suggest EE initiatives need to enable and encourage HR professionals and line managers to explore their own levels of engagement. This can be achieved through adopting techniques similar to those from our AE research, such as reviewing career timelines, assessing personal resource requirements and negotiating changes to address both individual and organizational needs, within the current context.
- *Change in HR Practice 2: Challenge the Assumption of an Engagement Deficit:* From conventional academic research we know that there is relatively high EE in the public sector. From our research we discovered that the public sector is a particularly tough place to maintain state EE or to demonstrate results from any device EE due to shocks, such as externally imposed budget cuts and control by external stakeholders (Jones, 2012). HR professionals need to question whether an "engagement deficit" really exists in their organization. The most realistic outcome for an organization in the public sector in the UK may be for levels of EE across a workforce to be acknowledged and maintained, rather than striving for endless increases in engagement which risk pressuring employees unsustainably.
- *Change in HR Practice 3: Employee Engagement at Multiple Levels in the Organization:* From conventional academic research we know more about state EE than we do about device EE. Our research has demonstrated the importance of making sure that device and state

engagement are integrated into action plans within organizations. HR professionals need to include an additional level in their device EE, that of the individual employee. An example of how they can do this is to ensure that the measurement of EE, which commonly focuses on workgroups and on the conditions for EE, is designed so that individuals can get feedback on their own state EE. In reality, device EE needs to take into account multiple levels of action and actors, especially the line manager, who has been found to be an important factor in state EE.

These three changes in HR practice can be combined, as illustrated in Table 3.1, to develop an holistic, balanced engagement plan.

Practice 1 involves HR professionals (and managers) discovering their own 'state' EE, and through Practice 2 then finding out how the organizational and wider contexts they occupy make a difference to their experiences of work. Through Practice 3 they are encouraged to implement an EE plan that combines both state and device approaches. HR professionals will learn to assess changes in EE at the individual level, the factors that are making a difference, the nature and scale of resources needed to enable changes that are intended to improve EE, as well as the difference, if any, that can be attributed to the activities undertaken to their sense of EE. As well as external evaluation of our approach that academic researchers can contribute, organizational support in the form of mentoring or groups, such as action learning sets, may be required to support individual HR professionals (and managers) to progress and measure the impact of their plans. Our approach to managing EE helps HR professionals design corporate EE initiatives that are sensitive to individual and organizational needs, request adequate resources to manage and measure initiatives, select context indicators of EE and of success that are appropriate to individual employees as well as the employing organization.

Why should HR professionals adopt these research-informed changes in HR practice? Senior decision makers often have a preference for device EE tools that enable them to benchmark their organization's performance with others and to adopt management consultancy-based products whose underlying theory can be unclear and with little evidence of impact. Public sector organizations are being urged to become more evidence informed and to base their decisions on knowledge about what works rather than on ideological or political grounds (Cabinet Office, 2015). The introduction of more transparent government means that the public sector is being judged in many more ways than was previously the case. Having evidence to inform decisions about how to invest in staff for maximum gain (for both parties) will become more, not less, important. HR professionals who adopt research-informed EE will be better placed to

**Table 3.1. Autoethnography-Inspired Employee Engagement in the Public Sector**

| *Practice 1: Diagnose your own EE (as an individual working in your organization, and as a member of an HR team)* | *Practice 2: Diagnose your organization's culture, and its wider context and its impact on your EE* | *Practice 3: Blend the diagnoses from Practice 1 and 2 to generate an EE plan for you as an individual, as an HR team, and organization* |
|---|---|---|
| • Check your own EE using an agreed framework (for example, we used Kahn, 1990).<br>• Analyze changes in EE and the likely reasons for these—what factors appear to be relevant?<br>• Come to a conclusion about your EE. How well is your EE doing, given past and current circumstances?<br>• What could be changed to better manage your EE (for example, job content, adequate resources, line manager support, organizational factors)? | • What is the policy context affecting your part of the public services?<br>• Using existing knowledge on what is known about factors that support EE (see McLeod and Clarke, 2009, for example, Section 4), assess through observation and discussion how these factors are performing in your organization.<br>• How do you "know" about EE in your organization? What evidence is this based on? For example, is this based entirely on organizational surveys?<br>• Challenge whether an "engagement deficit" really exists in your organization. | • Develop a personal EE plan—what does good EE look and feel like to you? What do you want to do about your state of EE?<br>• Compare what you need to build or maintain your own state EE with what is offered through any corporate device programs.<br>• Create and agree a set of success factors for your EE.<br>• Seek to implement your personal plan, stating what (resources) you need from others and the organization to make this happen.<br>• Evaluate progress toward meeting your plan.<br>• Assess implications of this approach for any organizational device approaches to EE. |
| AUTO | ETHNO | GRAPHY |

*Source:* Derived from Jones (2012).

demonstrate they are contributing to an agenda that is growing in importance in the public services, and they will be able to evidence their contribution at a time when HR services in the public sector are under threat (Jones, 2012).

So where does our approach leave the corporate EE program? If corporate EE initiatives are well designed according to the needs of the context (Jenkins & Delbridge, 2013), resourced and evaluated to demonstrate their impact on employees and organizations, and the benefits (or costs of implementation) are shared between employees and employers, there may be a case for undertaking such programs. We consider that the lack of impact from device EE that has been reported from the limited evidence available makes it difficult to justify organizationwide EE programs in the public sector as cuts to the public finances continue to be made. We think HR practices need to be reoriented toward our AE-based approach which provides a much-needed rebalancing of the EE agenda toward meeting employee as well as organizational needs that is sensitive to the contemporary public sector.

## CONCLUSION

In this chapter we have shown how HR practice needs to change if it is to be informed by evidence from academic research. Our research demonstrated the particular issues faced by the public sector and yet highlighted the dependence on evidence from the private sector. From our AE approach, we found that the public sector is a tough environment to "do" EE and to "be" engaged (Jones, 2012). HR practices to encourage EE need to be more holistic, more realistic and more aware of the constraints on EE imposed by the institutional conditions facing the public sector.

We know from (qualitative) research that EE is personal and dynamic, but current organizational initiatives do not reflect this knowledge. Surveys of EE have been recognized as a blunt tool for understanding EE (Purcell, 2010), yet many organizations rely on them as the single source of knowledge about EE in their organization. We demonstrate how our research, using an approach that blends the personal with the contextual, shows what needs to change in HR practice so that device EE is more context and people appropriate. Our AE-informed recommendations for HR professionals are more personal, emergent and small scale than has been the case with the more consultancy-informed or business-led EE initiatives. HR professionals will need to make the case for such an approach when more familiar consultancy-based approaches are on offer.

As the public sector is scrutinized continuously for its expenditures, we think that research-informed EE will help organizations demonstrate the evidence they need to deliver realistic and sustainable improvements in EE. We suggest HR practices need to be reoriented toward an approach that provides a much-needed rebalancing of the EE agenda toward meeting employee as well as organizational needs that is sensitive to the contemporary public sector. Until we research and practice EE in new ways, we will continue to depend on knowledge constructed in, and practices designed for, different sectors and different times. We encourage academic researchers to work with organizations and employ AE approaches with employees—and particularly HR professionals and line managers—to achieve this goal.

## NOTE

1. The "Engagement Index" (EI) is calculated as a weighted average of the responses to five questions in the survey, where a score of 100% represents all respondents giving a rating of strongly agree to all five questions and a score of 0% represents all respondents giving a rating of strongly disagree to all five questions. See Civil Service (2014) for more details. In 2009, the EI was 58%, which was also the case in 2013.

## REFERENCES

Albrecht, S. L. (2010). *Handbook of employee engagement*. Cheltenham, England: Edward Elgar.

Australian Public Service Commission. (2015). *Strategic directions 2011–2014*. Retrieved March 1, 2015, from http://www.apsc.gov.au/about-the-apsc/the-commission/strategic-directions-2011-14

Alfes, K., Truss, C., Soane, E. C., Rees, C., & Gatenby, M. (2010). *Creating an engaged workforce: Findings from the Kingston Employee Engagement Consortium Project*. Retrieved May 29, 2015, from http://www.cipd.co.uk/NR/rdonlyres/DD66E557-DB90-4F07-8198-87C3876F3371/0/Creating_engaged_workforce.pdf

Bach, S. (2011). *A new era of public service employment relations? The challenges ahead.* Retrieved May 29, 2015, from http://www.acas.org.uk/media/pdf/m/c/Future-workplace-relations-series-public-service-accessible-version-august-2011.pdf

Bakker, A. B., & Leiter, M. P. (2010). *Work engagement*. Hove, England: Psychology Press.

Cabinet Office (2015). *What works network*. Retrieved May 29, 2015, from https://www.gov.uk/what-works-network

Cameron, D. (2011). *Speech to the National Assembly for Wales, 12 July 2011*. Retrieved May 29, 2015, from http://www.number10.gov.uk/news/statement-to-the-national-assembly-for-wales/

Civil Service. (2013). *Civil Service People Survey 2012*. Retrieved May 29, 2015, from http://www.civilservice.gov.uk/wp-content/uploads/2013/01/csps2012_summary-of-findings_final.pdf

Civil Service. (2014). *Civil Service People Survey 2013*. Retrieved May 29, 2015, from http://www.civilservice.gov.uk/about/improving/employee-engagement-in-the-civil-service/people-survey-2013

Chartered Institute of Personnel and Development (CIPD). (2012). *Employee engagement*. Retrieved March 1, 2012, from http://www.cipd.co.uk/hr-topics/employee-engagement.aspx

Department for Business, Innovation and Skills. (2014): *Trade Union Membership 2013 Statistical Bulletin*. Retrieved May 29, 2015, from https://www.gov.uk/government/uploads/system/uploads/attachment_data/file/313768/bis-14-p77-trade-union-membership-statistical-bulletin-2013.pdf

Gregory, S., Dixon, A., & Ham, C. (2012). *Health policy under the coalition government*. London, England: The King's Fund.

Jenkins, S., & Delbridge, R. (2013). Context matters: Examining soft and hard approaches to employee engagement in two workplaces. *International Journal of Human Resource Management, 24*(14), 2670–2691.

Jones, N. (2012). *Full circle: Employee engagement in the Welsh Public Service* (Doctoral thesis). University of Bangor, Wales, UK.

Kahn, W. A. (1990). Psychological conditions of engagement and disengagement at work. *Academy of Management Journal, 33*(4), 692–724.

Kahn, W. A. (1992). To be fully there: Psychological presence at work. *Human Relations, 45*(4), 321–49.

Kinnie, N., Hutchinson, S., Purcell, J., Rayton, B., & Swart, J. (2005). Satisfaction with HR practices and commitment to the organisation: Why one size does not fit all. *Human Resource Management Journal, 15*(4), 9–29.

Luisis-Lynd, L., & Myers, P. (2011). *How, why and when organisations engage with employee engagement*. Retrieved May 29, 2015, from http://www.cipd.co.uk/NR/rdonlyres/C01B786F-563E-457A-A980-E2392041F1ED/0/LuisisLyndandMyers.pdf

Macey, W. H., Schneider, B., Barbera, K. M., & Young, S. A. (2009). *Employee engagement*. Chichester, England: Wiley Blackwell.

MacLeod, D., & Clarke, N. (2009). *Engaging for success*. London, England: Department for Business, Innovation and Skills.

Millard, B., & Machin, A. (2007). Characteristics of public sector workers. *Economic and Labour Market Review, 1*(5), 46–55.

Purcell, J. (2010): *Building employee engagement. ACAS policy discussion paper.* Retrieved May 29, 2015, from http://www.acas.org.uk/media/pdf/s/1/Building_employee_engagement-accessible-version-Jun-2012.pdf

Sambrook, S., Jones, N., & Doloriert, C. (2014). Employee engagement and autoethnography: Being and studying self. *Special Issue on Employee Engagement, Journal of Workplace Learning, 26*(3/4), 172–187.

Shuck, B., & Rocco, T. S. (2011). Exploring employee engagement from the employee perspective: implications for HRD. *Journal of European Industrial Training, 35*(4), 300–325.

Shuck, B., & Wollard, K. K. (2010). Employee engagement and HRD: A seminal review of the foundations. *Human Resource Development Review, 9*(1), 89–110.

Simpson, M. (2009). Engagement at work: A review of the literature. *International Journal of Nursing Studies, 46*(7), 1012–1024.

Truss, C., Soane, E., Edwards, C., Wisdom, K., Croll, A., & Burnett, J. (2006). *Working life: Employee attitudes and engagement 2006*. London, England: Chartered Institute of Personnel and Development.

Vance, R. (2006). *Effective practice guidelines: Employee engagement and commitment*. Alexandria VA: Society for Human Resource Management.

Wales Audit Office. (2011). *A picture of public services*. Cardiff, Wales Audit Office. Retrieved May 29, 2015, from http://www.wao.gov.uk/publication/picture-public-services-2011

Wall, S. (2006). An autoethnography on learning about autoethnography. *International Journal of Qualitative Methods, 5*(2), Article 9. Retrieved May 29, 2015, from www.ualberta.ca/~iiqm/backissues/5_2/html/wall.htm

Welsh Assembly Government. (2004). *Making the connections delivering better services for Wales*. Cardiff, Wales: Welsh Assembly Government.

Welsh Government. (2012). *Working differently, working together: A workforce and organisational development framework*. Retrieved May 29, 2015, from http://www.wales.gov.uk/topics/health/publications/health/strategies/working/?lang=en

CHAPTER 4

# EMPLOYEE COMMITMENT TO THE SUPERVISOR

## The Role of Side Bets

**Damian West**

Organizational commitment has become a much researched subject over the past 3 decades (Steijn & Leisink, 2006). Previous research has associated high commitment with increased productivity and decreased withdrawal behaviors such as turnover and absenteeism (Baba & Knoop, 1987; Mowday, Porter, & Steers 1982). Commitment to an organization has also been found to relate to a variety of desirable work outcomes including employee job satisfaction (Hackett, Bycio, & Hausdorf, 1994). Organizational commitment has been linked to absenteeism (Gellatly, 1995) and turnover intentions (Bateman & Stasser, 1984; Mathieu & Zajac, 1990; Mowday et al., 1982; Mowday, Steers, & Porter, 1979; Weiner & Vardi, 1980). Ostroff (1992) reported that committed employees are associated with better organizational performance. Recent research suggests there is a positive relationship between affective commitment and in-role performance (Allen & Meyer, 1996; McElroy, 2001).

This research examined the relationship between the traditional components of affective, normative and continuance commitment, including

*Human Capital Management Research: Influencing Practice and Process*
pp. 47–61
Copyright © 2016 by Information Age Publishing
All rights of reproduction in any form reserved.

the concept of side bets on the foci of employee commitment to the supervisor. The research was designed to develop a deeper understanding of how commitment works in practice from the perspective of the employee and extends our understanding of how employee commitment is fostered and works in large public sector organizations. A key finding of this research highlighted that employees believe they invest considerable effort into the development of the relationship with their supervisor. This is significant for Australian Public Service (APS) organizations and the 150,000 employees (Australian Public Service Commission, 2014) who work across these organizations.

According to side-bet theory, organizational commitment will increase with the accumulation of side bets (Cohen & Gattiker, 1992). Becker (1960) suggests that employees who devote time and effort in mastering tasks or skills are betting that the time and effort invested will pay off, but winning requires continued employment in the organization. This research explores the concept that "side bets" are transferable to the employee-supervisor relationship. What is found is that employees report a desire and willingness to invest in, and build, a strong relationship with their supervisor due to the fact that this investment is perceived to lead to positive outcomes for the employee.

The research provides considerable new insight and knowledge on how commitment works by providing empirical evidence on how the concept of side bets operate from the perspective of the employee. This research extends side-bet theory by introducing a two stage side bet decision-making process. The current paradigm of employee commitment is built on the concept that it is the relationship between the employee and the organization that forms the basis of employee commitment. This research has demonstrated that the size and structure of the organizational and the people management policies used by the organization can create the situation where the idea of a relationship or link between the employee and the organization has been brought into question. As a result there has been a change in the way that employee commitment is developed and works.

## WHAT IS KNOWN?

The current paradigm of employee commitment is built on the concept that it is the relationship between the employee and the organization that forms the basis of employee commitment. Most of the previous research undertaken on commitment explores the construct of commitment from the perspective of the impact of employee commitment on the organization, and organizational outcomes. There have been few studies which attempt to explore employee commitment from the perspective of the employee and which seek to identify how employee commitment works from the employee perspective.

Employee commitment to the organization has often been conceptualized as part of the exchange agreement between the individual and the organization (e.g., Angle & Perry, 1981; Rousseau, 1995). Social exchange theory (Blau, 1964) suggests that employees are motivated to seek a fair and balanced exchange with their organization (Homans, 1961). This research demonstrates that organizational size and management practices can lead to a change in the way the commitment works. As a result, an employee's ability to develop and maintain a relationship with their supervisor could become critical to the fulfilment of the exchange agreement and broader issues of retention and employee engagement. It may also suggest that employees will actively seek to link and remain working for a particular supervisor. It suggests that much of the literature on building employee commitment is incomplete.

## LOCATION OF THE RESEARCH

The Australian Government impacts the lives of all Australians. The APS plays a critical role in assisting the Government to implement its objectives and meet the responsibilities that are placed upon the government. The APS has over 150,000 employees (Australian Public Service Commission, 2014) who, in the main, work in policy, regularity, service delivery and implementation roles.

The APS was established as a bureaucracy (Parkin, Summers, & Woodward, 1994) with a set of instructions that directed and controlled activities with typical autocratic rule by management. The APS is a professional, nonpartisan service dedicated to assisting the government of the day to provide service to the citizen and meet forthcoming policy.

The research participants were drawn from one large APS organization. The organization was established to provide Australian Government services to the Australian public. The participant target group for the research was employees who work within the policy and/or service delivery implementation sections of the national support office in Canberra. The participant target group was chosen because of their level and the generalist nature of the work undertaken by the group (project, implementation, maintenance activities, etc.). The specific choice of the target group should assist the transferability of findings to other settings.

The nature of the research was inductive it aimed to demonstrate how and why employee commitment to supervisor is developed. The research focused on learning and inducting from the data to build understanding of the phenomena. The research design supported this explorative approach and allowed the researcher to build understanding in this manner, it included a contructivist research paradigm, case study approach, qualitative methodology and method (semistructured in-depth interviews) that comprise the research framework.

## HOW IS EMPLOYEE COMMITMENT DEVELOPED?

Currently, there is little empirical research that explores how continuance commitment and the concept of side bets are influenced by the relationship between the employee and the supervisor. The findings of this research indicated that the majority of employees have a desire and willingness to invest in, and build, a strong relationship with their supervisor. The underpinning premise is that this investment would lead to positive outcomes for the employee.

The literature on side bets and continuance commitment is best described by Becker (1960) who states that the term "side bets" refers to anything the individual has "invested" (time, effort, money) that would be lost if the individual was to leave the organization. Allen and Meyer (1990, p. 3) state that this commitment can be developed by "the individual's recognition of the costs associated with discontinuing the activity or leaving the organization." Fundamental to both of these definitions of side bets is the concept of leaving the organization. This research explored two aspects of the concept of side bets as they relate to the employee-supervisor commitment. First, whether the "side bets" that employees believe they invest in the development and maintenance of their relationship with the supervisor are consistent with those described by the literature on organizational commitment. Second, whether side bets are perceived to be lost if the individual leaves or fractures the employee-supervisor relationship?

The findings indicated that participants believed they invested considerable effort into the development of the relationship with their supervisor. The analysis identified that the side bets that employees invest in the development of the relationship with the supervisor included time, energy, physical and emotional effort. In several cases the side bet was reported as being available to do "whatever was required whenever it was required". This was done with the belief that this action would be recognized and that the employees effort would be rewarded.

The research confirmed the existence of side bets and the form that these side bets assume as described by the current literature. The findings confirm the work of Griffin and Batemen (1996) who suggested that side-bet theory is an exchange-based approach to commitment. This research has identified that employees believe that they would receive beneficial outcomes in recognition of the contribution they have made in the workplace. What is different from previous research is that the employees have linked the beneficial outcomes they receive directly to helping the supervisor.

This research expands the literature on commitment by identifying that side bets exist between employee and supervisor. This is a significant finding and provides further evidence of how the concept of employee commitment to supervisor works. It also provides evidence that employees in large public sector organizations perceive their investment of effort or side bets should be targeted toward the needs and requirements of the supervisor.

This finding has clear ramifications for large public sector organizations in terms of the potential to reduce or damage employee motivation if action is taken by the organization that has the potential to damage this relationship. This finding may also explain employment trends within the APS particularly pertaining to mobility, as employees will be less likely to fracture the relationship with the supervisor in order to seek opportunities elsewhere. Finally, the finding also suggests that organizational change initiatives and restructures have the potential to disenfranchise employees who perceive their side bets are lost as a result of a fractured employee-supervisor relationship.

The literature on side bets suggests that the consequences associated with leaving an organization increase with age and tenure due to the time and effort that an employee has invested within the organization. Hackett, Bycio, and Hausdorf (1994) reported a significant relationships between continuance commitment and both age and tenure. Analysis was undertaken to explore whether employees considered that the investment of time, effort and emotional energy required to develop and maintain the relationship with the supervisor increased the perceived side bets that would be lost if the relationship was fractured. The findings indicated that participants believed that the greater the investment they had made in building and maintaining the relationship with the supervisor, the more difficult it was to leave or fracture the relationship.

This finding provides strong evidence of the impact of side bets on employee commitment to the supervisor and the extent to which the supervisor has become the key figure in public service organizations. It also confirmed that side bets are transferable to the construct of employee-supervisor commitment.

Analysis also identified a supporting correlation whereby participants who did not believe they had invested a lot into the development of the relationship with the supervisor, or who thought that the investment had not resulted in positive outcomes found the decision to fracture the relationship easier. This result provides a clear example of the concept of the exchange approach to commitment in action, the failure of one party to fulfill the exchange agreement ultimately limiting the development of commitment from the other party.

> I believe I do invest a large amount, it takes a lot of my time and you have to give extra effort, where I feel I have not put so much into the relationship it is easier to leave.

> I have an example where I had put a lot into a previous relationship at work, this effort was not acknowledged so in the end it was an easy decision to go, I was not getting anywhere and I was putting in all the effort.

> I do put a lot into the relationship and I am not prepared to walk away quickly but once I get to the point where I feel this has not been recognized I don't care how much work that I have put in. I walk away.

The findings indicate that the level of the investment, or side bet, between supervisor and employees operates in the same manner as the traditional understanding of the concept in fostering commitment. It demonstrated that the accumulation of side bets have a direct impact on employee commitment to the supervisor. Moreover it has identified that the greater the perceived investment in the relationship the more employees considered they potentially stand to lose should the relationship with the supervisor be fractured. What has also been highlighted is that where the investment is not considerable or where there has been little beneficial outcome that the decision to leave the supervisor is much easier. This confirms the longstanding understanding of the impact of side bets on commitment. However an important question was raised: how much time will an employee invest in developing a relationship before deciding the relationship is not beneficial to them?

## EMPLOYEES INVEST THEIR TIME TO BUILD A RELATIONSHIP

The previous section identified that the concept of side bets was transferable to the construct of employee-supervisor commitment. Given the importance of the relationship between the employee and the supervisor participants were asked how long they believed it took to build a relationship with a supervisor, and what length of time would they invest in developing a relationship with a supervisor before making a decision that the relationship was likely or not to be beneficial.

The findings indicate that participants believed they could quickly identify and make a judgment on the likelihood that a relationship with the supervisor could be beneficial to them. For the majority of participants this decision could be made within 3 months.

The findings also demonstrate that employees will form a judgment about the potential of a relationship with the supervisor and, therefore make an early assessment and a decision to stay or leave, very early in the working relationship. This research identified that due to the devolved management practices employees in large public sector organizations recognize the employee-supervisor relationship has a critical impact on employee development, and the opportunities they receive in the workplace. The findings indicate that employees are less likely to invest significant effort if they consider the relationship is not likely to provide beneficial outcomes.

This is consistent with an exchange based approach to commitment and it suggests that employees are aware that the supervisor is critical to their experience in the workplace and that they will make a decision about the potential of a relationship with the supervisor to deliver positive outcomes within a short period of time. It also highlighted that once an employee had determined that they could develop an effective and beneficial relationship with a supervisor the employees were willing to invest a considerable period of time to build the relationship. Participants reported that it took 6 to 12 months to build a strong relationship with the supervisor.

Further exploration of this issue identified that participants believed their relationship with the supervisor needed to be tested across a range of situations and under varying degrees of work pressure before they would make a decision on the true worth of the relationship relative to the investment they had made.

This research adds to the knowledge on side-bet theory by introducing a two stage side-bet decision-making process as illustrated in Figure 4.1. The analysis has identified a new element to the commitment model which provides new insight into how commitment develops and the actions that support this process. The research indicated that an employee will invest a set amount of time to develop and test their relationship with the supervisor. After this period the employee will make an assessment and decision on the perceived worth of the relationship, and whether it is beneficial for them to stay or that they are best to leave. The decision to stay and, therefore, to invest further in the development of the relationship increases the side bets that the employee has invested in the relationship. Employees were aware that this also meant that they would have more to lose should the relationship not work out.

This provides new evidence into how concept of commitment to the supervisor works in practice, providing new insight into how the accumulation of side bets directly impacts the employee commitment to the

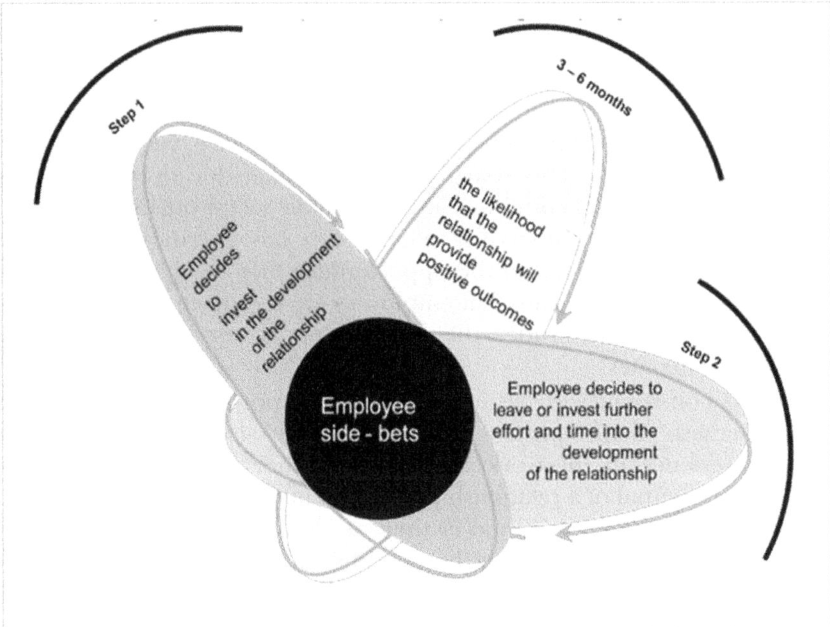


Figure 4.1. Two step side-bet process impacting employee-commitment.

supervisor. The greater the perceived investment in the relationship, the more employees considered they potentially stand to lose should the relationship be fractured.

The current understanding of side-bet theory, based on the concept of commitment to the organization, suggests that the accumulation of side bets will build continuance commitment and therefore commitment to the organization. The two stage process, as presented in Figure 1, emerged as a new concept resulting from the increased significance of the supervisor and the emergence of the concept of employee commitment to the supervisor. In the first stage, the employee quickly determines the likelihood of the development of a successful relationship with the supervisor. In the second stage the employee then makes a second side-bet decision to invest a further amount of time to develop and test the relationship.

This research has found that employees perceive that a return on their investment should start to occur from the 12-month mark. This finding raises the question: what is the impact of fracturing the employee-supervisor relationship? Is this the same as the traditional understanding of side bets which would suggest that these side bets are linked to the primary relationship? Therefore, from the perspective of the employee, maintaining the relationship with the supervisor is critical for realization of the side bet.

## THE IMPACT OF FRACTURING THE EMPLOYEE-SUPERVISOR RELATIONSHIP

There is little empirical evidence on the employee perception of the costs associated with fracturing the employee-supervisor relationship. In describing a traditional perspective of organization commitment Meyer and Allen (1984) state that side bets refer to anything of value the individual has invested that would be lost if he or she was to leave the organization. To explore whether the concept of a lost investment was transferable to the construct of commitment to the supervisor, participants were asked what they perceived were consequences of fracturing the employee-supervisor relationship. The findings indicated that if the relationship with the supervisor was fractured, all of the effort in developing the relationship with the supervisor and the potential for future benefits were lost.

> If you leave the supervisor, or they leave, you lose all the effort that you have put into that relationship.
>
> The effort is lost, this has happened to me when my last supervisor left the organization, they knew how I operated and had the history and knowledge of how I worked and what I had achieved.
>
> It becomes wasted effort. The fact is that only the current supervisor knows the amount of effort and the work that you have put into something. I think the biggest thing that you lose is the development opportunities that stem from a good relationship.
>
> I don't think that the knowledge they have on what you have done and the effort you have put is transferable to the next supervisor so the effort is lost.

This is a key finding as it suggests that the side bets that serve to strengthen commitment to the supervisor operate in the same manner as the traditional understanding of continuance commitment. Further analysis identified that, in addition to the perception that the effort invested in building the relationship was lost, participants also believed that access to future opportunities and, therefore, their career, was impacted when this occurred.

> "The effort is lost, but it is more than this as you also lose access to future opportunities. The supervisor knew exactly what you did and what you were

> capable of. When the change happens it is virtually a clean slate and you might not get the same sort of opportunities.

> All the effort is lost and in the situation of the supervisor leaving your career can stall for a period as it takes time to build a new relationship.

> I feel that if you leave a supervisor you lose a lot of the benefits that you have built up. I have seen a number of supervisors move on, each of who were good mentors and at the time were teaching me a lot, not being able to gain from their experience and what they can teach had an impact on my career development.

> What you have developed and the outcomes that you experience are not transferable. I think that you lose all of the intangibles, so it is a waste of your time and effort.

This finding has strong implications for employee motivation and engagement. It could result in higher turnover or lead to disengaged and disempowered employees. It suggests that when the employee-supervisor relationship is fractured employees feel that they have to start again from the beginning and build a relationship with the new supervisor. It highlights that employees believed that they were disadvantaged by this, and that they would have to invest greater effort into the new relationship to ensure that they limited the disadvantage experienced by the loss or fracture of the previous relationship.

This finding provides evidence of the importance of the employee-supervisor relationship and the implications of fracturing the relationship for employees. Analysis of the data identified that employees feared that any fracture of the relationship could create the situation where they could end up in a situation where they could not develop a relationship with the supervisor. This would result in wasted effort, and create the situation where they would need to move on and therefore invest even more effort to develop a relationship that provided the same level of outcomes that they currently received.

The research demonstrates that employees perceive there are clear consequences associated with the fracturing the relationship with a supervisor. This includes the perception that the side bets invested in building the relationship and the outcomes from this investment are lost. Furthermore, employees believe that there is a risk that they may have to invest considerable effort, at worst on a number of occasions, before they experience benefits similar to those they associated with their current supervisor. This research extends the concept of continuance commitment and side bets beyond the current definition of an attachment or linking of the employee to the organization, thereby indicating that the concept of continuance commitment and side bets is transferable to the construct of employee-supervisor commitment.

## SIDE BET REEMERGE IF THE EMPLOYEE RELINKS

The findings of this research indicated that if the employee-supervisor relationship was fractured the benefits that the employee received as a result of the effort they had invested in the relationship could be lost. In response to this finding participants were asked a supplementary question which explored the concept that if the employee relinked with the supervisor at a later stage would the benefits they had experienced during the previous relationship return? There is little, if any, literature on the concept of side-bet reemergence on the occasion of an employee relinking with a previous supervisor.

This research adds to the knowledge and literature by identifying the reemergence of side-bet outcomes if the employee relinks with a supervisor. The findings highlighted that the majority of participants believed, based on their own experience, that if they relinked with a supervisor with whom they had a strong relationship that many, if not all, of the positive outcomes that they had previously experienced, such as autonomy, trust, and high levels of communication would return. This finding suggests that employee side bets are not restricted to a point in time relationship with the supervisor. This is a significant finding in relation to our understanding of commitment and how commitment works in practice.

## INVESTING IN THE FUTURE

According to the traditional view of side-bet theory, organizational commitment will increase with the accumulation of side bets (Cohen & Gattiker, 1992). This research found that the concept of side bets is transferable to the employee-supervisor relationship. The research has also identified that employees perceive that they invest considerable effort (side bets) in developing and maintaining a relationship with their supervisor, and that this investment often can lead to beneficial outcomes for the employee. This research has also confirmed the importance of the supervisor in a large public sector organization in relation to the provision of development of career opportunities.

There is, however, little empirical research that explores the concept that an employee will invest effort into a relationship due to their perception that the supervisor is likely to be successful, which may, in turn, provide greater opportunities for the employee into the future. To explore this concept the participants were asked if they had assisted their supervisor in a manner which, as a result, would enhance the performance and standing of the supervisor and, if so, what was the motivation for this action?

The findings indicated that the majority of the participants believed they individually went well beyond the standard requirement and that they had directly assisted the supervisor to achieve outcomes that would increase the standing of the supervisor within the organization. The data highlighted that employees will invest effort that would as a result increase the performance and standing of the supervisor. However, it was also revealed that a large number of the participants had strategically aligned themselves with an identified supervisor due to their belief that this person would be successful. The analysis highlighted that the majority of participants believed that as they had invested considerable effort into building a strong relationship with the supervisor they had an interest in the continued success of the supervisor as this may provide opportunities for the employee.

This research has expanded the literature on continuance commitment by introducing the concept that employees actively invest effort (side bets) which the employees consider have the potential to provide both short and long-term outcomes. This finding provides further evidence of the perceived importance of the supervisor in a large public sector organization. It also clearly highlights the extent to which employees now believe that it is the supervisor, rather than the organization, which has the strongest influence on their career. This research introduces the concept that employees will actively target and invest effort into a relationship with a supervisor who they believe is likely to have a successful career as this could provide benefits and outcomes to the employee in the future. In this situation the employee is not only investing effort with the expectation of a return in the short term, the effort is considered to be an investment in future opportunities as well.

The concept of a form of employee commitment based on the idea that the employee will, at a later stage, receive a positive outcome from the investment (side bets) has not been explored in the literature. This research acknowledges that for this to occur it requires the supervisor to be successful and for the employee to relink with the supervisor at a later stage. The failure of either to occur will render the side bet as unrealized. Regardless, the findings of this section suggest that employees in large public sector organizations have low expectations of the organizations role in providing for future opportunities and will invest effort into building and strengthening the relationship that they have with their supervisor with the view that this investment will also provide future positive outcomes. The analysis has identified that employees believe that it is from a strong network of relationships that future opportunities will emerge.

## CONCLUSION

The objective of this research was to explore employee perception of the investment that is required to develop and maintain a strong relationship with the supervisor, and to identify the outcomes and impact of this investment on the employee-supervisor relationship. The research demonstrated that the concept of side bets was transferable to the employee-supervisor relationship and that the accumulation of side bets between employee and supervisor serves to strengthen employee commitment to the supervisor. The research also highlighted that time, effort and emotional energy were considered by employees as their investment (side bets).

The research found that the majority of participants reported a desire and willingness to invest in, and build, a strong relationship with their supervisor and that, in their view this will provide a range of outcomes including increased autonomy. Participants reported that they believe the strength of the relationship with the supervisor largely determines the opportunities and rewards that they received. The importance of feedback and trust between supervisor and employee were confirmed. The research also introduced a two stage framework for employee side bets. The first stage is the decision by the employee to invest up to 3 months to determine the likelihood of a strong relationship forming between the supervisor and the employee. The second stage requires a further decision to invest up to 12 months to build a strong relationship with the supervisor. It was reported that this was the point at which employees consider that they would start to experience benefits such as greater autonomy.

The research also identified that if the relationship with the supervisor is fractured the side bets and benefits are potentially lost. It was also highlighted that if the employee relinked with the supervisor the benefits and outcomes they previously experienced were likely to reemerge. Finally, the research highlighted that employees will target and invest considerable effort to build a strong relationship with supervisors who they feel have high potential. This decision is made with the view that if the supervisor is successful this could lead to greater opportunities for the employee into the future.

The implication of the findings of this research is that the construct of employee commitment in its present form is incomplete and it should be expanded. It also suggests that the way commitment is fostered within organizations needs to be reexamined to take into account the role of the supervisor. This research adds significant insight into the impact of organizational size and management practices on the development of employee commitment, which prior to this research had received little attention in the literature.

The research has explored the development of commitment from the perspective of the employee. The findings of this research provide new insight into how employee commitment works and how it is developed. The research has identified a range of drivers that support the development of employee commitment to the supervisor.

The fulfillment of the exchange agreement by the supervisor, for example the provision of recognition and rewards, has been reported to foster the development of employee commitment to the supervisor. However; there is a risk that should the supervisor fail to fulfill the exchange agreement in a manner acceptable by the employee, the employee's level of commitment and their performance is likely to be impacted.

The existence of the foci of employee commitment to the supervisor should be given deep consideration by the organizations due to the fact that employees who do not have a strong relationship with their supervisor may consider that they were disadvantaged. This could result in a reduction in the effort that they put into their work and increased absence and turnover. However, the benefits from the development of commitment to the supervisor could be used by the organization to achieve higher levels of performance and support a highly committed workforce.

## REFERENCES

Allen, N. J., & Meyer, J. P. (1990). The measurement and antecedents of affective, continuance and normative commitment to the organization. *Journal of Occupational Psychology, 63*(1), 1–19.

Allen, N. J., & Meyer, J. P. (1996). Affective, continuance and normative commitment to the organization: An examination of construct validity. *Journal of Vocational Behavior, 49*(3), 252–276.

Angle, H., & Perry, J. (1981). An empirical assessment of organizational commitment and organizational effectiveness. *Administrative Science Quarterly, 26*(1), 1–14.

Australian Public Service Commission. (2014). State of the Service Report, State of the Service Series 2013-14. *Australian Government, Canberra, Australia*. Retrieved from http://www.apsc.gov.au.

Baba, V. V., & Knopp, R. (1987). Organizational commitment and independence among Canadian managers. *Relations Industrielles, 42*, 325–343.

Bateman, T. S., & Strasser, S. (1984). A longitudinal analysis of the antecedents of organizational commitment. *Academy of Management Journal, 27*(1), 95–112.

Becker, H. S. (1960). Notes on the concept of commitment. *American Journal of Sociology, 66*(1), 32–40.

Blau, P. (1964). *Exchange and power in social life*. New York, NY: John Wiley.

Cohen, A., & Gattiker, U. E (1992). An empirical assessment of organization commitment using the side-bet theory approach. *Industrial Relations, 47*(3), 439–461.

Gellatly, I. R. (1995). Individual and group determinants of employee absenteeism: Test of a causal model. *Journal of Organizational Behavior, 16*(5), 469-485.

Griffin, R. W., & Bateman, T. S. (1986). Job satisfaction and organizational commitment. In C. L. Cooper & T. Robertson (Eds). *International review of industrial and organizational psychology* (pp. 157–188). New York, NY: John Wiley.

Hackett, R. D., Bycio, P., & Hausdorf, P. A. (1994). Further assessments of Meyer and Allen's (1991) three-component model of organizational commitment. *Journal of Applied Psychology, 79*(1), 15–23.

Homans, G. C. (1961). *Social behavior: Its elementary forms*. New York, NY: Harcourt.

Mathieu, J. E., & Zajac, D. (1990). A review and meta-analysis of the antecedents correlates, and consequences of organizational commitment. *Psychological Bulletin, 108*(2),171–194.

McElroy, J. C. (2001). Managing workplace commitment by putting people first. *Human Resource Management Review, 11*(3), 327–335.

Meyer, J. P., & Allen, N. J. (1984). Testing the "side bet theory" of organizational commitment: Some methodological considerations. *Journal of Applied Psychology, 69*(3), 372–337.

Mowday, R. T., Porter, L. W., & Steers, R. M. (1982). *Employee-organization linkages: The psychology of commitment, absenteeism, and turnover*. New York, NY: Academic Press.

Mowday, R. T., Steers, R. M., & Porter, L. W. (1979). The measurement of organizational commitment. *Journal of Vocational Behavior, 14*(2), 224–247.

Ostroff, C. (1992). The relationship between satisfaction, attitudes and performance: An organizational level analysis. *Journal of Applied Psychology, 77*(6), 963–974.

Parkin, A., Summers, J., & Woodward, D. (1994). *Government, politics, power and policy in Australia* (5th ed.). Melbourne, Australia: Longman Australia.

Rousseau, D. M. (1995). *Psychological contracts in organizations: Understanding written and unwritten agreements*. London, England: SAGE.

Steijn, B., & Leisink, P. (2006). Organizational commitment among Dutch public sector employees. *International Review of Administrative Sciences, 72*(2), 187–201.

Weiner, Y., & Vardi, Y. (1980). Relationships between job, organization and career commitments and work outcomes—An integrative approach. *Organizational Behavior and Human Performance, 26*, 81–96.

# CHAPTER 5

# A THREE-STAGE APPROACH FOR THE DIAGNOSIS AND REDUCTION OF EMPLOYEE TURNOVER

**Gerrit J. M. Treuren and Julie Goods**

## INTRODUCTION

Talent, skill, and labor shortage in some occupational groups and underemployment in others are features of modern employment (Smith, 2014). New technologies, the contraction of primary production and manufacturing, and the ongoing growth in services will see the growth in demand for some skills, and reduced demand for other skills (Healy, Mavromaras, & Sloane, 2012). Although fluctuating with the economy (Department of Employment, 2014), key employees with particular skills or high potential will be harder to find and keep. Consequently, employers will seek new and improved methods of retaining employees (Hays, 2014).

Until recently, the consensus held employee turnover to be a consequence of employee dissatisfaction (Holtom, Mitchell, Lee, & Eberly, 2008). This dissatisfaction may arise from job characteristics such as boring or unpleasant work, lack of autonomy, poor pay, or from managerial practices—such as abusive supervision, poor communication, or arbitrary decision making (Allen, Bryant, & Vardaman, 2010). In these accounts,

*Human Capital Management Research: Influencing Practice and Process*
pp. 63–80
Copyright © 2016 by Information Age Publishing
All rights of reproduction in any form reserved.

dissatisfied employees would seek out alternative jobs and leave when a suitable alternative is found (March & Simon, 1958).

Although intuitive, such accounts provide limited insight into the turnover seen in the workplace. For example, the dissatisfaction-job alternative theory does not explain why an employee might leave one employer to work for a similar employer down the road for similar pay and conditions or why a long-serving employee might suddenly quit with no job to go to. Further, Griffeth, Hom, and Gaertner's (2000) authoritative meta-analysis of employee turnover suggests that such accounts explain fewer than one in three job leavers.

A group of researchers based at the University of Washington have developed a set of turnover and retention theories that substantially overcome these deficiencies. The unfolding theory of turnover (UFT, Lee & Mitchell, 1994) supplements the traditional dissatisfaction-job framework by introducing several new concepts—employee shock, plans, and image violation—enabling a substantially more nuanced analysis of the turnover process. Job embeddedness theory (JET, Mitchell, Holtom, Lee, Sablynski, & Erez, 2001) provides an explanation of why one employee in an organization would stay in response to circumstances that would lead another employee to leave. Proximal withdrawal state (Hom, Mitchell, Lee & Griffeth, 2012) theory establishes a framework for identifying employees who have a higher likelihood of leaving.

This chapter will provide an introduction to these new approaches before outlining a way that employers can apply these theories to the diagnosis and minimization of their organization's voluntary turnover problems. Aspects of these theories will be illustrated using recent employee survey and exit interview data from a large, multisite aged care facility in South Australia.

## WHY DO PEOPLE LEAVE? THE UNFOLDING THEORY OF TURNOVER

Lee and Mitchell's UFT (1994) extends the traditional theory of turnover and explains why satisfied employees might leave a job or why an employee might leave with no job alternatives. The UFT recognizes the role of employee dissatisfaction and job alternatives, but with the three new components of employee shock, employee plans and image violation, identifies five distinct turnover paths (Table 5.1).

### Shocks, Plans, and Image Violation

The first new component is a *shock*. A shock is any event that prompts a re-appraisal of current employment circumstances. This event may be

**Table 5.1. Prototypes Associated With the Unfolding Model's Pathways**

| *Path* | *Shock* | *Plan* | *Image Violation* | *History of Dissatisfaction* | *Alternative Job Opportunity* | *Speed of Decision Making* | *Typical Examples* |
|---|---|---|---|---|---|---|---|
| 1 | ✓ Usually expected and nonjob related | ✓ | | | | Quick | A student works as a personal care worker while undertaking nursing studies, resigning to take up a registered nurse role after graduating. |
| 2 | ✓ Usually a negative organizational event | | ✓ | | | Quick | An unpleasant altercation with a client leaves the employee shocked and unwilling to continue working. |
| 3 | ✓ Usually an unexpected job offer | | ✓ | | ✓ | Medium | A registered nurse is offered a role as a nurse educator at a nearby aged care organization with better pay and more convenient hours. |
| 4a | | | ✓ | ✓ | | Long build up but quick decision to leave | After months of dreading coming to work, a personal care employee suddenly decides to resign without an alternative job. |
| 4b | | | ✓ | ✓ | ✓ | Slow | After several years of growing dissatisfaction, the employee realizes that he or she is unhappy with his or her job, initiates a job search, quitting when an acceptable alternative is found. |

*Source:* Kulik, Treuren, and Bordia (2012).

expected or unexpected, from inside or outside the organization and may be positive, negative or neutral in its personal significance (Holtom, Mitchell, Lee, & Inderrieden, 2005). Examples of shocks in our aged care sample include a partner being offered a job in a different city; becoming eligible for the pension; a drop in client numbers below a sustainable level; the announcement of a restructure; an altercation between the employee and client or manager; or the offer of a voluntary redundancy package. The shock prompts the employee to think about the relative merits of staying and leaving, and may lead to a decision to resign. UFT research suggests that up to two thirds of leaving decisions result from shocks (Kulik, Treuren, & Bordia, 2012).

The second new component is a *plan*. A plan is an employee's intention to carry out a particular activity when the right circumstances arise. Usually a plan is unrelated to an employee's current job, and is shaped by the employee's broader life—such as their family, their career, or their aspirations for their life. A plan is typically only activated after a shock occurs (Lee, Mitchell, Wise, & Fireman, 1996). Examples of plans include saving enough money to start a new business or start traveling, or to work until falling pregnant. In our aged care sample, plan-based leaving was mostly associated with the completion of studies: several personal care workers left once they had completed their registered nursing qualifications to take up a role that better used their new credentials.

The third new component is *image violation*. A shock prompts an employee to evaluate their current circumstances. This reevaluation involves the employee comparing their postshock view—their image—of their current circumstances with the preshock image of their work and their life. If the preexisting image is significantly threatened—violated, in the language of the UFT—the employee is prompted to reassess their commitment and ongoing employment within that organization, potentially leading to a turnover decision. The aged care exit interview reported several cases of image violation such as perceived unfair treatment during a restructuring, workplace bullying, negative feedback from a supervisor during a performance review, and an unwanted reduction in hours.

These three components are supplemented by the two features of the dissatisfaction-alternatives model. A history of *dissatisfaction* with the job or organization is clearly an important reason for leaving a job, as is the existence of an *alternative job opportunity*.

## Separation Paths

Table 5.2 shows the distribution of these turnover paths in our aged care example. Three of these pathways are initiated by shocks. In the first,

**Table 5.2. Length of Service and Time Taken to Decide to Leave, in Months and Pathway**

| | | | *Months of Thinking About Leaving Before Resigning* | |
|---|---|---|---|---|
| | *Mean* | *%* | *Mean* | *SD* |
| Pathway 1 | Shock based | 5.8 | — | — |
| Pathway 2 | Shock based | 15.4 | 1.9 | 2.2 |
| Pathway 3 | Shock based | 19.2 | 2.7 | 2.6 |
| Pathway 4a | Dissatisfaction based | 15.4 | 6.9 | 11.9 |
| Pathway 4b | Dissatisfaction based | 17.3 | 4.4 | 4.0 |
| Retirement | Other | 15.4 | 7.8 | 5.9 |
| Unclassifiable | Other | 11.5 | 5.2 | 4.1 |
| | | 100% | 4.8 | 6.2 |

*Source:* Unpublished data, Centre for Human Resource Management, University of South Australia.

*Notes:* $n = 53$; Pathway 1 mean and standard deviation unable to be calculated because of missing data.

*Pathway 1*, the shock takes the form of an event that triggers a preexisting plan that involves leaving the organization. Typically, the shock is expected and unrelated to the organization and does not involve dissatisfaction or image violation. Examples of Pathway 1 include leaving after having graduated from one's nursing or physiotherapy studies and then taking up a role that requires those qualifications, or retiring having reached the age of pension eligibility. As the employee has clearly established the various steps within their plan, once a plan is activated, the employee usually decides to leave very quickly, with little further deliberation.

The other two shock-based paths depend on the existence of a shock and an image violation. In Pathway 2, the shock event creates an image violation that *pushes* the employee from their job very quickly. Usually the shock was so sudden and distressing that the employee felt obliged to leave, without arranging a new position. Examples from our aged care sample of shocks leading to Pathway 2 turnover include an allegation of misbehavior, negative feedback following a promotion application and disappointment at management's handling of a grievance. For these leavers, Pathway 2 leavers took an average of 1.9 months to decide to leave after the shock.

In Pathway 3, an employee is *pulled* toward a new and better opportunity. Here the shock is an event—commonly a job offer, often unsolicited—that prompts the employee to compare the new option with their current circumstances. The employee then decides to leave. Unlike Pathway 2, this event is usually positive. Typically the employee is not unhappy with their job before the shock event; dissatisfaction only emerges *after* the shock, sparked by the image violation created by the comparison of the new opportunity with the current job. The classic Pathway 3 departure is the unexpected offer of a new, superior role in another organization.

Pathway 3 exits usually take longer than Pathway 2, as the employee needs to choose between the current job and the new opportunity. In the aged care sample, Pathway 3 leavers took an average of 2.7 months to decide to leave after the shock.

Turnover is driven by dissatisfaction in Pathways 4a and 4b. This dissatisfaction builds over time. In Pathway 4a, the employee suddenly decides to leave without having found an alternative job. In Pathway 4b, the decision to leave is only made when there is a clear alternative—a job or the perceived likelihood of another suitable role—to go to. This pathway is the UFT equivalent of the March and Simon (1958) account of turnover. In some cases, an employee may decide to leave because of a "final straw"—a shocklike event that confirms previous dissatisfaction and prompts the employee to finally resign (Kulik et al., 2012). Turnover through Pathways 4a and 4b is likely to be the slowest of all UFT departure pathways, as the intention to leave grows over time with mounting dissatisfaction. In the aged care sample, Pathway 4a leavers left after 6.9 months of deliberation and Pathway 4b leavers left after 4.4 months of deliberation.

## WHY DO PEOPLE STAY? JOB EMBEDDEDNESS THEORY

Mitchell et al.'s (2001) JET holds that employees stay with an organization because of a unique set of affective, cognitive and material attachments that exists between them, their organization and their life outside of work that binds them to the organization. Highly embedded employees are less likely to leave an organization due to a shock or dissatisfaction compared to less highly embedded employees as employee embeddedness buffers the leaving intention and effect of a shock (Burton, Holtom, Sablynski, Mitchell, & Lee, 2010) (Figure 5.1).

The buffering effect of employee embeddedness is apparent in our aged care sample. Employees with higher levels of on-the-job embeddedness reported a lower intention to leave than employees with lower levels of embeddedness when experiencing psychological contract breach (Figure 5.2).

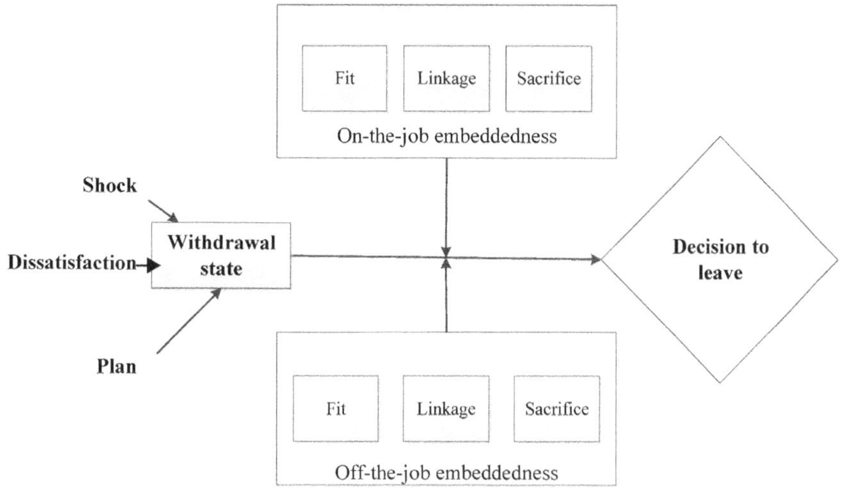


Figure 5.1. Employee embeddedness as a buffer to shock, dissatisfaction, and plan.

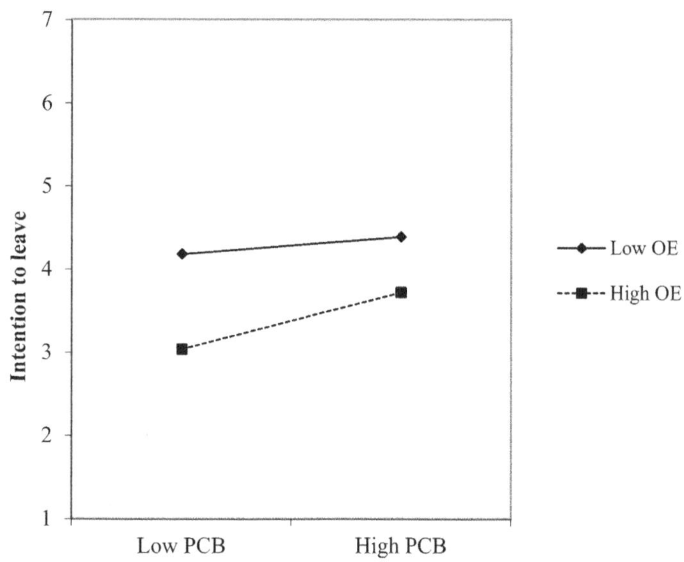


*Source:* Unpublished data, Centre for Human Resource Management, University of South Australia

Figure 5.2. Employee organizational embeddedness (OE) as a buffer to the negative effect of psychological contract breach (PCB) on leaving intention.

An employee's embeddedness has three dimensions. The first dimension is the *fit* of the employee to the job and the organization. Here fit is understood as the extent to which the employee's skills, attitude, approach and values are congruent with those of the organization, the work and other employees. The greater the fit, the greater the embeddedness.

The second dimension relates to the level of *linkage*—the level of involvement, connection and incorporation of the individual into the organization. This can be formal, such as the level of responsibility the individual has for decisions within the organization, or the number of people the employee is responsible for. The linkage could be informal or social, relating to one's immediate work responsibilities and the social connection resulting from one's work, the number of people they work with, whether they socialize outside of work, or their feeling of belonging. In our aged care sample, community program employees—who provide home-based care—reported a lower level of connection to other employees and the organization than personal care workers who worked in the residential facilities. The greater the linkage, the greater the embeddedness of the individual into the organization.

The third dimension—*sacrifice*—is concerned with the real or perceived loss the employee would experience if they left the organization. Management can develop organizational practices that increase the employee's cost of leaving the organization (Table 5.2). These practices may be financial (such as salary sacrificing provisions, entitlements that are linked to length of service, career development opportunities that come through internal promotion), as well as social (such as the development of social networks through organizationally supported out-of-work activities such as sport or recreational activities); quality of life issues (such as on-site or subsidized childcare, superior work-life balance arrangements, healthcare and gym membership sponsorship). Table 5.3 also points to the variety of ways that managements can increase employee fit and linkage embeddedness.

Each organization has its distinct embeddedness profile due to the organization's specific policies and procedures, people and leadership approach, reflecting the type of work, the state of the industry and the history of the organization. Table 5.4 summarizes the job embeddedness profiles of a range of organizations.

## Ready to Leave or Wanting to Stay? Employee Proximal Withdrawal States

Finally, employees also may be classified in terms of their *withdrawal state* (Hom et al., 2012). Proximal withdrawal state theory suggests that

**Table 5.3. Management Activities Aimed at Increasing Embeddedness**

| *Organizational Embeddedness Components* | *Management Activities Influencing Embeddedness* |
|---|---|
| Fit | • Recruiting for fit: person-job, person-workgroup, person-organization<br>• Job design and training to improve person-job fit<br>• Development of internal labor markets<br>• Development of organizational-community involvement |
| Linkage | • Mentoring schemes<br>• Team-based work design<br>• Career development<br>• Employee referral schemes<br>• Emphasis on organizational communication and consultation |
| Sacrifice | • Incentives linked to length of service<br>• Work-based community activities<br>• Workplace facilities such as childcare, gym, subsidized healthcare<br>• Succession planning processes |

*Source:* Based on Mitchell, Holtom, and Lee (2001).

**Table 5.4. Employee Embeddedness Scores**

| | *Aged Care* | | | *Public Sector* | | *Manufacturing* | |
|---|---|---|---|---|---|---|---|
| | *2014 Wave 3* | *2012 Wave 2* | *2011 Wave 1* | *2012 Wave 2* | *2011 Wave 1* | *2010 Wave 2* | *2010 Wave 1* |
| On-the-job embeddedness | 5.3 | 5.5 | 5.3 | 4.8 | 4.8 | 4.9 | 4.9 |
| On-the-job fit | 5.4 | 5.5 | 5.5 | 4.7 | 4.6 | 4.7 | 4.8 |
| On-the-job links | 5.6 | 5.7 | 5.6 | 5.6 | 5.9 | 5.7 | 5.7 |
| On-the-job sacrifice | 5.0 | 4.8 | 4.9 | 4.1 | 3.8 | 4.3 | 4.3 |
| Intention to leave | 3.6 | 3.6 | 3.6 | 3.8 | 4.1 | 4.0 | 4.3 |
| Job satisfaction | 5.6 | 5.7 | 5.7 | 4.9 | 4.8 | 5.0 | 5.1 |
| $n$ = | 476 | 340 | 490 | 56 | 58 | 125 | 154 |

*Source:* Unpublished data, Centre for Human Resource Management, University of South Australia.
*Note:* All items measured on 1–7 scale (1 = *lowest score*, 7 = *highest score*).

currently employed staff can be categorized according to (1) the employee's wish to leave; (2) the availability of a viable alternative job for the leaving employee; and (3) whether management wants them to leave. In one simpler version of this theory, an employee can be classified into one of several categories: as an *enthusiastic stayer* (the employee is keen to

**Table 5.5. Employee Withdrawal States**

| | *Employee Wants to Stay* | *Employee Wants to Leave* |
|---|---|---|
| Employee is able to choose whether they stay or leave | • Enthusiastic stayer/ happy stayer | • Enthusiastic leaver |
| Employee unable to find alternative role | • Enthusiastic stayer/ happy stayer | • Reluctant stayer |
| Management wants the employee to leave | • Reluctant leaver/ happy stayer | • Enthusiastic leaver |

*Source:* Based on Hom, Mitchell, Lee, and Griffeth (2012).

**Table 5.6. Employee Withdrawal States in Five Organizations (%)**

| | *Aged Care* | | | *Public Sector* | *Manufacturing* | *Disability* | *Security* |
|---|---|---|---|---|---|---|---|
| | *2014 Wave 3* | *2012 Wave 2* | *2011 Wave 1* | *2011* | *2010* | *2009* | *2008* |
| Reluctant stayers | 5.2 | 5.9 | 5.9 | 0.5 | 13.7 | 8.7 | 4.3 |
| Enthusiastic leavers | 45.9 | 45.3 | 45.6 | 20.5 | 33.1 | 23.5 | 41.1 |
| Happy stayers | 48.8 | 48.8 | 48.5 | 59.1 | 53.2 | 67.8 | 54.6 |
| *n* = | 476 | 340 | 491 | 68 | 121 | 152 | 125 |

*Source:* Unpublished data, Centre for Human Resource Management, University of South Australia.

remain employed with the organization), a *reluctant stayer* (the employee wants to leave, but cannot find an alternative), a *reluctant leaver* (the employee wants to stay but management wishes the employee to leave) or as an *enthusiastic leaver* (where the employee is keen to leave and is optimistic about finding alternative employment) (Table 5.5). Table 5.6 reports on the distribution of these withdrawal states in several organizations that distinguishes between reluctant stayers and enthusiastic leavers, and that combines enthusiastic stayers and reluctant leavers into one group ("happy stayers").

Each of these withdrawal states has a different implication for an employer and requires a different response (Table 5.7). Enthusiastic stayers present the least difficulty for an employer. These employees like their job and the organization, and intend to stay. These employees are still susceptible to Pathway 2 and Pathway 3 shocks. Reluctant stayers present a much larger risk to the organization, potentially demonstrating low performance

**Table 5.7. Employer Risk and Management Response**

| | | *Risk to Employer* | *Management Response* |
|---|---|---|---|
| Enthusiastic stayer | | Negligible | Further embed employee |
| Reluctant stayer | Regrettable | Medium | Use staying interview to investigate opportunities for embedding employee |
| Reluctant stayer | Not regrettable | High | Provide job search assistance. Cultivate post-leaving relationship. |
| Reluctant leaver | Not regrettable | Low | Provide job search assistance. Cultivate post-leaving relationship. |
| Enthusiastic leaver | Regrettable | Medium | Use staying interview to investigate opportunities for embedding employee. Cultivate postleaving relationship. |
| Enthusiastic leaver | Not regrettable | Low | Provide job search assistance. Cultivate postleaving relationship. |

*Note:* Regrettable – Management regrets the employee wishing to leave

or having a demoralizing influence on co-workers. Reluctant leavers may require assistance in finding alternative employment. With some care from management, enthusiastic leavers could be cultivated to be ambassadors for the organization after leaving the organization, potentially referring future employees or clients (Somaya & Williamson, 2008).

The relevance of withdrawal states can be seen when applied to our aged care sample (Table 5.8). Enthusiastic leavers surveyed in 2011 and 2012 were twice as likely to leave by 2014 as happy stayers. Enthusiastic leavers and reluctant stayers reported lower scores for job satisfaction, employee engagement, affective commitment and organizational identification.

## Integrating UFT, JET and Proximal Withdrawal State Into a Retention Strategy

Taken together, these theories enable practitioners to diagnose and remedy voluntary turnover, enabling the development of organizationally relevant retention strategies (Figure 5.3). The first stage uses UFT-based exit interviews to understand why employees are *currently* leaving the organization. The second stage uses regular JET-based surveys to identify

**Table 5.8. Percentage of Proximal Withdrawal State Cohort in 2011 and 2012 who had Left by 2014 and Selected Attitudinal Scores**

| | *Voluntary Turnover* | | | | |
|---|---|---|---|---|---|
| | *2011 (%)* | *2012 (%)* | *Satisfaction* | *Affective Commitment* | *Employee Engagement* |
| Happy stayers | 16.9 | 12.0 | 4.4 | 3.9 | 4.0 |
| Reluctant stayers | 14.3 | 20.0 | 4.0 | 3.4 | 3.7 |
| Enthusiastic leavers | 31.1 | 30.3 | 3.6 | 2.9 | 3.5 |
| *n*= | 130 | 144 | 476 | 477 | 477 |

*Source:* Unpublished data, Centre for Human Resource Management, University of South Australia.
*Notes:* Happy stayers are people who are either enthusiastic stayers or reluctant leavers; satisfaction, affective commitment, and employee engagement measured at 2012; measured on 1–7 scale (1 = *lowest score*, 7 = *highest score*).

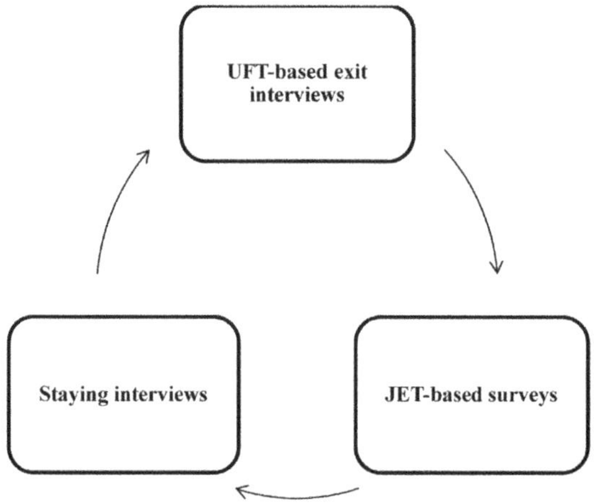


Figure 5.3. Three stages of diagnosis and reduction of turnover.

employee withdrawal states and the *emerging* causes of leaving. In the third stage, staying interviews are used to assess employee satisfaction, career progression and developments, the likelihood of leaving and better ways of embedding employees.

## Stage 1: Diagnosing an Organization's Turnover

The first stage enables management to identify an organization's turnover, enabling management to develop appropriate remedial measures to minimize and potentially prevent voluntary turnover. A well designed and properly implemented exit interview program will enable an organization to identify *how* employees leave and *why* they leave. It enables an organization to answer immediately relevant questions such as: how much of an organization's turnover results from *shock* (Pathways 1, 2, and 3) or from *dissatisfaction* (Pathways 4a and 4b)? How often are unpleasant, unexpected shocks from within the organization cited in cases of immediate leaving (Path 2 and 4a)? Does the organization experience systematic poaching from rival employers (Path 3)? What proportion of people are leaving for reasons beyond the influence of management (Path 1)? Was there a spike in turnover following a particular management decision?

Exit interviews are the main source of information about actual turnover, but are often haphazardly organized, providing infrequently analyzed information (HCA, 2013). A 2010 study of 374 Australian and New Zealand employers found that 92% of these organizations routinely undertook exit interviews but only 15% analyzed the resulting data (The Interview Group, 2010, 2012).

The literature identifies two sets of concerns about the implementation of exit interviews. First, departing employees may find candidly providing their reasons for leaving confronting and unpleasant (Lefkowitz & Katz, 1969). A frank explanation of the reasons for leaving may lead to a poor recommendation, a reputation as a difficult employee, or may prevent an employee returning at a later date (Hinrichs, 1975) or have repercussions for friends remaining with the organization (Zaradona & Camuso, 1985). Hinrichs (1971) found leavers were more likely to emphasize personal reasons for leaving when exit interviews were undertaken by management representatives, compared to exit interviews conducted by people external to the organization. This is more likely if the leaver experienced conflict with management or feels embarrassed by the circumstances of their leaving, which may lead them to disguise the real reasons for leaving (Giacalone, Knouse, & Montagliani, 1997). This is particularly relevant for our aged care employees. Many employees work for more than one aged care provider in order to maximize their working hours and a leaver may need to return sometime later in search of additional hours.

The second reason is that follow-up interviews taken sometime after departure report different, more truthful explanations to those given by the employee at the time of departure (Lefkowitz & Katz, 1969). Exit interviews should be undertaken sometime after departure to improve the reliability and usefulness of the data, with 4 to 6 months considered to be optimal. However response rates are likely to decline the longer the time since the employee left (Hinrichs, 1975). Thus, there is a trade-off: the *usefulness* of exit data increases with time after leaving, but the *likelihood* of actually arranging the interview falls quickly in the weeks after leaving.

Research and practitioner experience has pointed toward more effective approaches to collecting exit interview data. First, the exit interview should be conducted by people independent of the work situation of the departing employee. Exit interview response rates increase the more distant the interviewer is from the former employee, especially if the departure was the result of conflict with other employees or management (The Interview Group, 2010).

Second, the exit interviewer should provide clear information about how the responses will be used by the organization and who will see the leaver's data, as well as providing clear assurances about the confidentiality of the data. Third, the exit interview process should be promoted as a regular part of the employment process, based on a standardized set of questions, with a clear and explained purpose (Hinrichs, 1971, 1975; Kulik et al., 2012; Lefkowitz & Katz, 1969). The occasional or random use of haphazardly designed exit interviews is likely to exacerbate leaver concerns about the purpose and merit of the exit interview (Hinrichs, 1971, 1975).

## Stage 2: Surveying for Employee Embeddedness

Exit interviews provide evidence of the reasons why people have left the organization, but give no insight into the *emerging* reasons why employees might leave in the future. The second stage uses regular JET-based surveys to identify the level of employee embeddedness and the distribution of withdrawal states across the workforce. Regular tracking of employee embeddedness enables management to identify specific deficiencies in job embeddedness and the distribution of employee withdrawal states. Management can influence job embeddedness through its policies and practices (Bergiel, Nguyen, Clenney, & Taylor, 2009). By identifying the actual levels of employee embeddedness and the connection between that embeddedness and employee intention to leave, management is able to devise appropriate interventions for a business unit or organization. For example, it may become apparent that leavers have lower than average organizational-fit and organization-linkage scores than those not leaving. Management could counter this by adopting recruitment techniques aimed at increasing person-job and person-organization-fit for new recruits, developing more effective onboarding programs aimed at cultivating organizationally-appropriate values and attitudes, introducing mentoring schemes to increase linkage, and using training and development to improve skill levels. Table 5.3 highlighted possible management interventions in response to an organization's specific embeddedness characteristics.

To catch changes in employee attitudes about their relationships with their job, other employees and the organization, embeddedness data needs to be collected at least annually. In cases of high levels of turnover, or where the seasonality of work leads to big shifts in the workforce, such as beachside or snowfield accommodation, three or six monthly data collection may provide better tracking of employee sentiment.

Our research into employee embeddedness in aged care, as well as the public sector and manufacturing sectors, suggests that an employee's and an organization's average level of embeddedness is relatively stable over time within that organization (Table 5.4). However, employee embeddedness can be affected by organizational policy and practice changes, changes in personnel, as well as by external factors, such as the state of the broader labor market.

## Stage 3: The "Staying Interview"

Stages 1 and 2 are concerned with understanding turnover behavior and retention characteristics at the organizational level. Organizations that introduce changes in policies and practices based on Stages 1 and 2 will see a gradual improvement in employee retention, as management identifies and removes systematic causes for turnover.

Stage 3 involves the line manager, or a nearby manager, holding regular face-to-face discussions with employees about their career plans and their experiences in working with the organization. The immediate purpose of these staying interviews is to discuss the employee's career development, including the employee's plans for staying with the company, and as described earlier, the employee's withdrawal status (Groth, 2009; Miller-Merrill, 2012).

Staying interviews provide the opportunity for line managers and employees to redesign roles to better suit the employee's capabilities, talents, interests and needs, and in so doing, increase the employee's embeddedness (Berg, Wrzesniewski, & Dutton, 2010). Regular staying interviews could enable the negotiation of individual work arrangements—flexible working time, for example—which could lead to increased employee embeddedness, through better employee fit (resulting from improved work-life balance), linkage (as the employee is now better able to commit to out-of-work activities), and increased sacrifice (what other employer would match this arrangement?).

A "staying intention" interview has all of the problems of data collection and analysis of an exit interview- and it requires more candor from for the employee. The success of the interview requires the employee to make potentially controversial comments about their manager and the organization, while remaining within the organization. In order to be implemented, the employee's comments must be disclosed to other people within the organization. The medium-term success of the staying interviews requires management to act on the information provided by the employees, and to give clear evidence that management will not punish employees who provide controversial insights into the organization. These interviews will only succeed where there is trust between the employee and manager.

## The Three Stages Together or Separately

Taken together, organizations that adopt these three approaches will reduce turnover. The first stage identifies the reasons why employees are currently leaving, enabling the organization to develop and implement appropriate remedies to the causes of voluntary, regrettable and avoidable turnover. The second stage identifies the causes of potential turnover, enabling management to develop and implement appropriate remedies before turnover occurs. The third stage develops a closer relationship between the employer and employee, and—hopefully—enables the organization to develop more personalized employment and development arrangements for that employee. Each of these stages could be undertaken independently. Undertaken together, however, the organization is likely to substantially improve its employee retention.

## REFERENCES

Allen, D. G., Bryant, P. C., & Vardaman, J. M. (2010). Retaining talent: Replacing misconceptions with evidence-based strategies. *Academy of Management Perspectives, 24*, 48–64.

Berg, J. M., Wrzesniewski, A., & Dutton, J. E. (2010). Perceiving and responding to challenges in job crafting at different ranks: When proactivity requires adaptivity. *Journal of Organizational Behavior, 31*, 158–186.

Bergiel, E. B., Nguyen, V. Q., Clenney, B. F., & Taylor, G. S. (2009). Human resource practices, job embeddedness and intention to quit. *Management Research News, 32*, 205–219.

Burton, J. P., Holtom, B. C., Sablynski, C., Mitchell, T. R., & Lee, T. W. (2010). The buffering effects of job embeddedness on negative shocks. *Journal of Vocational Behavior, 76*, 42–51.

Department of Employment. (2015, June 6). National, state and territory skill shortage information. Retrieved from https://employment.gov.au/national-state-and-territory-skill-shortage-information

Giacalone, R. A., Knouse, S. B., &Montagliani, A. (1997). Motivation for and prevention of honest responding in exit interviews and surveys. *Journal of Psychology, 131*(4), 438–448.

Griffeth, R. W., Hom. P. W., & Gaertner, S. (2000). A meta-analysis of antecedents and correlates of employee turnover: Update, moderator tests, and research implications for the millennium. *Journal of Management, 26*(3), 463–488.

Groth, P. (2009, August 12). Stay interviews versus exit interviews. Retrieved from http://anthillonline.com/stay-interviews-vs-exit-interviews

Hays. (2014). Hays Global Skill Index 2014. Retrieved from http://www.hays-index.com/wp-content/uploads/2014/09/Hays-GSI-Report-2014.pdf

HCA. (2013, January 10). Conduct an exit interview or remain in the dark. Retrieved from http://www.hcamag.com/article/conduct-an-exit-interview-or-remain-in-the-dark-147800.aspx

Healy, J., Mavromaras, K., & Sloane, P. J. (2012). *Skill shortages: Prevalence, causes, remedies and consequences for Australian businesses*. Adelaide, South Australia, Australia: National Centre for Vocational Educational Research.

Hinrichs, J. (1971). Employees coming and going. *Personnel, 48*(1), 30–35.

Hinrichs, J. (1975). Measurement of reasons for resignation of professionals: Questionnaire versus company and consultant exit interviews. *Journal of Applied Psychology, 60*(4), 530–532.

Holtom, B., Mitchell, T., Lee, T., & Inderrieden, E. (2005). Shocks as causes of turnover: What they are and how organizations can manage them. *Human Resource Management, 44*(3), 337–352.

Holtom, B. C., Mitchell, T. R., Lee, T. W., & Eberly, M. B. (2008). Turnover and retention research: A glance at the past, a closer review of the present, and a venture into the future. *The Academy of Management Annals, 2*(1), 231–274.

Hom, P., Mitchell, T., Lee, T. W., & Griffeth, R. (2012). Reviewing employee turnover: Focusing on proximal withdrawal states and an expanded criterion. *Psychological Bulletin, 138*(5), 831–858.

The Interview Group. (2010). Exit, stay and on-boarding interviews in Australia and New Zealand: Current practices and untapped value. Retrieved from http://www.interviewgroup.biz/download/SampleReport.pdf

The Interview Group. (2012). *Endings matter. Making exit interviews powerful* (2nd ed.). Retrieved from http://www.interviewgroup.biz/downloadForm.aspx?rd=White_Paper-EndingsMatter

Kulik, C., Treuren, G., & Bordia, P. (2012). Shocks and final straws: Using exit-interview data to examine the unfolding model's decision paths. *Human Resource Management, 51*(1), 25–46.

Lee, T. W., & Mitchell, T. (1994). An alternative approach: The unfolding model of voluntary employee turnover. *Academy of Management Review, 19*(1), 51–89.

Lee, T., Mitchell, T., Wise, L., & Fireman, S. (1996). An unfolding model of voluntary employee turnover. *Academy of Management Journal, 39*(1), 5–36.

Lefkowitz, J., & Katz, M. (1969). Validity of exit interviews. *Personnel Psychology, 22*(4), 445–455.

March, J., & Simon, H. (1958). *Organizations*. New York, NY: John Wiley.

Miller-Merrell, J. (2012, May 29). Stay interviews: Free employee retention program that doesn't suck. Retrieved from http://www.blogging4jobs.com/hr/stay-interviews-powerful-employee-retention-program

Mitchell, T. R, Holtom, B. C., & Lee, T. W. (2001). How to keep your best employees: Developing an effective retention policy. *Academy of Management Executive, 15*(4), 96–108.

Mitchell, T. R, Holtom, B. C., Lee, T. W., Sablynski, C., & Erez, M. (2001). Why people stay: Using job embeddedness to predict voluntary turnover. *Academy of Management Journal, 44*(6), 1102–1121.

Somaya, D., & Williamson, I. O. (2008). Rethinking the 'War for Talent'. *MIT Sloan Management Review, 49*(4), 29–34.

Smith, J. (2014, June 1). Struggling to fill roles? You're not alone. Retrieved from http://www.hcamag.com/hr-news/struggling-to-fill-roles-youre-not-alone-188229.aspx

Zaradona, J. L., & Camuso, M. A. (1985). A study of exit interviews: Does the last word count? *Personnel, 62*, 47–48.

CHAPTER 6

# RECRUITING FOR COMMITMENT AND PERFORMANCE

**Samantha Johnson**

In this chapter I present the psychological state of organizational commitment in a new light and link it to both employee performance and employee recruitment. Drawing from my research into commitment in a public sector environment, I present findings that encourage (human resource management) HRM professionals to do three things. First, to reconsider what commitment to an employer looks like and be open to the idea that it is more complex than may be realized. Second, to consider how commitment is linked to individual performance and how understanding a person's commitment state can give helpful insight into their performance levels. Third, explore how it is developed in an employee and the role that HR practices may play in its development.

The complex nature of commitment was first identified by leading researchers Allen and Meyer (1990a, 1990b), and yet some 25 years on many of us may remain unaware of how complex commitment states actually are. Research dating back to the mid-1980s identified the paradoxical link between high commitment and low performance (Allen & Meyer, 1996; Allen & Smith, 1987; Becker, Billings, Eveleth, & Gilbert, 1996; Blau, 1986; Blau & Boal, 1987, 1989; Chen & Francesco, 2001; Kibeom,

*Human Capital Management Research: Influencing Practice and Process*
pp. 81–97
Copyright © 2016 by Information Age Publishing
All rights of reproduction in any form reserved.

Carswell, & Allen, 2000; Meyer, Bobocel, & Allen, 1991; Mathieu & Zajac, 1990; Meyer, Paunonen, Gellatly, Goffin, & Jackson, 1989; Petersen & Dietz, 2008; Siders, George, & Dharwadkar, 2001; Wright & Bonnett, 2002). Despite this, in general conversations with managers and HRM professionals, there remains a tendency to assume that high commitment equates to high performance.

The research I present here supports the literature that identifies the combination of high commitment and low performance and my findings encourage HRM professionals to rethink the way an employee becomes committed to their employer and how this ultimately affects their performance. I hope that gaining a deeper understanding of the links between HR practices, such as recruitment, the state of organizational commitment and performance levels brings new insight into managing and addressing performance in the workplace.

In this chapter, I present a multidimensional construct of commitment and the concept of commitment profiles. I present links between commitment, high performance and underperformance. I present research into how commitment is experienced by a group of Australian public servants and why I believe their commitment profile might be directly influenced by the department's recruitment practices. Finally, I will discuss why understanding the complex nature of commitment and its links to recruitment and performance are important in the HRM profession.

## THE STATE OF ORGANIZATIONAL COMMITMENT: A DEFINITION

"Organizational commitment" was originally, and quite simply, defined as the "strength of an individual's identification with and involvement in a particular organization" (Porter, Steers, Mowday, & Boulian, 1974, p. 604). Almost 20 years later, leading researchers Allen and Meyer presented commitment as a multidimensional construct that has three separate elements or states of commitment: *affective* commitment, *normative* commitment and *continuance* commitment. Understanding these separate states of commitment is important because each influences performance in different ways and each state of commitment forms in different situations and with different influences (Allen & Meyer, 1990a, 1991).

**Affective commitment** relates to the employee's emotional attachment to, identification with and involvement in an organization—or an attitude of "*wanting*" to work there because of a connection between individual and organizational values. Affective commitment is values based and is an emotional commitment to an organization. We see this type of commitment in welfare organizations such as the Red Cross, Greenpeace, et cetera.

**Normative commitment** relates to the employees' feelings of obligation or loyalty to remain with the organization—or a feeling that they *"ought to"* work there. Normative commitment generates a sense of loyalty to the organization, staying is the "right" thing to do to be loyal.

**Continuance commitment** relates to a state of commitment that is based on the perceived costs associated with leaving the organization and the number of investments people have made in an organization—or perceiving that they *"need to"* work there because there is too much to lose if they leave. Losses can include income, comfort in knowing the job and the organization, stability of employment, conditions of employment, location of employment, et cetera.

Sometime later, two additional dimensions of commitment were added to Allen and Meyer's model, which were "low alternatives" and "high sacrifice" as elements of the state of continuance commitment. The state of low alternatives relates to the perception that one must stay with their employer because there is nowhere else to go for similar employment. The state of high sacrifice occurs when the individual believes that there is too great a sacrifice to leave the organization.

## Commitment Profiles

According to Allen and Meyer (1990a), individuals experience each of these states of commitment to varying degrees. That is, someone may experience affective, normative and continuance commitment simultaneously; or different degrees of each of these states simultaneously. The "net sum" of their states of commitment forms what is called a "commitment profile." Commitment profiles, therefore, reflect the overall commitment state that a person experiences toward their employing organization.

There are two key commitment profiles worth mentioning because of their links to performance. The first profile occurs when the combination of *affective* and *continuance* commitment leads to a sense of being "devoted" to the organization. This means that the individual experiences the combined psychological states of *wanting* to work in their current place of employment, while also feeling that they *need to* work there and would lose too much if they were to leave (Gellatly, Hunter, Currie, & Irving, 2009).

The second profile is one based entirely on *continuance* commitment that can lead to a state of feeling "trapped" in the organization (Gellatly et al., 2009). This means that the individual does not experience a state of *wanting to* work in their current organization, nor do they feel a sense of loyalty or obligation to work there. Rather, their state of commitment is based only on *needing to* work in the organization because of a perception that if they were to leave they would lose too much, or they may believe that there are insufficient alternatives to allow them to leave the organization.

It is the trapped profile that is the most problematic, because it has the highest tendency to lead to lower levels of performance, relative to the levels of performance experienced by someone with a devoted profile. In other words, the link between the commitment profile and performance levels suggests that when an employee has a devoted commitment profile, they are also likely to be higher performers. Likewise, where an employee has a trapped commitment profile, they are less likely to be a high performer (Gellatly et al., 2009).

## THE LINK BETWEEN COMMITMENT AND PERFORMANCE

Commitment forms the basis of retention. Being committed means staying with an organization, but it does not necessarily mean performing well. At any given stage, everyone is committed to their employer in some way until they physically leave. For some people, their commitment profile is such that they will perform to a high level. For others, their commitment profile will present the paradoxical combination of high retention and low performance (Allen & Smith, 1987; Meyer et al., 1989; Shore, Barksdale, & Shore, 1995). An employee who: displays a positive response to change; greater organizational citizenship behaviors; higher job satisfaction; better in-role performance, time management and teamwork; high levels of innovation and creativity; and has greater chances of promotion, is likely to have a devoted commitment profile (Allen & Smith, 1987; Bateman & Strasser, 1984; Bishop & Scott, 2000; Chen & Francesco, 2001; Cohen, 1993; Curry, Wakefield, Price, & Mueller, 1986; Iverson & Buttigieg, 1999; Meyer et al., 1989; Shore et al., 1995; Stevens, Beyer, & Trice, 1978; Vandenberg & Lance, 1982). An employee with higher levels of absenteeism, who presents in a tardy fashion, can be discriminative and generally performs at a lower level is more likely to have a trapped commitment profile (Allen & Meyer, 1996; Becker et al., 1996; Blau & Boal, 1989; Kibeom et al., 2000; Mathieu & Zajac, 1990; Petersen & Dietz, 2008).

## COMMITMENT, PERFORMANCE AND HRM PRACTICES

HRM practices can influence the development of a commitment profile (Conway & Monks, 2009; Gong, Law, Change, & Xin, 2009; Grant, Dutton, & Rosso, 2008; Guest, 2002; Kinnie, Hutchinson, Purcell, Rayton, &

Swart, 2005; Meyer & Smith, 2000; Ouchi, 1981; Peters & Waterman, 1982; Steijn & Leisink, 2006). In particular, HRM practices have been seen to influence the development of continuance commitment (Meyer & Smith, 2000), which means that HR practices can potentially impede the achievement of high performance. This is an important finding. It is not unreasonable for HR practitioners to expect that the HR practices they put into place ultimately improve performance—something that has been supported in the literature (Schuler & Jackson, 1987). Over the years, however, scholars have noted that it is bundles of HRM practices that are most effective for performance improvement (Dyer & Reeves, 1995), along with complete HR systems (Becker & Gerhart, 1996), and that stand-alone HR practices will not necessarily bring performance improvement (Ulrich, 1998). The research presented here supports Ulrich's (1998) premise that single HR practices may not improve performance. Indeed, the findings of this research take this one step further and suggest that it is possible for single HR practices to *reduce* individual and organizational performance. The relationship between certain HR practices and the development of continuance commitment in individuals as a dominant commitment state may be an example of where a single HR practice ultimately, and unexpectedly, reduces performance.

To explain further, the way an employee is recruited to an organization is likely to have a direct influence on the development of their state of commitment. As a consequence, the recruitment process may directly influence long-term employee performance because it influences the development of a commitment state. Somewhat ironically, the very practice that is designed to bring high performers into an organization may be influencing employees in such a way that their potential for high performance is reduced, and their actual performance levels fall below expectations (Iles, Mabey, & Robertson, 1990).

The findings of research presented in this chapter illustrate these links. This study identified a commitment profile that is unique to the context of employment and which is likely to directly influence performance levels. A theoretical argument is presented to show how this particular commitment profile is influenced by a popular large-scale recruitment process. Through this research and its findings, the relationship between recruitment, commitment and performance can be better understood.

## METHODOLOGY

This study explored how organizational commitment was experienced by a group of generalist officers in an Australian federal government department. The research was designed to determine if continuance commitment, the state of commitment most likely to result in lower levels of performance, was the dominant state of commitment, as the literature suggests is likely in public sector environments (Abbott, White, & Charles, 2005; Goulet & Frank, 2002; Liou & Nyhan, 2004; Lyons, Duxbury, & Higgins, 2006). The study was also designed to explore the state of continuance commitment to see if it was influenced by the employment context and, therefore, if it was varied in its form. Finally, it sought to identify implications for HRM practice.

The research took place in the corporate services group of a Commonwealth government department with a departmental total employment figure of 950. Respondents were drawn from a small population of 98 permanent, full-time and part-time staff employed in nonexecutive, generalist positions in information technology, HR and corporate support. These officers could be employed in any government department in similar generalist corporate management roles, and thus it was more likely that their commitment to the organization was being measured, rather than their commitment to a particular profession or occupation. The population size led to only 44 employees taking part in this project. Nevertheless, despite the small numbers, a reasonable insight into commitment was deemed possible through a qualitative research process, as this offered deep insights into how commitment was experienced by this particular group of employees.

The research questions posited in this study required the use of a mixed methodology. In the first part of the study, a quantitative approach was used to measure the levels of continuance commitment experienced by a small group of employees. Following this, a qualitative approach was used to explore possible variations in the form of continuance commitment that was experienced. Three research questions were:

1. What levels of continuance commitment are experienced by a group of Australian federal public servants?
2. In what way, if any, does continuance commitment differ for this group of public service employees?
3. What implications are evident for HRM practices in the Australian public sector context?

Allen and Meyer's (1990a) organizational commitment questionnaire, modified by Chen and Francesco (2001), was used in the first part of the study to measure the levels of commitment. A series of interviews and focus group discussions were used in the second part of the research to explore possible variations in continuance commitment. The third research question was addressed through theoretical discussion.

## WHAT COMMITMENT LOOKED LIKE IN THIS SETTING

A number of themes identified in this study suggested that, overall, low levels of affective commitment were experienced by these employees. This was not unexpected, as the literature suggests affective commitment is low in public sector organizations (Liou & Nyhan, 2004). However, what was unexpected was the variation seen in the form that affective commitment took. In Allen and Meyer's (1990a, 1990b) model, affective commitment is presented as an emotional connection to the organization that reflects at attitude of *wanting to* work in the organization. For these employees, the only clear emotional connection expressed was related to respondents' team mates and work colleagues, rather than toward the organization. Statements to reflect this included: "I feel an emotional connection to my team; not emotional to the department, but to the people in my team"; "Not passionate about the work, but interested in it"; "I feel passion and commitment to the work these guys [in the department do] and I can assist them to do their job."

When normative commitment was explored there appeared to be a clear sense of obligation or loyalty. However, in a similar vein to affective commitment, normative commitment was directed to respondents' work colleagues rather than to the organization itself. The themes identified were that people enjoyed working with their colleagues, they felt a sense of loyalty to their team mates and managers, felt part of the team and felt appreciated by others in the department, but did not feel loyal to the organization itself. Comments that reflected this included: "I stay because I would feel disloyal to my manager, but if she left I don't think I would worry. That might decrease the loyalty"; "I feel a sense of obligation to the department; [it] gave me a job and paid me good money so I feel obligated—to the group of people I think."

Continuance commitment was dominant and particularly easily seen in the focus group sessions, where employees spoke mostly of pay and conditions and comfort and complacency as key reasons for their commitment. Interestingly, this state of commitment was also not typical of Allen and Meyer's (1990a) model. Thus, although this study sought to explore possible variations in the form of continuance commitment, it actually identified variations in all three states of commitment and this was unexpected.

In Allen and Meyer's (1990a) model, continuance commitment relates to the perception of loss and the number of investments people have made in an organization as well as a perceived lack of alternative places to work. However, for these employees, perceived losses related to loss of stability, job comfort, pay and conditions, but were not necessarily based on investments into the organization. There was also no apparent perception of an absence of alternative employment options. Finally, continuance commitment was not focused entirely on the organization, as is expected in Allen and Meyer's (1990a) model, but was split between the organization and the broader Australian Public Service.

Some of the comments that reflected this varied form of continuance commitment were: "I really like the public service superannuation. Money was the driver ..."; "Stability, holidays, sick leave, this is the first time I've had paid sick leave. Super etc., so for me [it's] like heaven. So this is wonderful. Flexitime"; "Our conditions of leave are really good. The certified agreement is an enticing factor"; "I like the style of the public service"; "[The] conditions of service in the public service are very good ..."; "It's a comfort thing. Why leave?"; "The pay is good compared to the private sector"; "Why leave? It's good here ..."; "I think I would probably put off looking for other work because I am comfortable here, and I would need to start over."

The atypical commitment states seen in this study formed a unique commitment profile that, arguably, was consistent with performance levels experienced, directly reflective of the public sector employment context and influenced by the recruitment process. The links between the recruitment process, the formation of a unique commitment profile and its direct influence on performance gave interesting insight into how certain HRM practices can—via commitment—influence performance.

## IDENTIFICATION OF A UNIQUE COMMITMENT PROFILE

In this study I identified a commitment profile consisting of a varied and atypical combination of the psychological states of affective, normative and continuance commitment. This finding was both surprising and important. The dominance of continuance commitment, albeit in a varied form, suggests that a trapped profile remains relatively common in public sector environments. This matters, because a trapped profile is not the most likely to result in high performance. Ideally, for an organization to have a high performance culture, trapped profiles should not be dominant. For the highest levels of performance, organizations should strive to develop devoted commitment profiles. Employees with devoted profiles *need to work*, but they also *want to work in the organization*, and it is this combination of attitude that has a positive influence on performance levels. This combination brings both high retention and high performance.

The combined effect of all three varied forms of commitment that forms an individual's commitment profile is worth considering, particularly when identifying the impact of attitude on performance. In other words, it is not just the low levels of affective commitment and the high levels of continuance commitment that should be considered in exploring the relationships between commitment and performance. For example, what influence does the state of normative commitment have, when combined with affective and continuance commitment, on an individual's performance level? Is it possible that when an individual experiences both affective and normative commitment and when both of these states of commitment are focused on colleagues rather than the organization, that this combination reduces the negative impact on performance of continuance commitment? The answer is "yes." This may be possible because of the relationship between the state of normative commitment and performance. The commitment research shows that, although the state of affective commitment is *most* conducive to high performance in an individual, the state of normative commitment only moderates this and as such, does *not* reduce performance to the same degree that continuance commitment does (Chen & Francesco, 2001). Therefore, where an individual experiences normative commitment along with either affective or continuance commitment, the addition of the state of normative commitment is likely to have a positive influence on performance. When an individual's commitment to their employer is based on positive and healthy relationships with colleagues, their performance is likely to be relatively high. In contrast, those individuals whose commitment is based entirely on their perception of loss should they leave, and who have little or no commitment to their colleagues, are less likely to perform to the same level. Given this, HRM professionals may find improvements to performance occur through relationship-building activities in the workplace. Strong relationships and a dominant state of normative commitment are likely to enhance what may be a unique aspect of a public sector commitment profile that improves overall performance levels.

There is considerable value for HRM professionals to understand how commitment profiles develop and how HRM practices, such as recruitment practices, influence these profiles. This knowledge has the potential to offer a deeper understanding of the drivers of performance and underperformance. This knowledge also offers insight into which HRM practices to change, and perhaps how to change them, to enhance performance levels.

## ORGANIZATIONAL COMMITMENT AND PERFORMANCE—LINKED TO LARGE-SCALE RECRUITMENT

The unique commitment profile identified in the employees involved in this study reflected a dominance of continuance commitment. In considering the implications of this, certain HRM practices were reviewed in this study. The practice of large-scale recruitment stood out as offering a potential influence on the development of this profile and the dominance of the psychological state of continuance commitment.

Large-scale recruitment is readily practiced in Australia and in other countries (Synnerstrom, 2007). This type of recruitment is most effective when organizations seek significant cost savings (Bergmann & Martin, 1987). Large-scale recruitment refers to recruitment activities whereby organizations seek to fill multiple positions by recruiting several people in a single recruitment drive. In doing so, the recruitment and selection practice tends to invite candidates to apply for one of many positions which are often, but not always, at similar employment levels. Interested candidates present themselves as competent in various generalist positions or in positions at a particular employment level. Those successful candidates selected through the recruitment process tend to be placed into one of many vacant positions. Successful candidates may or may not have a choice in the position they are eventually offered or placed into.

## RECRUITMENT AS AN INFLUENCE ON COMMITMENT

There is considerable research that identifies recruitment processes as key influences in the development of commitment profiles. For example, scholars have identified a link between the perception of fairness and accuracy in recruitment and the development of commitment (Ogilvie, 1986, cited in Meyer & Smith, 2000, p. 320). Other scholars have also linked recruitment practices and commitment, showing that HRM practices that seek to promote commitment may have an unintended and paradoxical effect that may lead to high retention but reduced performance. Iles et al., for example, suggest that: "Organizations which seek to bind employees through [specific benefits such as financial gains] may find that they end up with employees who may not wish to leave but who merely perform at a minimum level sufficient to retain their jobs and benefits" (1990, p. 153). Moreover, Caldwell, Chatman, and O'Reilly state that: "[an] individual's commitment to an organization may be shaped by the process through which he or she enters the organization" and "factors related to an individual's decision to accept a job offer can influence his or her subsequent commitment" (1990, p. 246).

The link between recruitment practices and the development of continuance commitment, or a trapped profile, was supported by some scholars claiming that: "HRM practices might also affect continuance commitment by making it costly for employees to leave" and "continuance commitment might be influenced by specific practices that increase the cost of leaving" (Meyer & Smith, 2000, pp. 327–328).

It is possible that continuance commitment in employees may develop where job candidates are encouraged to seek general employment in an organization rather than employment into a specific role. That is, applying for consideration against numerous positions in an organization may very well contribute to the development of a state of continuance commitment. This is because candidates are asked to prove their abilities in relation to general competencies or capabilities in order to be found suitable to operate in a generalist role or at a particular employment level. If successful, they are employed into a role and they gain the benefits of the pay, status and conditions set for that role. The focus of employment during the recruitment process tends to be on a level of competency that may lead to greater rewards including remuneration, permanency of employment, opportunity, employment conditions and stability, rather than on employment into a specific job or role. As such, the recruitment process tends to promote an attitude of continuance commitment from the onset. Where there is no single role that is a focus of the recruitment process, the focus invariably becomes the employment level or job family and this general focus perpetuates an attitude of continuance commitment rather than affective or normative commitment.

Developing affective or normative commitment in an individual may need to be done after employment is secured and once they have settled into a new role. This can be through teamwork, management practice and leadership prowess and it seeks to balance the continuance commitment developed through the recruitment process with affective and normative commitment developed in the workplace.

If a recruitment process were to focus on the value of the work of a particular role and allow candidates to express their emotional and values-based connection to that particular role, then affective commitment might be encouraged in the interested candidate from the outset. That is, where the value and purpose of a role are promoted and a candidate seeks to be employed in that role because they feel an emotional and values-based connection to the role, they may begin employment with stronger affective commitment and weaker continuance commitment. Likewise, a recruitment campaign that focuses on developing long-term reciprocal relationships and that offers enticements that generate a sense of obligation or loyalty may encourage an attitude of normative commitment, which is less detrimental to high performance than an attitude of continuance commitment. Paying for studies toward formal qualifications where successful candidates agree to be employed for a minimum of five years is an example of an enticement that may generate normative commitment and a sense of obligation and loyalty.

In line with this, there are two key ways to consider the effectiveness of a recruitment process. On the one hand, the activity and process itself can be assessed. If a competent and capable person is recruited into a vacant role and, indeed, if several such people are recruited to fill several vacant roles, then the recruitment process has succeeded. The measure of success is the efficiency and effectiveness of the recruitment *activity* itself—vacant roles are filled and quite likely filled in a cost- and time-efficient manner.

On the other hand, the recruitment process has had a direct influence on the psychological state of the individual and, in particular, on their state of commitment and their commitment profile. It may be that this psychological state is not conducive to high performance, as is the case when a dominance of continuance commitment is experienced or a trapped commitment profile is developed. This *outcome* of the recruitment process may not be recognized and, therefore, it is neither accurately assessed nor effectively managed. Consider Ulrich's premise that for HRM to truly improve performance, practices must be measured according to their *outcomes* rather than the *activities* they include (1998, p. 133). Given this approach, large-scale recruitment must be measured according to the *outcomes* gained, rather than the immediate effectiveness of the *activity* itself. It is likely that large-scale recruitment activity is successfully meeting requirements. That is, the recruitment *activity* is resulting in the efficient recruitment of capable employees. However, while the focus of review and the measurement of success remains on the *activity* itself, the *outcome* of a dominance of continuance commitment, which leads to a trapped commitment profile and a reduction in performance, is likely to be missed.

The challenge with large-scale recruitment processes is to get the balance between efficiency and effectiveness right. These processes are popular because they are efficient and cost effective. The question is: is it possible that they are contributing to lower levels of performance and that this contribution has, until now, been missed? If it is likely that a recruitment campaign that focuses on general aspects of performance or performance at a particular level can promote continuance commitment to the detriment of the other components of commitment, then the HRM professional must balance this with postrecruitment practices that build affective commitment and, therefore, promote devoted commitment profiles and encourage higher levels of performance.

HRM professionals, along with managers and leaders, can counteract a dominance of continuance commitment developed through large-scale recruitment processes by enhancing affective commitment in teams and individuals once new recruits are settled into their positions. This can be done by encouraging candidates to choose the position they are most interested in, once selected for employment in the organization. Professionals and managers can also speak explicitly about the purpose and value of the work of a specific role and encourage employees to develop a personal connection to the work, a belief in the importance and value of a role. They can also enhance normative commitment, which can inhibit the development of a trapped profile, by building strong, positive and supportive relationships in workplaces.

The worst-case scenario, and one that is most likely to inhibit the development of a strong performance culture, is the overuse of large-scale recruitment, offering people little or no choice in the position they are given, locking them into that position for significant periods of time and assuming that capability alone will bring high levels of performance. Where employees find themselves with trapped commitment profiles, they are likely to experience the reality of high retention and lower levels of performance. In other words, where trapped profiles are not managed and reduced, organizations may be filled with employees who neither leave nor perform exceptionally well. The greatest risk with large-scale recruitment, where the outcomes of trapped profiles are not recognized and managed, is the active employment of people who may ultimately find themselves trapped. These people can become disengaged from the working group or team, unable to perform at their best, and may be unresponsive to other HRM activities designed to improve performance, such as performance management processes.

## CONCLUSION

Understanding current research into the complex state of organizational commitment and commitment profiles is valuable; likewise, understanding how these may be formed through recruitment processes and how they influence overall performance levels. Helping HRM practitioners understand this could influence many other HRM activities, such as the way management and leadership training is conducted, the way managers and leaders behave in general and the HRM practices adopted by an organization. The commitment-organizational link is complex and closely related to performance and managers, leaders, trainers, and HRM specialists are encouraged to explore this relationship further; the starting point may be to explore it within their own organization and, indeed, within themselves.

Performance management is challenging for managers and HRM practitioners most of the time. If it happens that an HRM practice such as large-scale recruitment is inadvertently perpetuating a commitment profile that is reducing performance and inhibiting a performance culture, then there is an added dimension to performance management that may not be clearly understood. Over the years HRM research continues to provide insight into organizational life and the link between HRM activities and organizational performance is becoming better understood. HRM practitioners would benefit greatly from staying on top of the academic work in universities all over the world and through this improve their understanding of the impact of their work on the overall performance of an organization.

To remain strong, viable and successful, HRM practitioners must develop a deeper understanding of the *outcomes* of HRM activities on organizations and must look to HRM and organizational behavior research to test their assumptions and fill their knowledge gaps. Understanding the complexity of organizational commitment, its link to performance and the influence of HRM practices on commitment is strong in the academic field but weak in the practitioner field. It's time for this to change and for HRM practitioners to understand more thoroughly the complex nature of organizational commitment, it's influence on performance and the influence that HRM practices can have on its development.

## REFERENCES


Abbott, G. N., White, F. A., & Charles, M. A. (2005). Linking values and organizational commitment: A correlational and experimental investigation in two organizations. *Journal of Occupational and Organizational Psychology, 78*, 531–551.

Allen, N. J., & Meyer, J. P. (1990a). The measurement and antecedents of affective, continuance and normative commitment to the organization. *Journal of Applied Psychology, 63*, 1–18.

Allen, N. J., & Meyer, J. P. (1990b). Organizational socialization tactics: A longitudinal analysis of links to newcomers' commitment and role orientation. *Academy of Management Journal, 33*(4), 847–858.

Allen, N. J., & Meyer, J. P. (1991). A three-component conceptualization of organizational commitment. *Human Resource Management Review, 1*(1), 61–89.

Allen, N. J., & Meyer, J. P. (1996). Affective, continuance and normative commitment to the organization: An examination of construct validity. *Journal of Vocational Behavior, 49*(1), 252–276.

Allen, N. J., & Smith, J. (1987, June). *An investigation of 'extra-role' behaviours within organizations.* Paper presented at the annual meeting of the Canadian Psychological Association, Vancouver, British Columbia, Canada.

Bateman, T. S., & Strasser, S. (1984). A longitudinal analysis of the antecedents of organizational commitment. *Academy of Management Journal, 27*(1), 95–112.

Bishop, J. W., & Scott, K. D. (2000). An examination of organizational and team commitment in a self-directed team environment. *Journal of Applied Psychology, 85*, 439–450.

Becker, T., Billings, R., Eveleth, D., & Gilbert, N. (1996). Foci and bases of employee commitment: Implications for job performance. *Academy of Management Journal, 39*, 464–82.

Becker, B., & Gerhart, B. (1996). The impact of human resource management on organizational performance: Progress and prospects. *Academy of Management Journal, 39*(4), 779–801.

Bergmann, T. J., & Martin, G. E. (1987). Optimal large-scale manpower recruitment policies. *Human Resource Planning, 10*(2), 93–101.

Blau, G. J. (1986). Job involvement and organizational commitment as interactive predictors of tardiness and absenteeism. *Journal of Management, 12*(4), 577–584.

Blau, G. J., & Boal, K. B. (1987). Conceptualizing how job involvement and organizational commitment affect turnover and absenteeism. *Academy of Management Review, 12*, 288–300.

Blau, G.J., & Boal, K. B. (1989). Using job involvement and organizational commitment interactively to predict turnover. *Journal of Management, 15*(1), 115–127.

Caldwell, D. F., Chatman, J. A., & O'Reilly, C. (1990). Building organizational commitment: A multifirm study. *Journal of Occupational Psychology, 63*, 245–261.

Chen, Z. X., & Francesco, A. (2001). The relationship between the three components of commitment and employee performance in China. *Journal of Vocational Behaviour, 62*, 490– 510.

Cohen, A. (1993). Organizational commitment and turnover: A meta-analysis. *Academy of Management Journal, 36*(5), 1140–1157.

Conway, E., & Monks, K. (2008). HR practices and commitment to change: An employee-level analysis. *Human Resource Management Journal, 18*(1), 72–89.

Conway, E., & Monks, K. (2009). Unravelling the complexities of high commitment: An employee-level analysis. *Human Resource Management Journal, 19*(2), 140–158.

Curry, J. P, Wakefield, D. S., Price, J. L., & Mueller, C. W. (1986). On the causal ordering of job satisfaction and organizational commitment. *Academy of Management Journal, 29*(4), 847–858.

Dyer, L., & Reeves, T. (1995). Human resource strategies and firm performance: What do we know and where do we go? *International Journal of Human Resource Management, 6*, 656–670.

Gellatly, I. R., Hunter, K. H., Currie, L. G., & Irving, P. G. (2009). HRM practices and organizational commitment profiles. *The International Journal of Human Resource Management, 20*(4), 869–884.

Gong, Y., Law, K. S., Change, S., & Xin, K. R. (2009). Human resource management and firm performance: The differential role of managerial affective and continuance commitment. *Journal of Applied Psychology, 94*(1), 263–275.

Goulet, L. R., & Frank, M. L. (2002). Organizational commitment across three sectors: Public, non- profit, and for-profit. *Public Personnel Management, 31*(2), 201–210.

Grant, A. M., Dutton, J. E., & Rosso, B. D. (2008). Giving commitment: Employee support programs and the prosocial sensemaking process. *Academy of Management Journal, 51*(5), 898–918.

Guest, D. (2002). Human resource management, corporate performance and employee wellbeing: Building the worker into HRM. *Journal of Industrial Relations, 44*(3), 335–358.

Iles, P., Mabey, C., & Robertson, I. (1990). HRM practices and employee commitment: Possibilities, pitfalls and paradoxes. *British Journal of Management, 1*(3), 147–157.

Iverson, R. D., & Buttigieg, D. M. (1999). Affective, normative and continuance commitment: Can the 'right kind" of commitment be managed? *Journal of Management Studies, 36*(3), 307–333.

Kibeom, L., Carswell, J., & Allen, N. (2000). A meta-analytic review of occupational commitment: Relations with person and work-related variables. *Journal of Applied Psychology, 85*(5), 799–811.

Kinnie, N., Hutchinson, S., Purcell, J., Rayton, B., & Swart, J. (2005). Satisfaction with HR practices and commitment to the organization: Why one size does not fit all. *Human Resource Management Journal, 15*(4), 9–28.

Liou, K., & Nyhan, R. C., (1994). Dimensions of organizational commitment in the public sector: An empirical assessment. *Public Administration Quarterly Spring, 18*(1), 99–118.

Lyons, S. T., Duxbury, L. E., & Higgins, C. A. (2006). A comparison of the values and commitment of private sector, public sector and parapublic sector employees. *Public Administration Review, 66*(4), 605–616.

Mathieu, J. E., & Zajac, D. (1990). A review and meta-analysis of the antecedents, correlates, and consequences of organizational commitment. *Psychological Bulletin, 108*, 171–194.

Meyer, J. P., Bobocel, D. R., & Allen, N. J. (1991). Development of organizational commitment during the first year of employment: A longitudinal study of pre and post entry influences. *Journal of Management, 17*(4), 716–736.

Meyer, J. P., Paunonen, S. V., Gellatly, I. R., Goffin, R. D., & Jackson, D. N. (1989). Organizational commitment and job performance: It's the nature of the commitment that counts. *Journal of Applied Psychology, 74*(1), 152–156.

Meyer, J. P., & Smith, C. A. (2000). HRM practices and organizational commitment: Test of a mediation model. *Canadian Journal of Administrative Sciences, 17*(4), 319–331.

Ouchi, W. G. (1981). *Theory Z*. Reading MA: Addison-Wesley.

Peters, T. J., & Waterman, R. H. (1982). *In search of excellence*. New York, NY: Harper and Row.

Petersen, L. E., & Dietz, J. R. (2008). Employment discrimination: Authority figures' demographic preferences and followers' affective organizational commitment. *Journal of Applied Psychology, 93*, 1287–1300.

Porter, L. W., Steers, R. M., Mowday, R. T., & Boulian, P. V. (1974). Organizational commitment, job satisfaction and turnover among psychiatric technicians. *Journal of Applied Psychology, 59*(5), 603–609.

Schuler, R. S., & Jackson, S. E. (1987). Linking competitive strategies with human resource management practices. *The Academy of Management Executive, 1*(3), 207–219.

Shore, L. M., Barksdale, K., & Shore, T. H. (1995). Managerial perceptions of employee commitment to the organization. *Academy of Management Journal, 38*(6), 1593–1615.

Siders, M. A., George, G., & Dharwadkar, R. (2001). The relationship of internal and external commitment foci to objective job performance measures. *Academy of Management Journal, 44*(3), 570–579.

Steijn, B., & Leisink, P. (2006). Organizational commitment among Dutch public sector employees. *International Review of Administrative Services, 72*(2), 187–201.

Stevens, J. M., Beyer, J. M., & Trice, H. M. (1978). Assessing personal role, and organizational predictors of managerial commitment. *Academy of Management Journal, 18*, 74–81.

Synnerstrom, S. (2007). The civil service: Towards efficiency, effectiveness and honesty. In R. McLeod & A. MacIntyre (Eds.), *Indonesia: Democracy and the promise of good governance* (pp. 159–177). Singapore: Institute of Southeast Asian Studies.

Ulrich, D. (1998). A new mandate for human resources. *Harvard Business Review, Jan-Feb*, 124–134.

Vandenberg, R. J. & Lance, C. E. (1992). Examining the causal order of job satisfaction and organizational commitment. *Journal of Management, 18*(1), 153–168.

Wright, T. A., & Bonnett, D. G. (2002). The moderating effects of employee tenure on the relation between organizational commitment and job performance: A meta-analysis. *Journal of Applied Psychology, 87*(6), 1183–1190.

CHAPTER 7

# TECHNOLOGY-BASED TRAINING

## Connecting HR Research With HR Practice

**Adam M. Kanar, Matisha Montgomery, Rebecca L. Fraser, and Tara S. Behrend**

Several recent trends, including rapid advances in technology, limited and uncertain budgets, growing skill gaps, and demand for just-in-time training have led organizations to increasingly embrace technology-based training (TBT) interventions such as e-learning (Patel, 2010). Technology-driven instruction brings many changes to the traditional training and development process. For example, once TBT programs such as e-learning have been developed, they can be administered broadly, potentially removing cost, geographic, and time constraints faced by traditional training delivery modes. Trainers also have more options for instructional design than ever before, and have seen their role change from expert to facilitator. In addition, learners have the potential to become responsible and active drivers of their own learning, making decisions regarding the content, timing and sequence of instruction.

Unfortunately, greater use of technology has also created several significant challenges for learners and trainers. First, although learners tend to

*Human Capital Management Research: Influencing Practice and Process*
pp. 99–116
Copyright © 2016 by Information Age Publishing
All rights of reproduction in any form reserved.

prefer the increased flexibility and control offered by technology-based interventions, evidence suggests that more learner control does not always lead to desirable learning outcomes (Kraiger & Jerden, 2007). For example, learners are frequently overconfident and unable to self-assess their current levels of knowledge and skills, and make poor decisions such as exiting training too early (DeRouin, Fritzsche, & Salas, 2004). Second, the implementation of technology-based interventions tends to outpace evidence-based recommendations for using technology to support effective training design. However, as the recent emergence of such trends as gamification, social learning, mobile learning, and immersive learning exemplify, this pattern will continue. Practitioners face a plethora of training design decisions driven by technological capabilities and practical constraints, leading to instructional design decisions that are decoupled from targeted learning processes and outcomes. As a result, studies of the effectiveness of TBT programs have been mixed (for example, Sitzman, Kraiger, Stewart, & Wisher, 2006).

The goal of this chapter is to review the current state of science and practice of TBT design, and then illustrate and apply key principles to a case study of a U.S. federal agency seeking to transition from traditional classroom learning to e-learning. The first section provides an overview of TBT system design from a research and practical perspective, and then outlines best practice for theory-based TBT design. Rather than focusing on the specific technologies that are effective or ineffective, the recommended design process involves choosing technology only when it is deemed the best method to help achieve learning goals (Kozlowski & Bell, 2007). We describe similarities across TBT interventions in terms of their underlying psychological elements (for example, interactivity, immersion, richness), discuss mechanisms by which these elements are thought to affect learning processes and link these design elements with key engagement and learning outcomes when possible (see Bell, Kanar, & Kozlowski, 2008).

The second section presents a case study illustrating many of the fundamental considerations related to implementing technology-based learning systems and details how these matters were addressed. The U.S. Office of Personnel Management's Human Resources Solutions (HRS) division invested time and resources expanding the accessibility of its training offerings by transitioning one of its critical courses for federal human resource (HR) specialists from the classroom to online training. The classroom training included lecture, discussion and hands-on exercises with special attention to increasing learner interactivity. We discuss their approach according to the recommended TBT design model.

## TBT DESIGN: THEORY VERSUS PRACTICE

Ideal approaches based on theory versus those that are adopted in practice are often very different, and TBT is no exception. Desire to reduce training costs is at the heart of typical practice-based technology-based learning systems (Kraiger, 2003). Organizations typically aim to reduce costs while achieving the same level of training effectiveness as classroom training. Resource limitations often determine the training that is selected for conversion from in-person to TBT. Once training is selected, the technology to be utilized is selected primarily based on an organization's existing technology and the cost of upgrade, employee access and the ability of the technology to present the existing training materials. New training content is often mapped onto the existing technology (often termed "repurposing"). Alternatively, organizations with greater resources may implement technology-based programs not based on cost but instead based on a "best practice" approach, where they adopt the latest technology using evidence that the technology was effective for another organization. Overall, practice-based systems tend to be designed around resource constraints or a specific technology.

A theory-based approach, in contrast, represents the ideal approach; it differs from practice-based training design in several critical ways. Kozlowski and Bell (2007) propose a framework stating that systems should be designed so that they best facilitate the attainment of learning goals, and the choice of technology should be one of the last steps in the training design process. Learning goals refer to the knowledge, skill, and behavioral competencies targeted by the training program and they define success for the training program. Rather than beginning with potential cost savings or a way to implement a new technology, the design approach should instead begin with the desired outcome (learning goals) and work backwards toward the processes and inputs necessary to reach the outcomes. For example, the instructional systems design (ISD) model is a common theory-based approach that comprises five stages, including analysis, design, development, implementation and evaluation (e.g., Craig, 1996). The ISD model uses a systems approach to instructional design, in that it views human organizations and activities as systems in which inputs, outputs, processes (throughputs), and feedback and control elements are salient features.

As described in more detail below, the design process should, therefore, begin with a needs assessment (i.e., task, person and organization analysis) and the identification of instructional goals. A full needs assessment is often overlooked in practice, and beginning with this step is one of the clearest ways organizations can improve the effectiveness of their training systems (Goldstein, 1986). Needs analysis answers the questions:

Who needs training?, What do they need to learn?, What supports and methods will be most effective for them?, What constraints exist that may hamper training efforts? Importantly, needs assessment determines the learning goals that ultimately define success for the system and, therefore, the entire training system should be designed around these objectives. Beginning with these goals is important because different goals have implications for the processes of learning that must occur in order to reach the goals. For example, trainees rely on certain motivational and cognitive processes when trying to master certain types of knowledge and skills. A theory-based approach attempts to incorporate instructional design features that can facilitate these key processes. The aim is to create an instructional experience that stimulates the learning processes necessary to reach the instructional goals. Training technologies are, therefore, chosen to create the desired instructional experience rather than for cost savings.

Broadly, training systems may be evaluated based on effectiveness and efficiency; practice-based systems often fail at both of these criteria. Effectiveness has been defined in many ways but ultimately refers to whether the training program has achieved the goals defined during the needs analysis. Because many practice-based training systems are rooted in cost-savings rather than designed in a way to best meet the instructional goals, practice-based systems are often ineffective. Alternately, practice-based systems that are not rooted in cost savings but are designed around implementing a newly available and novel training technology often ignore the mismatch between the technology and learning objectives. Specifically, training is designed based on an approach that was effective in a very *different* setting, with different trainees, and different training content and, therefore, may not generalize to the target setting. Practice-based systems may be effective based on chance, which can lead to false conclusions and the attempted replication or scale-up of a system that will not be effective in the future. Although practice-based systems are often designed to be efficient, they are not always effective. An efficient but ineffective system has little value to an organization. However, practice-based training designs that are effective may also be inefficient because the amount invested in mapping the technology to the existing content may be more than is necessary to achieve the instructional goals of the training program. Finally, practice-based systems rarely achieve the cost savings they intend to achieve (Kraiger, 2003; Patel, 2010) and, therefore, practice-based systems may be inefficient.

The practice-based approach designs TBT intending to replicate learning outcomes that were previously achieved in classroom settings. However, the theory-based approach has the potential to create a TBT program that is *more* effective than the initial in-person training program it intended to replace. Many technologies have the ability to create more effective instructional experiences than can be accomplished through face-to-face training. For example, difficult-to-recreate situations can be simulated effectively; trainees can be connected with remote resources and mentors; and feedback can be delivered instantaneously. The theory-based approach described next has the potential to be both effective and efficient because it is designed to directly link instructional goals with training design in an efficient way.

## THEORY-BASED INSTRUCTIONAL DESIGN PROCESS

We describe the recommended approach based on Kozlowski and Bell's (2007) model of TBT design process. According to Kozlowski and Bell (2007), the instructional design process begins with needs assessment through task, person and organization analyses. Identifying instructional goals is accomplished through task analysis (for observable behaviors) or cognitive task analysis (for mental aspects of the job). In order to design a training system that is theoretically grounded, it is critical to define instructional goals in terms that are consistent with learning theory. Substantial evidence supports the notion that when training is designed around the science of learning, it leads to positive results (Salas, Tannenbaum, Kraiger, & Smith-Jentsch, 2012). Learning theory specifies that all knowledge and skills range on a continuum from basic to adaptable (Kozlowski & Bell, 2007). Basic knowledge and skills are those rooted in declarative knowledge (for example, knowledge of facts, concepts and simple rules). Procedural knowledge and skills are more advanced and involve context-specific rules for application of knowledge. Strategic knowledge and skills involve an understanding of the contingencies that drive shifts in prioritization and allocation of attention and effort; they involve seeing the "big picture." Adaptable knowledge and skills are the most advanced and involve generalizing knowledge and skills to new situations and tasks. Specifying instructional goals as declarative, procedural, strategic and/or adaptable knowledge and skills is important because it helps to identify the learning processes necessary to develop and sustain these skills and ultimately the technology tools that can facilitate these processes (Kolzowski & Bell, 2007).

The needs assessment also includes organizational analysis, which addresses organization-level factors, such as the fit between the distributive learning system and the organization's culture, and person analysis, which evaluates trainees' knowledge, skills and abilities and the fit between trainees and the training program. Person analysis is critical in the technology-based instructional design process because: (1) TBT programs have the capability to adapt to individual differences in knowledge, skills, and abilities; and (2) most TBT programs involve extensive learner-control (Patel, 2010). By adapting to individual differences, TBT programs can help overcome trainees' weaknesses and enhance their strengths. Some learners, such as those with high levels of cognitive ability, metacognitive skills and adequate prior knowledge, are better at navigating learner-controlled training programs. It is important to design programs to facilitate self-regulation in learners lacking these knowledge and skills. For example, Kanar and Bell (2013) show the effectiveness of different forms of adaptive guidance for reaching different instructional goals depending on learners' level of cognitive ability and motivation to learn. Learner preferences for control over their learning experience, and their ability to correctly assess their own skill level, are essential parts of whether they will make the best use of TBT. Past research has shown that low-ability learners often use the flexibility afforded by e-learning to terminate the training too soon, missing important knowledge and skills (DeRouin et al., 2004). Other learners may use that flexibility to complete training in a distraction-heavy environment, similarly harming learning. At the same time, other learners are able to use the self-paced learning to their advantage; following up with difficult topics and seeking additional assistance in a ways that is much more difficult in classroom training.

Different learning processes are required to achieve the different learning goals described above, and any training design will only be effective to the extent that it stimulates and supports these learning processes. Therefore, the next step in the theory-based TBT design process described by Kozlowski and Bell (2007) involves describing the key learning processes necessary to achieving instructional goals. For example, basic knowledge and skills rely on declarative knowledge and require learning processes based on repetition and practice. More advanced knowledge and skills, such as adaptability, require extensive learner self-regulation of motivation and attention, and the development of adaptable knowledge structures. In addition, more advanced levels of knowledge and skill require sufficient acquisition of basic knowledge and skills. Therefore, learning goals must proceed in a way that basic skills are taught before more advanced skills (e.g., Bell & Kozlowski, 2002). It is also important to note that instructional design that stimulates learning processes related to the acquisition of the wrong learning goal can inhibit the attainment of a targeted learning goal.

After specifying key learning processes, the next step involves connecting those learning processes to training design features. Different instructional technologies stimulate and sustain different learning processes. For example, CD-ROMs and intranet sites may be best for teaching facts and figures, while high-fidelity simulations may be best for teaching complex skills. Kozlowski and Bell (2007) note that it is important to look beyond the surface features of the technologies and instead look at the instructional design characteristics that are embedded in the technologies which can stimulate and support key learning processes. They highlight four instructional design features—content, immersion, interactivity and communication—that underlie TBT design and are important for linking technology with learning processes and instructional goals. Content refers to the richness of information delivered to trainees. For example, content may be conveyed via text, video and graphics. Immersion is the realism, or the extent to which the training captures important psychological and contextual characteristics of the performance domain. For example, high-fidelity simulations may closely replicate a job situation. Interactivity refers to the collaboration potential between trainees, trainers and the system itself. For example, teams of individuals may collaborate across settings. Communication refers to the extent that users of the system (trainees, trainers) can communicate via verbal and nonverbal means. For example, communication may be in real-time video and audio, or may have a time delay. Any technology will have a certain level of each of these four features. The combination of the levels of these features inherent in the technology results in a learning experience that stimulates learning processes. Choice of technology must be based on the levels of these features that stimulate the learning processes necessary to reach instructional goals. More complex learning goals, such as adaptive skills and knowledge, generally require richer instructional experiences and, therefore, high levels of content, immersion, interactivity and communication. On the other hand, declarative knowledge does not require a rich experience, as simple repeated exposure to text can often suffice.

In the past few years, training technologies, such as virtual reality, serious games, intelligent agents, massive open online courses and others, have been deployed as means of increasing engagement and delivering training materials effectively. Within each of these broad categories, levels of content, immersion, interactivity and communication can vary widely. For example, a "serious game" may make use of sophisticated and immersive graphics in order to convey a realistic training environment for the purposes of training emergency medics how to respond in a crisis. A different serious game may have little to no immersion, but use a system of badges to reward trainees for progress, thus increasing their engagement in a very different way. Choosing technology based on the content, immersion, interactivity and communication necessary to activate learning processes can ultimately facilitate the achievement of instructional goals and lead to an effective training system. The next section illustrates the instructional design process through a case study.

## CASE STUDY

HRS, a division of the U.S. Office of Personnel Management, provides HR consulting services, including technical training, to help position agencies and individuals across the federal government for maximum performance. Like many other private and public organizations, the U.S. federal government has begun a transition from classroom- to web-based instruction (for example, live virtual training, recorded webinars, online self-paced learning modules). In response to tightening budgets across the federal government, advanced training technologies and an overwhelming demand, HRS transformed one of its popular classroom trainings to an online TBT.

Similar to the theory-based approach to instructional design discussed earlier, an ISD model was employed for the TBT. HRS first conducted a needs assessment and established clear learning objectives and instructional goals to guide the design of the training. Next, HRS selected the most appropriate technologies to achieve learning outcomes based on their availability in the online platform selected. Finally, HRS evaluated the TBT to determine whether learning and instructional goals were achieved. This case study details the development process and key considerations that guided the TBT design to replicate classroom training learning outcomes and advance training effectiveness where possible.

## NEEDS ASSESSMENT

Across the federal government, assessment questionnaires (also known as training and experience questionnaires) are the most widely used assessment for selection of employees. Assessment questionnaires are administered via web-based talent acquisition systems, which enable users (that is, agency HR specialists) to manage job announcements and automate portions of the hiring process, including assessments. HRS's classroom training on assessment questionnaire development introduces learners to the importance of valid assessment practices and equips them with the knowledge and skills to design effective assessment questionnaires.

Over time, the expanding and worldwide customer base and demand for delivery of the assessment questionnaire training exceeded the capabilities of HRS staff to deliver the course. Online TBT was an appealing alternative. This option afforded HRS the opportunity to train large numbers of federal HR professionals without an instructor present. Further, the online TBT would reduce coordination time associated with in-person classes and eliminate employee travel to training locations. Thus, developing the TBT to mirror the classroom training would provide multiple modes of delivery and allow HRS to provide guidance to a broader audience of federal employees and agencies on the development of quality assessments.

HRS undertook transforming the popular 2-day in-person, classroom-based, assessment questionnaire development training into a self-paced TBT. The classroom training is a blend of lecture presentation, hands-on exercises and classroom discussion. The training covers assessment and measurement topics as well as federal laws, regulations and professional standards. The first day of classroom training is primarily lecture based, including a series of presentations covering foundational topics; the second day covers more advanced topics. The second day also devotes a significant amount of time to hands-on exercises and practical application, as well as classroom discussion.

Several important considerations guided HRS in developing the self-paced TBT. First, the technical content and exercise-heavy training design of the classroom training demanded serious consideration and a thoughtful online-learning design to ensure achievement of learning objectives. Table 7.1 displays the learning objectives addressed by the course.

Trainees' understanding is particularly critical for this course, given the potential legal ramifications associated with misunderstanding. To reinforce the content and practical application of best practices, the classroom-based assessment questionnaire development training devotes significant time to hands-on exercises. Two types of exercises are completed during the training: (1) short basic comprehension and identification exercises that reinforce new concepts (that is, declarative and procedural knowledge); and (2) challenging real-life exercises to offer hands-on application of best practices, enabling development of adaptable knowledge. While some classroom exercises focused on declarative or procedural knowledge were amenable to online administration given their definitive right and wrong answers, creating opportunities to develop strategic and adaptable knowledge were more difficult in the absence of an instructor. The training also involved extensive classroom discussion to promote application of knowledge and skills on the job; for example, discussion of agency-specific policy or guidelines that directly affect the implementation of concepts and methods taught by instructors. Adult learners retain approximately 10% of what they see; 30 to 40% of what they see *and* hear; and 90% of what they see, hear, *and* do. The goal was to maintain as much of the classroom-based training practical applications as possible.

Second, a lack of prerequisites for the course in conjunction with the limited knowledge and experience levels further complicated online development. As a whole, the target audience has a broad range of knowl-

**Table 7.1. Learning Objectives**

| *Lesson* | *Objectives* |
|---|---|
| Course Overview | • State the purpose of the course.<br>• Describe the role of assessment in federal hiring. |
| Research the Position | • Define key terms related to job analysis.<br>• Identify ways in which a job analysis supports human resource (HR) functions, including hiring.<br>• Identify reasons for conducting a job analysis.<br>• Identify roles of subject matter experts.<br>• Identify the purposes and uses of job analysis documents.<br>• List the methods for conducting a job analysis.<br>• List steps in the job analysis process.<br>• Identify legal considerations and professional standards relevant to employee hiring.<br>• Identify procedures for evaluating a job analysis. |
| Identify & Write Screen Out Items | • Define minimum qualifications.<br>• Identify why minimum qualifications are needed.<br>• Identify resources which provide guidance and standards for minimum qualifications.<br>• Determine how minimum qualifications should be assessed.<br>• Describe practices for assessing minimum qualifications.<br>• Write minimum qualifications questions, including specialized experience descriptions for automated delivery.<br>• Describe the types of questions that can be used to screen out unqualified or ineligible applicants using an automated assessment questionnaire. |
| Identify Competencies & Write Ranking Items | • List criteria to be considered when identifying competencies/KSAs to be assessed for hiring purposes.<br>• Define competencies/KSAs.<br>• Identify criteria for developing assessment questionnaire items.<br>• List the three parts of the item writing formula.<br>• Identify tips and pitfalls for writing quality assessment questionnaire items.<br>• Correct improperly written assessment questionnaire items.<br>• List the types of rating scales used in automated assessment questionnaires.<br>• Identify the pros and cons of different rating scale options.<br>• Describe why knowledge-based items would be used in assessments.<br>• Identify an appropriate rating scale to measure an assessment questionnaire item response. |
| Develop Scoring Procedures | • Explain the role of the assessment questionnaire developer in the scoring process.<br>• Describe the USA Staffing scoring process.<br>• Identify options and procedures for scoring assessment questionnaires in USA Staffing.<br>• Describe the purpose and impact of weighting ranking factors. |

*(Table continues on next page)*

**Table 7.1. (Continued)**

| *Lesson* | *Objectives* |
|---|---|
| Ensure Quality | • Identify the reason why quality review is important.<br>• Identify necessary actions in both internal and external reviews.<br>• List the steps in testing an assessment tool in USA Staffing.<br>• List reasons why the assessment tool development process should be documented.<br>• Describe the importance of using and storing templates in a standardized format.<br>• Identify factors to be considered when verifying applicant qualifications.<br>• Identify why, when, and how to adjust an applicant's score.<br>• Identify considerations and methods for evaluating the assessment process.<br>• Identify ways to overcome challenges in developing an assessment tool. |
| Learn More About Assessment | • Describe the importance of effective assessments.<br>• List considerations for developing assessment strategies.<br>• Define validity and reliability.<br>• Identify ways to gather and demonstrate validity evidence.<br>• Identify alternate assessment tools (those other than the assessment questionnaire).<br>• Define a multiple hurdles approach.<br>• Describe which assessment tools are best used for first, second, and subsequent hurdles. |

edge and experience with HR and federal HR, but the majority has little or no experience with developing assessments. In addition, the varied learning styles of the training audience necessitated a flexible design capable of adapting to individual differences.

Finally, the transition of the training from an instructor-led training to a self-guided learning demanded consideration of adult learning and instructional system design principles. Adults are capable of succeeding in TBT, but they often succumb to distractions in their training environment, procrastinate, fail to devote enough time to training, fail to accurately assess their knowledge levels and utilize ineffective learning strategies, which prevent them from achieving their full learning potential. Despite this self-concept and need for responsibility, once learners enter a classroom or log on to an online course many revert back to their time in school and become passive learners.

## COURSE DESIGN AND DEVELOPMENT PROCESS

HRS undertook the development of the TBT as a research and development (R&D) initiative. The R&D team was comprised of HRS's Industrial/

organizational psychologists and HR specialists who served as subject matter experts. These groups developed the training material and deliver the classroom training. The R&D team also collaborated with a vendor specializing in online learning and instructional system design (ISD) to assist with the transition from classroom instruction to technology-based instruction.

In accordance with the theory-based approached to TBT design, the R&D team used a collaborative and iterative process centered on traditional ISD methodology. The course design elements are shown in Table 7.2.

The ISD model links instructional strategies and content to specific learning objectives (Craig, 1996). Thus, the instructional systems designers (that is, the vendor) were charged with organizing and presenting the training content in a logical fashion to facilitate learner achievement of the learning objectives. The design provided a foundation or blueprint upon which all development was based, as well as the audience, learning objectives, course content, evaluation strategies and interactive capabilities of the final course. The R&D team worked closely with the vendor's instructional designers to identify and approve content sources, specifying the information from each source to be included in the course. The TBT, learning assessment and evaluation process were designed to maximize participation, facilitate learning and increase motivation for completion.

## LEVERAGING TECHNOLOGY TO ACHIEVE LEARNING GOALS

The TBT was designed for self-paced learning (without instructor facilitation). The course structure is displayed in Table 7.3.

The classroom training includes 14 hours of instruction, hands-on exercises and feedback. Due to the complex technical content and need for practice opportunities, the TBT requires approximately 8–12 hours of learner contact time. This translates to more than 400 screens and links to secondary information, animations and demonstrations. Therefore, several steps were taken to ensure a balance of guidance, structure, and flexibility in the training.

First, learner progress and record of completion is tracked via a learning management system. The course requires learners to complete the lessons in order. Learners advance to the next lesson once they have completed the previous lesson. However, a bookmark feature is available at any point in the course. If learners choose to exit a lesson before completing it, they are asked if they wish to bookmark the page to return to it later.

**Table 7.2. Course Design Elements**

| *Element* | *Description* |
|---|---|
| Introduction | The introduction begins by providing the learner with the overall goal of the lesson and how it fits into the bigger picture of the course. A motivational statement is presented regarding how this lesson relates to the audience.<br>In addition, a cognitive instructional strategy known as an "advance organizer" is used to promote the acquisition and retention of new information. This is accomplished by providing an overview of what will be taught, or a graphical representation of the structure so that learners can build upon prior knowledge and mentally organize their thoughts before being introduced to details of the new concepts. |
| Objectives | Presents the learning objective(s) for the lesson. |
| Presentation | The instructional segments present the informational text and graphics, and are interspersed, as appropriate, with embedded questions and other learner interactions. In order for learning to occur, the lesson presents facts, concepts and rules, and describes and demonstrates the tasks.<br>The material is presented in an orderly, highly structured form that is meaningful to the learners. Extraneous information is kept to a minimum. Lessons with several topics use transitional statements and advance organizers throughout the presentation. |
| Knowledge checks and exercises | Unscored knowledge appraisals and feedback responses are integrated into the instruction to enhance learning and promote success. The learner is informed that the knowledge checks are unscored and will receive feedback on each. The learner is not required to complete the knowledge checks.<br>Lessons also include exercises where appropriate to reinforce concepts and to allow the learner to apply some of the new concepts to a real-life scenario. All exercise practice situations have relevance to the content. |
| Summary | The instructional presentation concludes by summarizing the key learning points of the lesson, why the lesson is important and how the learner will use this newly acquired information on the job. |
| Additional resources | Each lesson contains links to additional resources pertinent to the information being taught. These are provided in separate screens or integrated into the lesson content and listed in the "Resources" button on the interface. |

Second, to engage learners, the course was designed to avoid "electronic page-turning" and promote interactivity between the learner and the system. Electronic page-turning refers to a situation when the learner reads numerous text screens in a row. In contrast, the TBT screens contain a mix of media, including audio, digitized photographs, graphics,

**Table 7.3. Course Structure**

| *Lesson* | *Lesson Description* | *Number of Screens* |
|---|---|---|
| Help (button on interface) | Course navigation and structure | 20 screens |
| Course Overview and Getting Started | Introduction to the course, along with course overview, motivation for taking the course, introduction to important course topics, and background information | 32 screens |
| Research the Position | Process for performing a job analysis; HR manager demonstration/animation; description of all other types of information that should be reviewed prior to developing the assessment questionnaire; legal requirements for a job analysis hands-on, interactive exercise to reinforce process | 62 screens |
| Identify & Write Screenout Items | Description of what minimum qualification standards are, why they are used and where and how to find them; real-world examples; screen-out factors; and exercises for determining good and bad standards and for writing minimum qualification standards | 60 screens |
| Identify Competencies & Write Ranking Items | Process for developing competencies/KSAs; criteria, instructions, and guidelines; three parts of the item writing formula; tips and pitfalls for writing quality assessment items; key components of an assessment questionnaire; types of rating scales and their pros and cons; of the different rating scales; knowledge-based items in assessments; and, interactive exercises | 62 screens |
| Develop Scoring Procedures | Role of questionnaire developer in the scoring process; scoring process; screen out and rating and ranking; points and weighting factors; Manual scoring and USA Staffing scoring; warnings and verification statements; hands-on exercise to reinforce skills. | 51 screens |
| Develop a Questionnaire for Federal Wage System Position | Optional lesson; differences between wage grade and general service assessments; categories of job elements; and, how to change job elements. Interactive exercises. | 29 screens |
| Ensure Quality | Importance of quality reviews; procedures for ensuring results and questionnaires are getting the expected results | 57 screens |
| Learn More About Assessment | Alternative assessment options, multiple hurdles, customized rating scales, reliability and validity | 46 screens |
| Course Summary & Evaluation | Review of topic areas covered; obtain course certificate | 6 screens |
| Course Assessment | End-of-course test – scored | NA |

animation, or video, to increase the richness of information, enhance and reinforce instruction and hold the learner's interest. Each media type is used to facilitate the best presentation of course content and the needs of the visual, auditory and kinesthetic learner. Graphics, including diagrams, drawings and animations are used to illustrate concepts and procedures within the course. Simple and flash animation is used to emphasize or clarify concepts. For particularly complex content and to ensure immersion, learners are presented with simulations of the processes through screen capture recordings.

Further, the course aims to assist the learner in assessing his/her performance and level of engagement by providing knowledge checks to stimulate retention, maintain motivation and facilitate self-regulation. Knowledge checks and practice exercises focus on lesson objectives as outlined in the course, and attempt to help the learner summarize and apply what has been taught to that point and to provide real-world relevance. Finally, they aim to promote learner interaction with the training, keep learners involved in the course and extend the course beyond page-turning, computer-based instruction. A variety of exercise types is used as knowledge checks throughout the online training, including multiple-choice questions, matching, sequencing and fill in the blank. The type of exercise depends on the content being tested and which option is appropriate to stimulate and support the learning process. The learner is provided at least two chances to select the correct answer for each item and provided feedback following each attempt. Feedback is tailored to each response as well as to the attempt. The subject matter experts and instructional designers carefully developed feedback and remediation to reinforce learning as the learner progresses. Following each exercise, the learner receives positive and upbeat feedback that, when appropriate, provides additional help/hints for an incorrect learner response. For example, if the learner answers correctly, he/she is congratulated as potential reinforcement. If the learner answers incorrectly after first attempt, he/she is told the answer is incorrect, encouraged to try again and is provided a hint to help solve the particular problem. Thus, the course aims to reinforce correct answers and remediate incorrect answers.

Finally, an end-of-course assessment launches at the completion of the course. Each assessment is a random 10-item assessment linked to the learning objectives from each of the training modules. Some questions measure learners' capacity to recall factual (declarative) information presented during training, whereas others measure learners' capacity to recall sequences of actions (procedural) for executing functions or how such actions affect the quality of assessment questionnaires (strategic). Learners who receive less than 70% on the end-of-course assessment must retake and pass the assessment. Upon completion, learners receive a report identifying the questions that are incorrect so they can focus on those particular content areas for improvement. Learners who achieve 70% or more on the assessment can print a Certificate of Completion. The average learner score on the end-of-course assessment is 69.4%, which includes first-time and repeat test takers. This suggests the assessment challenges learners to reflect on knowledge learned during the training and signals to learners where additional review is required to ensure understanding.

## EFFECTIVENESS OF THE TBT PROGRAM

In accordance with instructional system design, the training is accompanied by a robust evaluation approach. The evaluations are based on Kirkpatrick's model (Kirkpatrick & Kirkpatrick, 2006) and aligned with other successful evaluation approaches. Prior to beginning the course, all learners complete a questionnaire to assess their perceived knowledge in the content areas addressed in the training (Kirkpatrick Level II). Immediately following course completion, learners respond to the same questions on perceived knowledge (Kirkpatrick Level II) in addition to questions assessing their satisfaction with the course (Kirkpatrick Level I). Finally, 6 months following course completion, learners receive an evaluation that asks whether they have had an opportunity to demonstrate their new skills, how often they use the skills they learned on the job (Kirkpatrick Level III), and how they would rate the training. Two years since the TBT launched, 1592 individuals registered for the voluntary training; and 644 (40.5%) learners completed the training. Results for Kirkpatrick Level I and Level II evaluations show that nearly half (47.4%) of learners rated the online course as very good or excellent. In addition, 54.1% of learners agreed the course was easy to use and effective, and 64.7% of learners agreed it was beneficial to take the course online.

Approximately half (53%) of learners indicated they would prefer to take the course in a classroom rather than online. For 23% of learners, this was the first online course they had ever taken. Thirty-two percent of learners had taken at least one other course online and 45% had taken three or more courses online prior to this course. Thus, the shift and widespread comfort level with self-paced TBT has not yet been seen with this audience. Overall, for questions related to perceived learning, both pre- and posttraining, learners reported higher levels of perceived knowledge following the course. Results for the 6-month evaluation (Kirkpatrick Level III) are not provided due to a limited response rate. Only 2% of the 644 learners who have completed the course have completed this follow up evaluation. In the future, we hope to identify opportunities for increasing this response rate.

## LESSONS LEARNED AND RECOMMENDATIONS FOR THE FUTURE

- Although the TBT course was designed in a careful and deliberate manner from an instructional design standpoint, the majority of people in the intended audience did not complete the course. There may have been a mismatch between person needs and organization needs and the program design and delivery. For example, needs analysis can consider the necessary supports for learner-controlled training such as sustaining motivation over time or providing supervisor support for learners completing the training (for example, distraction-free environment).
- It is likely that the density and cognitive demand of the course resulted in a majority of learners not completing the entire course. In the future, training such as this may be better received if broken up into more manageable or bite-size topics. Platform capabilities could allow for a prerequisite or fixed order by allowing full immersion in the topic at hand without the overwhelming nature of all topics at once.
- While the majority of the content in the course seemed to be presented effectively in an online format, a blended solution may have been ideal for complete student attainment of the knowledge needed for this course's topics. Specifically, treating the online course as an introduction and then participating in an 'advanced' in-person class for custom, specific issue exploration may be more effective.
- In the future, as changes are made in legislation or updates are implemented in the online software that supports federal hiring, the content of this course will have to change as well. These will likely be opportunities to implement a better or more appropriate approach to presenting the content and introducing self-regulation checks to ensure learners have not "checked-out."
- Furthermore, training was just the first step in assisting agencies with improving the quality of their assessment questionnaires. HRS could offer a more expanded training approach that couples technical coaching and advisory services with the implementation of the training course to improve interactivity and communication. Training learners often feel the content is clear in the classroom or online setting but then do not have a resource on the job. HRS con-

sultants can serve as assessment reviewers during a scheduled time frame following training to ensure consistency in the application of the techniques taught during training.

## REFERENCES

Bell, B. S., Kanar, A. M., & Kozlowksi, S. J. (2008). Current issues and future directions in simulation-based training in North America. *International Journal of Human Resource Management, 19*(8), 1416–1434.

Bell, B. S., & Kozlowski, S. W. J. (2002). Adaptive guidance: Enhancing self-regulation, knowledge and performance in technology-based training. *Personnel Psychology, 55*, 267–306.

Craig, R. L. (1996) *The ASTD training & development handbook: A guide to human resource development* (4th ed.). New York, NY: McGraw Hill.

DeRouin, R. E., Fritzsche, B. A., & Salas, E. (2004). Optimizing e-learning: Research-based guidelines for learner-controlled training. *Human Resource Management, 43,* 147–162.

Goldstein, I. L. (1986). *Training in organizations: Needs assessments, development, and evaluation* (2nd ed.). Monterey, CA: Brooks/Cole.

Kanar, A. M., & Bell, B. S. (2013). Guiding learners through technology-based instruction: The effects of adaptive guidance design and individual differences on learning over time. *Journal of Educational Psychology, 105*, 106–1081.

Kirkpatrick, D. L., & Kirkpatrick, J. L. (2006). *Evaluating training programs* (3rd ed.). San Francisco, CA: Berrett-Koehler.

Kozlowski, S. W. J., & Bell, B. S. (2007). A theory-based approach for designing distributed learning systems. In S. M. Fiore & E. Salas (Eds.), *Toward a science of distributed learning* (pp. 15–39). Washington, DC: American Psychological Association.

Kraiger, K. (2003). Perspectives on training and development. In W. C. Borman, D. R. Ilgen, & R. J. Klimoski (Eds.), *Handbook of psychology: Vol. 12. Industrial and organizational psychology* (pp. 171–192). Hoboken, NJ: Wiley.

Kraiger, K., & Jerden, E. (2007). A new look at learner control: Metaanalytic results and directions for future research. In S. M. Fiore & E. Salas (Eds.), *Where is the learning in distance learning? Towards a science of distributed learning and training* (pp. 65–90). Washington, DC: APA.

Patel, L. (2010). *ASTD state of the industry report 2010.* Alexandria, VA: American Society for Training & Development.

Salas, E., Tannenbaum, S., Kraiger, K., & Smith-Jentsch, K. A. (2012). The science of training and development in organizations: What matters in practice. *Psychological Science in the Public Interest, 13*, 74–101.

Sitzman, T., Kraiger, K., Stewart, D., & Wisher, R. (2006). The comparative effectiveness of web-based and classroom instruction: A meta-analysis. *Personnel Psychology, 59*, 623–664.

CHAPTER 8

# CURRENT THEMES IN BEHAVIORAL BUSINESS ETHICS

## Implications for Human Resources Training and Development

**Sheldene Simola**

The spate of corporate scandals that occurred during the last 2 decades resulted not only in increased demands for corporate legal compliance, but also in more emphasis on ethical business practice as a foundation for regaining and maintaining stakeholder trust (Sloan & Gavin, 2010). In keeping with these trends, the use of ethics and compliance training programs has steadily increased in the last decade, such that in the United States some form of training is now used in approximately 81% of private sector organizations (Ethics Resource Centre, 2014). Additionally, a growing responsibility for ethics training and development has been ascribed to human resource (HR) professionals, not only by global human resource management (Garavan & McGuire, 2010; Sloan & Gavin, 2010; Valentine, Hollingworth, & Francis, 2013) and business ethics scholars (Treviño & Brown, 2004; Weaver & Treviño, 1999; Wells & Schminke, 2001), but also,

*Human Capital Management Research: Influencing Practice and Process*
pp. 117–130
Copyright © 2016 by Information Age Publishing
All rights of reproduction in any form reserved.

within organizations themselves (Martin & Woldring, 2001; Parkes & Davis, 2013; Society for Human Resource Management & Ethics Resource Centre, 2008). However, despite the actual or expected involvement of HR professionals in selecting, designing, or implementing ethics-related training and development initiatives, ethics coverage has typically been quite limited within human resource management textbooks (Deckop, 2008). Moreover, even when HR scholars have tried to ameliorate this gap (e.g., Deckop, 2008), the information provided has not necessarily reflected the novel, significant and often counterintuitive insights that have emerged through recent research in behavioral business ethics (e.g., De Cremer & Tenbrunsel, 2012).

Therefore, the purpose of this chapter is twofold. First, in order to fill the gap in content coverage of business ethics that often occurs in human resource management texts, an overview of recent themes from behavioral business ethics will be provided, many of which challenge conventional and commonly held beliefs about workplace ethical decision making and action. Second, the chapter will also offer contextual guidance for HR professionals on the provision of ethics-related training and development.

## WHY BEHAVIORAL BUSINESS ETHICS?

There are two key approaches to business ethics. The first is the philosophical or normative approach, which, historically, has been dominant in the field of business ethics (Pamental, 1991). It focuses on the use of moral philosophical theories such as consequentialism, deontology, and virtue ethics for evaluating ethical dilemmas and distinguishing good courses of action that "should" be implemented. This approach is highly valued because it shifts decision making away from ad hoc, idiosyncratic, or opinion-based strategies toward more methodical and scrupulous forms of reasoning through which morally justifiable decisions can be made (Buchholz & Rosenthal, 2001). The second approach is the behavioral or descriptive approach, which since the beginning of the current millennium has become increasingly influential. It identifies and describes the psychological processes through which individuals actually make and implement ethical decisions (De Cremer & Tenbrunsel, 2012).

Despite the value of the normative philosophical approach for identifying morally justifiable courses of action (Buchholz & Rosenthal, 2001) and for serving as a foundation upon which corporate values statements and ethics codes can be built (Van Gerwen, 1996), its use and benefits are predicated on the ability of individuals to deploy certain skills. For example, individuals must first be able to recognize that an ethical dilemma has emerged, and upon recognition, engage in conscious, intentional, and rational evaluation of the dilemma to determine a good or right course of action. Subsequently, the individual must be able to choose and actually implement that good course of action (e.g., Rest, 1986, 1994). However, despite the common assumption that individuals will implement these skills predictably and with relative ease, a plethora of research from within behavioral ethics has identified that this is not the case (e.g., Banaji, Bazerman, & Chugh, 2003; De Cremer & Tenbrunsel, 2012; Messick, 2008; Reynolds, 2006; Welsh & Ordóñez, 2014). Rather, individuals often respond to ethical situations not in conscious, intentional, and rational ways required by normative philosophical approaches, but in unconscious, automatic, and intuitive ways that preclude intentional and active use of formal moral deliberation (Haidt, 2001; Reynolds, 2006). Additionally, these automatic, intuitive tendencies are reflected in a large range of individual and group-level processes that can significantly inhibit or impede ethical recognition, evaluation, and action (Banaji et al., 2003; Messick, 2008). Therefore, the development of skills aimed at recognizing these tendencies and implementing strategies for overcoming their potentially deleterious effects on ethical decision making and action is critical. Indeed, it has been noted that training and development programs that overlook or discount behavioral influences on ethical decision making and action will be unsuccessful in achieving positive gains, regardless of how well intentioned these programs might be (Banaji et al., 2003; Bazerman & Tenbrunsel, 2011; Tenbrunsel & Messick, 2004). Consider, therefore, an overview of recent findings from within behavioral ethics, summarized by theme.

## RESEARCH IN BEHAVIORAL ETHICS: SOME KEY FINDINGS

**1. When it comes to ethical issues, human beings are not nearly as conscious, intentional, and rational as they think they are.** In groundbreaking research on ethical judgment, Haidt (2001) identified that human beings often engage in highly automatic and intuitive responses that occur below the level of conscious awareness. These intuitive responses involve "the sudden appearance in consciousness of a moral judgment, including an affective valence (good-bad, like-dislike) without any conscious awareness of having gone through steps of searching, weighing evidence, or inferring a conclusion" (Haidt, 2001, p.818). Although these intuitive responses do not preclude conscious, rational forms of reflection or reasoning, they are seen as much more frequent in occurrence. Indeed, behavioral business ethicists (e.g., Bazerman & Tenbrunsel, 2011; Shu, Gino, & Bazerman, 2012) often conceptualize the two approaches to ethical judgment within the System 1 and System 2 processing framework first articulated by Stanovich and West (2000), or within the X-system and C-system processes described by Reynolds (2006). Within these frameworks, System 1 or X-system processing is that which is rapid, automatic, effortless, implicit, nonconscious, and visceral or emotionally laden. System 2 or C-System processing is that which is slower, intentional, effortful, explicit, conscious, and rational. In neurocognitive terms, it is argued that X-system processing involves reflexive attempts at matching the electrochemical patterns formed by incoming data with the electrochemical patterns of previously established prototypes for various ethical situations. When pattern matching is successful, associated normative judgments and prescriptive courses of action automatically emerge. In contrast, C-system or conscious, deliberate processing is used only when pattern matching fails, or when individuals deliberately invoke its use in an effortful way, in order to reconsider or override automatic judgments. Although less common than X-system processing, C-system processing is thought to be more likely to result in good ethical judgment (Reynolds, 2006).

Practical examples of the ways automatic or intuitive processes can impact ethical decision making are multiple and varied. For example, with regard to discrimination, training, and development often focuses on the legal requirements of human rights codes, assuming that if employees are aware of requirements for fairness, then they will act accordingly. However, a large body of research has demonstrated that racism and other types of discrimination come in various forms, not all of which are reduced simply by increasing conscious awareness of legal requirements. Rather, individuals often hold implicit stereotypes that occur below the level of conscious awareness (Greenwald & Banaji, 1995), and that have significant potential to result in subtle and insidious yet unintentional forms of bias in employment-related processes and decisions. These implicit stereotypes are particularly concerning because they are pervasive, even among those individuals who on a conscious level are firmly committed to egalitarian principles (Dovidio & Gaertner, 2004). For example, although individuals might be highly trained in and consciously intending to use fair selection practices such as behavior description interviews (Janz, 1982), they might unintentionally give fewer prompts or less informal encouragement to interviewees from certain ethnic or racial groups. Similarly, interviewers might unintentionally give weaker ratings to ambiguous answers provided by interviewees from certain groups. Moreover, because implicit processes are more likely to exert influence under conditions involving time pressure, distraction or ambiguity, their impact might be greater in organizational settings where these conditions are common (e.g., Banaji et al., 2003; Chugh, 2004).

In terms of conflict of interest, it is widely acknowledged that when such situations arise, intentional self-serving choices are common (Banaji et al., 2003). However, notwithstanding the role that conscious deliberation plays in self-serving choices, an accumulating body of empirical research also supports an important role for implicit processes (Bazerman, Loewenstein, & Moore, 2002). In this regard, it has been argued that in many cases when professional responsibilities and self-interest are in conflict, professional responsibilities tend to be processed intentionally, whereas self-interest tends to be processed automatically (Moore & Loewenstein, 2004), thereby increasing the potential for unintentional, self-preferential decisions. For example, empirical investigation of a commonly recommended strategy for managing potential conflict of interest situations, that of disclosure, has demonstrated that disclosure is associated not only with higher (versus lower) levels of self-interested behavior on the part of the individual declaring the conflict of interest, but also with failure by those receiving the disclosure to discount information from the person making the disclosure (Cain, Loewenstein, & Moore, 2005, 2011). Moreover, the higher levels of self-serving behavior associated with disclosure might well reflect a moral licensing or compensation effect in which unethical (i.e., self-serving) behavior follows ethical behavior (i.e., disclosure) (Bazerman & Tenbrunsel, 2011; Cain, Loewenstein, & Moore, 2011).

**2. Individuals are not as skilled at recognizing emerging ethical issues as is often believed.** In framing difficulties with ethical awareness or recognition, Tenbrunsel and Messick (2004) used the term "ethical fading" to denote situations where ethical considerations are excluded from analysis due to a lack of awareness about the underlying, nonconscious processes through which individuals often respond to ethical situations. In particular, they argued that: "individuals do not 'see' the moral components of an ethical decision, not so much because they are morally uneducated, but because psychological processes *fade* the 'ethics' from an ethical dilemma" (Tenbrunsel & Messick, 2004, p. 224).

Although it is beyond the scope of this chapter to elaborate the full range of contexts in which individuals may have difficulty recognizing emerging ethical issues, several examples are offered here. First, a number of authors have noted that failure to recognize unethical behavior is often associated with the predicament in which individuals and groups gradually "slide down a slippery slope" into unethical behavior without realizing that this is occurring (Bazerman & Tenbrunsel, 2011; Gino & Bazerman, 2009; Tenbrunsel & Messick, 2004). Indeed, empirical research demonstrates that individuals find it much more difficult to notice ethical violations that happen as a result of a series of small deviations compared to ethical violations that occur suddenly through a single large deviation (Gino & Bazerman, 2009). Tenbrunsel and Messick (2004) argue that two important mechanisms through which incremental movement toward unethical behavior occurs are a gradual and nonconscious induction process related to subtle and therefore unrecognized shifts in behavior, combined with psychological numbing associated with repeated exposure to incremental shifts in ethical standards. Welsh, Ordóñez, Snyder, and Christian (2015) empirically demonstrated not only that gradually changing ethical decisions over time resulted in larger lapses, but also, that gradual rather than sudden changes occurring across ethics-related decisions resulted in both diminished self-regulation and increased moral disengagement.

A second example of conditions that can inhibit our ability to recognize emerging ethical issues is the manner in which language is used to describe those issues. In particular, Bandura (1999) found that in many settings commonly used phrases often describe harmful behaviors in ways that make them seem benign. In business and organizational settings, there are many such phrases, and they have significant potential to obscure the ethical dimensions of situations. For example, as noted by Tenbrunsel and Messick (2004), it is not uncommon to speak of aggressive (versus illegal) accounting practices or to speak of externalities (versus injurious environmental practices) or rightsizing (versus placing people out of work). An additional linguistic tool through which business language can obscure the ethical dimensions of a situation is that involving the use of sports or other metaphors. Although metaphors can be powerfully inspiring to individuals in organizational settings, they also pose a number of risks. For example, individuals might begin to perceive not just that business is *in some ways like* a game, but rather, that business *actually is* a game (Hamington, 2009). When business is conceptualized as a game, ethical recognition can be obscured because it compartmentalizes business as separate from the normative standards endorsed in broader society, and also restricts ethical considerations to the relatively narrow procedural rules of the game which might be inconsistent with ethical guidelines that apply in society more generally. Additionally, business as game metaphors have potential to trivialize stakeholder concerns and to promote highly adversarial, win at all costs, mindsets (Hamington, 2009).

**3. Social context exerts substantial influence on ethical decision making and action.** Treviño and Brown (2004) identified that contrary to common belief, ethical problems are typically not the result of a few 'bad apples' with weak intraindividual standards. Rather, social or contextual factors can lead normal adults to make ethically troubling decisions. Examples from within classic social psychological research include harmful actions undertaken during obedience to authority (Milgram, 1974);

diffusion of responsibility that occurs as group size increases (Darley & Latané, 1968); social conformity in which individuals (often knowingly) give inaccurate answers that match those of others (Asch, 1956); and the rapid deterioration of civil behavior into abuse that has been associated with deindividuation in social roles (Zimbardo, 2007). In contemporary workplaces, a range of other contextual factors can also exert influence. These include organizational leadership and culture, as well as reward systems that promote unethical behavior (Treviño & Brown, 2004). Contemporary researchers have also identified the ways in which contextual factors, such as corporate culture or leader directives, can interact with implicitly held beliefs to increase unethical behavior. In particular, when individuals who hold implicit beliefs that conventional business practices are inherently moral are presented with contextual cues consistent with this assumption, they are more likely to behave in ways that reflect these implicitly held beliefs. This suggests that relevant contextual cues can strengthen preferences for highly competitive, stockholder versus stakeholder-driven practices that could exacerbate unethical action (Reynolds, Leavitt, & DeCelles, 2010). However, interestingly and in contrast, subconscious priming of individuals' moral standards has been found to both increase their propensity to categorize morally ambiguous situations as unethical, as well as to result in less unethical behavior, even in situations in which individuals are left unmonitored and assigned challenging performance goals previously linked to unethical behavior (Welsh & Ordóñez, 2014).

**4. Good moral judgment will not necessarily result in moral action.** A common concern within the field of behavioral business ethics is the gap that often exists between moral judgment and moral action, such that even when ethically sound judgments are made, the corresponding ethical actions are not necessarily implemented (Aquino & Reed, 2002; Hannah, Avolio, & Walumbwa, 2011). An important area of research in this regard is that of moral identity (Aquino & Reed, 2002; Blasi, 1984), and more specifically, the centrality or importance of an individuals' moral identity to overall concept of self. When moral identity is highly central or important to individuals, they will be more likely to engage in various moral behaviors (Aquino & Reed, 2002), particularly when social consensus about the ethicality of a situation is not high (Reynolds & Ceranic, 2007) or when moral identity is made particularly salient by situational cues (Aquino & Freeman, 2009). Moral identity is, therefore, likely to be a critical concept in understanding why some individuals, despite significant risks of ostracism or other forms of social censure, still act in morally courageous ways by giving voice to ethical concerns (Simola, 2014). Indeed, "professional moral courage" (Sekerka, Bagozzi, & Charnigo, 2009, p. 565) is seen as an important area in which organizations can facilitate proactive movement toward "moral strength" and "virtue excellence" that can serve as important aspects of training aimed at prevention of ethical problems.

**5. Individuals are not necessarily always and primarily self-motivated and self-serving.** Although the themes summarized above might on first review appear to suggest that the possibilities of human ethical behavior are relatively bleak, there are also important bodies of knowledge that provide encouraging perspectives on human ethical behavior. For example, research on the "ultimatum game" emerging from within behavioral economics sheds important light. Within the ultimatum game, a participant called 'the proposer' is asked to split a sum of money between himself or herself and a second participant called "the responder." If the responder accepts the offer, both parties keep their portion of the money. However, if the responder rejects the split, neither receives their portion of money. Under classical economic assumptions, any amount of money should be accepted by the responder, because even a small amount of money makes that individual better off than before the money was offered. However, research demonstrates not only that most individuals offer what is perceived to be a "fair" split (50-50 or close to it), but also that responders often reject what are perceived to be nonfair offers, even though these might be lucrative to them (see Bazerman & Moore, 2009), thereby drawing into question traditional economic assumptions about the nature of human decision making.

## CONTEXTUAL GUIDELINES FOR HUMAN RESOURCES TRAINING AND DEVELOPMENT

Five current themes in behavioral business ethics were described above, along with some specific activities that can be used in training and development. Below, some contextual guidelines for the provision of ethics-related training and development are provided.

### Contextual Guidelines

1. In order for the positive effects of ethics-related training and development to be fully realized, the organization itself must be committed to an ethical culture. If ethics are peripheral rather than central to organizational strategy, then ethical action by employees is much less likely to occur even when high quality training has been provided (Parkes & Davis, 2013; Sekerka, 2009; Sloan & Gavin, 2010). In terms of establishing or maintaining an

ethical organizational culture, there is broad support for HR practitioners to serve various roles. These include roles in raising ethical consciousness and promoting ethical practices throughout organizations (Society for Human Resource Management & Ethics Resource Centre, 2008; Sloan & Gavin, 2010; Valentine et al., 2013), often within various HR functions such as recruitment, selection, orientation, training, performance management, compensation and ethics-related change management (Craft, 2010; Garavan & McGuire, 2010; Parkes & Davis, 2013; Sloan & Gavin, 2010).

2. In terms of actual implementation of ethics-related training and development, it should be noted that one size does not fit all (Garavan & McGuire, 2010). Rather, different HR roles and approaches might emerge through consideration of a range of variables such as industry and institutional context, size of the organization, and the historical and current status of HR in the organization. Consideration should, therefore, be given to particular needs and possibilities as suggested by these factors.
3. A needs assessment is often a useful starting point. Although research within behavioral ethics suggests various areas on which training and development initiatives might fruitfully focus, it is also important to understand the unique concerns and learning needs that employees within a given organization might have. Once these are assessed, they can be addressed within various HR functions, including training and development (Society for Human Resource Management & Ethics Resource Centre, 2008; Wells & Schminke, 2001).
4. Include information not only on *compliance* to legal requirements, but also on the use of *values* in ethical decision making and action. Research on the relationship between employee perceptions of training program orientations and employee attitudes and behaviors has found that although perceptions of both compliance-based and values-based programs were positively related to various favorable outcomes, perceptions of values-based programs were associated with additional favorable outcomes not found in compliance-based programs (Weaver & Treviño, 1999). Moreover, perceptions of a values- (versus compliance-) based orientation had more explanatory power relative to favorable outcomes. Indeed, as Sloan and Gavin (2010) suggest, compliance is often facilitated by extrinsic factors and is unlikely to be sufficient to achieve the full range of organizational ethical goals. However, values are intrinsically

motivating such that facilitating employee reliance on them might well support a broader range of ethical outcomes.

5. Use training and development techniques that are likely to be effective. Although ethics-related training often occurs as part of orientation for new employees (Sekerka, 2009), it has been noted that development of ethics-related skills is often a longer term process. Hence, a single training program should be complemented by ongoing opportunities for development and dialogue, and ethical considerations integrated into training programs on other topics (Craft, 2010). Characteristics of ethics training identified as particularly desirable are: the inclusion of face-to-face (versus online only) training which includes interactive and reflective components (Craft, 2010; Sekerka, 2009); training relevant to workplace responsibilities, possibly through the use of realistic vignettes (Frisque & Kolb, 2008); training grounded in theory (Wells & Schminke, 2001); and, the use of active, experiential activities, such as role playing and discussion of video vignettes (Wells & Schminke, 2001). Importantly, ethics-related training programs also need to facilitate not simply awareness about important findings from recent research in behavioral ethics, but rather skills for overcoming potentially deleterious tendencies that often happen outside of conscious awareness. Conventional strategies that exclude the influence of situational factors, situational cues and unconscious processes will be insufficient.
6. It is also important to use training that promotes subsequent transfer of newly acquired skills into the actual work of participants. Transfer of training can be facilitated in various ways, including through the use of meta-cognitive strategies in which participants learn skills for monitoring and adjusting their own application of new knowledge, as well as through a focus on mastery goals aimed at improved abilities rather than a focus on performance goals aimed simply at demonstrating that new skills can be performed. Posttraining support is also useful, particularly when it occurs in a culture that supports and models not only desired ethical outcomes but also continuous learning (Frisque & Kolb, 2008; Wells & Schminke, 2001).
7. In order to have a strategic impact, outcomes should be assessed (Sloan & Gavin, 2010). However, assessment of outcomes, such as trainee satisfaction, knowledge or skill acquisition, are likely to be insufficient. Rather, assessing the extent to which individuals demonstrate ethics-related competencies or best practices

(Sekerka, 2009) as well as any improvements in organizational-level ethics-related results is important (Wells & Schminke, 2001).

## SUMMARY

The purpose of this chapter was twofold. First, in order to fill the gap in content coverage of business ethics that often occurs in human resource management texts, it provided an overview of recent themes from behavioral business ethics, many of which challenge conventional and commonly held beliefs about workplace ethical decision making and action. Second, the chapter also provided contextual guidance for HR professionals on the provision of ethics-related training and development. Future research should focus on the evaluation of behaviorally based ethics training and development programs, including assessment not just of trainee satisfaction and knowledge or skill acquisition, but also of the extent to which participants actually demonstrate ethics-related competencies (Sekerka, 2009) and any improvements in organizational-level ethics-related results (Wells & Schminke, 2001).

## REFERENCES

Aquino, K., & Freeman, D. (2009). Moral identity in business situations: A social cognitive framework for understanding moral functioning. In. D. Narvaez & D. K. Lapsley (Eds.), *Personality, identity and character: Explorations in moral psychology.* Cambridge, England: Cambridge University Press.

Aquino, K., & Reed, A. (2002). The self-importance of moral identity. *Journal of Personality and Social Psychology, 83*(6), 1423–1440.

Asch, S. E. (1956). Studies of independence and conformity. A minority of one against a unanimous majority. *Psychological Monographs, 70*(9), 1–70.

Banaji, M. R., Bazerman, M. H., & Chugh, D. (2003). How un(ethical) are you? *Harvard Business Review, 81*(12), 56–65.

Bandura, A. (1999). Moral disengagement in the perpetration of inhumanities. *Personality and Social Psychology Review, 3*(3), 193–209.

Bazerman, M. H., Loewenstein, G., & Moore, D. A. (2002). Why good accountants do bad Audits. *Harvard Business Review, 80*(11), 96–102.

Bazerman, M. H., & Moore, D. A. (2009). *Judgment in managerial decision-making* (7th ed.). Hoboken NJ: John Wiley & Sons.

Bazerman, M. H., & Tenbrunsel, A. E. (2011). *Blindspots: Why we fail to do what's right and what to do about it.* Princeton NJ: Princeton University Press.

Blasi, A. (1984). Moral identity: Its role in moral functioning. In W. M. Kurtines & J. L. Gewirtz (Eds.), *Morality, moral behavior, and moral development* (pp. 128–139). New York, NY: John Wiley & Sons.

Buchholz R. A., & Rosenthal, S. B. (2001). A philosophical framework for case studies. *Journal of Business Ethic, 29,* 25–31.

Cain, D., Loewenstein, G., & Moore, D. (2005). The dirt on coming clean: Perverse effects of disclosing conflicts of interest. *Journal of Legal Studies, 34*(1), 1–25.

Cain, D., Loewenstein, G., & Moore, D. (2011). When sunlight fails to disinfect: Understanding the perverse effects of disclosing conflicts of interest. *Journal of Consumer Research, 37,* 836–857.

Chugh, D. (2004). Societal and managerial implications of implicit social cognition: Why milliseconds matter. *Social Justice Research, 17*(2), 203–222.

Craft, J. L. (2010). Making the case for ongoing and interactive organizational ethics training. *Human Resource Development International, 13*(5), 599–606.

Darley, J. M., & Latané, B. (1968). Bystander intervention in emergencies: Diffusion of responsibility. *Journal of Personality and Social Psychology, 8*(4), 377–383.

Deckop, J. R. (2008). Conceptual tools for studying the ethics of human resource management. In V. G. Scarpello (Ed.), *The handbook of human resource management: Promoting an effective and efficient curriculum* (pp. 185–200). Thousand Oaks, CA: SAGE.

De Cremer, D., & Tenbrunsel, A. E. (Eds.). (2012). On understanding the need for a behavioral business ethics approach. In *Behavioral business ethics: Shaping an emerging field* (pp. 3–16). New York, NY: Routledge-Taylor & Francis Group.

Dovidio, J. F., & Gaertner, S. L. (2004). Aversive racism. *Advances in Experimental Social Psychology, 36,* 1–52.

Ethics Resource Center. (2014). National business ethics survey of the U.S. workplace. Arlington, VA: Author. Retrieved on November 22, 2014, from http://www.ethics.org/resource/national-business-ethics-survey%C2%AE-us-workplace

Frisque, D. A., & Kolb, J. A. (2008). The effects of an ethics training program on attitude, knowledge, and transfer of training of office professionals: A treatment- and control-group design. *Human Resource Development Quarterly, 19*(1), 35–53.

Garavan, T. N., & McGuire, D. (2010). Human resource development and society: Human resource development's role in embedding corporate social responsibility, sustainability, and ethics in organizations. *Advances in Developing Human Resources, 12*(5), 487–507.

Gino, F., & Bazerman, M. (2009). When misconduct goes unnoticed: The acceptability of gradual erosion in others' unethical behavior. *Journal of Experimental Social Psychology, 45,* 708–719.

Greenwald, A. G., & Banaji, M. R. (1995). Implicit social cognition: Attitudes, self-esteem, and stereotypes. *Psychological Review, 102*(1), 4–27.

Haidt, J. (2001). The emotional dog and its rational tail: A social intuitionist approach to moral Judgment. *Psychological Review, 108,* 814–834.

Hamington, M. (2009). Business is not a game: The metaphoric fallacy. *Journal of Business Ethics, 86,* 473–484.

Hannah, S. T., Avolio, B. J., & Walumbwa, F.O. (2011). Relationships between authentic leadership, moral courage, and ethical and pro-social behaviors. *Business Ethics Quarterly, 21*(4), 555–578.

Janz, T. (1982). Initial comparisons of patterned behavior description interviews versus unstructured interviews. *Journal of Applied Psychology, 67*(5), 577–580.

Martin, G., & Woldring, K. (2001). Ready for the mantle? Australian HR managers as stewards of ethics. *Journal of Human Resources Management, 12*(2), 243–255.

Messick, D. M. (2008). What can psychology tell us about business ethics? *Journal of Business Ethics, 89,* 73–80.

Milgram, S. (1974). *Obedience to authority.* New York, NY: Harper & Row.

Moore, D. A., & Lowenstein, G. (2004). Self-interest, automaticity, and the psychology of conflict of interest. *Social Justice Research, 17*(2), 189–202.

Pamental, G. L. (1991). The course in business ethics: Why don't the philosophers give business students what they need? *Business Ethics Quarterly 1,* 385–393.

Parkes, C., & Davis, A. J. (2013). Ethics and social responsibility—Do HR professionals have the 'courage to challenge' or are they set to be permanent 'bystanders'? *The International Journal of Human Resource Management, 24*(12), 2411–2434.

Rest, J. R. (1986). *Moral development: Advances in research and theory.* New York, NY: Praeger.

Rest, J. R. (1994). Background: Theory and research. In. J. R. Rest & D. Narvaez (Eds.) *Moral development in the professions: Psychology and applied ethics* (pp. 1–26). Hillsdale, NJ: Erlbaum.

Reynolds, S. J. (2006). A neurocognitive model of the ethical decision-making process: Implications for study and practice. *Journal of Applied Psychology, 91*(4), 737–748.

Reynolds, S. J., & Ceranic, T. L. (2007). The effects of moral judgement and moral identity on moral behaviour: An empirical examination of the moral individual. *Journal of Applied Psychology, 92*(6), 1610–1624.

Reynolds, S. J., Leavitt, K., & DeCelles, K. A. (2010). Automatic ethics: The effects of implicit assumptions and contextual cues on moral behavior. *Journal of Applied Psychology, 95*(4), 75–760.

Sekerka, L. E. (2009). Organizational ethics education and training: A review of best practices and their application. *International Journal of Training and Development, 13*(2), 77–95.

Sekerka, L. E., Bagozzi, R. P., & Charnigo, R. (2009). Facing ethical challenges in the workplace: Conceptualizing and measuring professional moral courage. *Journal of Business Ethics, 89,* 565–579.

Simola, S. (2014). Understanding moral courage through a feminist and developmental ethic of care. *Journal of Business Ethics,* Advance online publication. doi:10.1007/s10551-014-2203-y

Society for Human Resource Management & Ethics Resource Center. (2008). *The ethics landscape in American business: Sustaining a strong ethical work environment.* Alexandria VA: Ethics Resource Center. Retrieved May 30, 2015, from http://www.shrm.org/research/surveyfindings/documents/08-0449_ethics_landscape.pdf

Sloan, K., & Gavin, J. H. (2010). Human resource management: Meeting the ethical obligations of the function. *Business and Society Review, 115,* 157–174.

Stanovich, K. E., & West, R. F. (2000). Individual differences in reasoning: Implications for the rationality debate. *Behavioral & Brain Science, 23*, 645–665.

Shu, L. L., Gino, F., & Bazerman, M. H. (2012). Ethical discrepancy: Changing our attitudes to resolve moral dissonance. In D. De Cremer & A. E. Tenbrunsel (Eds.), *Behavioral business* (pp. 221–239). New York NY: Routledge-Taylor & Francis Group.

Tenbrunsel, A. E., & Messick, D. M. (2004). Ethical fading: The role of self-deception in unethical behavior. *Social Justice Research, 17*(2), 223–236.

Treviño, L. K., & Brown, M. E. (2004). Managing to be ethical: Debunking five business ethics myths. *Academy of Management Executive, 18*(2), 69–81.

Valentine, S., Hollingworth, D., & Francis, C. A. (2013). Quality-related HR practices, organizational ethics and positive work attitudes: Implications for HRD. *Human Resources Development Quarterly, 24*(4), 493–523.

Van Gerwen, J. (1996). Three methods in applied ethics. *A Critical Review Ethical Perspectives, 3*(4), 184–193.

Weaver, G. R., & Treviño, L. K. (1999). Compliance and values oriented ethics programs: Influences on employees' attitudes and behavior. *Business Ethics Quarterly, 9*(2), 315–335.

Wells, D., & Schminke, M. (2001). Ethical development and human resources training: An integrative framework. *Human Resource Management Review, 11*, 135–158.

Welsh, D. T., & Ordóñez, L. D. (2014). Conscience without cognition: The effects of subconscious priming on ethical behavior. *Academy of Management Journal, 57*(3), 723–742.

Welsh, D. T., Ordóñez, L. D., Snyder, D. G., & Christian, M. S. (2015). The slippery slope: How small ethical transgressions pave the way for larger future transgressions. *Journal of Applied Psychology, 100*(1), 114–127.

Zimbardo, P. (2007). *The Lucifer effect: Understanding how good people turn evil.* New York NY: Random House.

CHAPTER 9

# PERFORMANCE MANAGEMENT

## Common Practice, Unique Practice, and Effective Practice

**Alan Colquitt**

### INTRODUCTION

There is perhaps no topic in human resource management that has been more written about in the popular business press in the past few years than performance management. At the time of this writing, an Amazon search reveals 55,871 books available and a Google search results in 250,000,000 hits on the term "performance management" alone.

In this chapter, I examine why performance management fails to address important business needs and propose an alternative framework based on sound research. Central to this failure is the reliance on benchmarking information over rigorous research to guide performance management design decisions and the failure of business leaders and (human resource) HR professionals to critically examine the theories, assumptions, and beliefs that underlie their practices. Challenging existing assumptions and leveraging the scientific research literature will enable

*Human Capital Management Research: Influencing Practice and Process*
pp. 131–147
Copyright © 2016 by Information Age Publishing
All rights of reproduction in any form reserved.

companies to identify the next generation of performance management practices.

Benchmarking research reveals organizations approach performance management in similar ways (Mercer, 2011, 2012b; Gorman et al., 2012; Institute for Corporate Productivity, 2011):

- 95% of companies set individual goals;
- 65% conduct performance feedback sessions between official performance reviews;
- 95% of companies have formal year-end reviews; 63% have midyear or quarterly reviews
- Over 90% use performance ratings;
- As many as 65% of companies give supervisors guidance on the expected distribution of performance ratings;
- 91% link pay to performance to at least some extent;
- 82% link individual performance ratings and compensation decisions; and
- 71% differentiate rewards at least to a "moderate" amount and 69% are working to increase differentiation. Only 1% are working to reduce differentiation.

Experts recommend companies adopt many of these same practices (see, e.g., Aguinis, 2013; Pulakos, 2009). There are however others who have been critical of many of these practices (see, e.g., Coens & Jenkins, 2002; Manzoni, 2008; Pfeffer & Sutton, 2006; Pink, 2009) and this criticism appears to be well founded (McCann, 2013):

- Up to 58% of companies are planning to make major changes to their process;
- Only 20% are pleased with it;
- Only 35% feel their process significantly helps them improve their business performance;
- Respondents to a Conference Board survey rated their performance management system in 11 areas. The average across the 11 was only 28% favorable (McCann, 2013).

Why have companies adopted practices that do not appear to be working? Why are the changes companies are making to their systems not making things better? I would propose two key reasons. First, organizations rely heavily on benchmarking information from consulting firms and HR think tanks for guidance in designing their performance management systems. Although there is rigorous research available on performance management practices, companies tend to look at what other companies are doing instead. They favor information on "common" practices instead of "effective" practices and these two are not always the same. Second, organizations have a penchant for "single-loop learning" (Argyris, 1990). They try something and if it does not work they try something else. When faced with failure, they rarely step back and question the assumptions, beliefs and values that underlie their practices ("double-loop learning").

Common performance management practices like those presented above have well-documented roots in theories from psychology, economics and management. While there is not space here to discuss these theories in depth; suffice it to say the positions they take form the basis of many of the assumptions behind these practices. Table 9.1 summarizes common performance management practices from the benchmarking literature and traces their origins to relevant theories and research in the academic literature, highlighting the key assumptions and positions taken by these theories.

I believe it is these assumptions and the theories that underpin them that represent the greatest barrier to fundamental change in performance management. They are taken as truths and they can blind companies to alternative practices and solutions. In the next section I examine the research support for these theories and assumptions.

## RESEARCH SUPPORT—THEORIES AND ASSUMPTIONS UNDERLYING PERFORMANCE MANAGEMENT PRACTICES

***"Goals motivate individuals and help align employee efforts with company goals."*** There have been hundreds of studies on the effectiveness of goal setting and there are several reviews of this research available, including three meta-analysis studies (for the latest reviews see Kleingold, van Mierlo, & Arends, 2011; Locke & Latham, 2013).

This research clearly indicates people (and groups) who set goals tend to perform better than those who do not and those who set specific and challenging goals perform better than those with no goals, general goals or easy goals. For goals to motivate however, employees need to commit to them, they need to believe they can achieve them ("self-efficacy"), and they need feedback on their progress (Locke & Latham, 2013). Goals also need to be manageable. When they become too complex, strategies for accomplishing them become complicated and they are less likely to be accomplished (see, e.g., Wood, Mento, & Locke, 1987). Finally, there is less support for other practices such as cascading goals (Pulakos &

**Table 9.1. Performance Management Practices, Assumptions, and Theories**

| *Practice* | *Assumption* | *Theoretical Foundation* |
|---|---|---|
| Employees set objectives at the beginning of the year | • Goals motivate individuals and help align employee efforts with company goals | • Goal setting (Locke, 1968)<br>• Conscious regulation of behavior (Locke, 1968)<br>• Functions of management (Drucker, 1954; Fayol, 1917) |
| Supervisors provide feedback and coaching to employees during the year | • Feedback helps employees improve their performance | • Goal setting (Locke, 1968)<br>• Conscious regulation of behavior (Locke, 1968)<br>• Control theory and self-regulation of behavior (Carver & Scheier, 1981; Klein, 1989; Kluger & DeNisi, 1996)<br>• The law of effect (Thorndike, 1927) |
| Supervisors evaluate the performance of employees at the end of the year | • Supervisors can (and will) objectively and consistently rate the performance of their employees<br>• Performance ratings or rankings motivate employees to improve or maintain their performance | • Psychological measurement (O'Boyle & Aguinis, 2012)<br>• Labor economics, tournament theory (Connelly, Tihanyi, Crook, & Gangloff, 2014) |
| Organizations base rewards employees receive on evaluations of their performance | • People are motivated by financial rewards<br>• Tying individual rewards to individual performance will motivate behavior change and higher levels of performance | • The law of effect, reinforcement theory, and behavior modification (see, e.g., Luthans & Kreitner, 1975)<br>• Expectancy theory (Vroom, 1964)<br>• Scientific management (Taylor, 1911)<br>• Classical economics (Hollander, 1987)<br>• Agency theory (Eisenhardt, 1989; Rynes & Gerhart, 2003)<br>• Tournament theory (Connelly et al., 2014; Rynes & Gerhart, 2003) |

O'Leary 2011) and linking goal achievement to incentives (more on this below).

***"Feedback helps employees improve their performance."*** Based on research from several areas (goal-setting, feedback, education, neuroscience, and positive psychology), the effectiveness of feedback in changing behavior and improving performance is at best "equivocal." Feedback does not necessarily improve performance—it is not this simple. Other factors moderate the relationship between feedback and performance (for excellent reviews of this literature, see Hattie & Timperley, 2007; Kluger & DiNisi, 1996).

Feedback helps improve performance when it is related to the work or tasks employees are doing. When feedback becomes more personal, it can feel threatening and interfere with performance. Delivering feedback using less personal channels can help avoid these problems and generally leads to improved performance and achievement. When feedback is framed relative to a specific goal, it also has a more positive impact on performance. Positive feedback is generally more effective in improving performance than negative feedback and a more positive ratio/offset is associated with better performance (Baumeister et al., 2001; Losada & Heaphy, 2004). Negative feedback tends to be more effective for prevention or avoidance goals like safety or compliance (Van Dijk & Kluger, 2011).

***"Supervisors can (and will) objectively and consistently rate the performance of their employees."*** A review of research across multiple disciplines (psychology, statistics, and economics) shows little support for this assumption. Research from perceptual psychology shows people's observations and judgments can be very inaccurate (Goldstein, 2014). Decision making and performance appraisal research indicates people display many biases and take shortcuts that interfere with their judgments (see, e.g., Aguinis, 2013; Kahneman, 2012). Making matters worse, supervisors have many motives for their judgments and are not always motivated to make them accurately (Spence & Keeping, 2011). Finally, other factors beyond the control of the employee influence their performance, leading to errors in performance judgments (Coens & Jenkins, 2002). For these reasons, estimates of the reliability, validity and accuracy of supervisor ratings of performance ratings is generally low. A review by O'Neil, Carswell, and McLarnon (2012) suggests that only between 8% and 32% of the variation in performance ratings is due to individuals and their achievements. Efforts to improve performance ratings through scale improvements, rater training, calibration processes, 360 degree feedback, and forced distributions have been marginally effective at best (Conway & Huffcutt, 1997; Dominick, 2013; Hauenstein, 1999; Landy & Farr, 1980).

***"Performance ratings or rankings motivate employees to improve or maintain their performance."*** This assumption comes from labor economics, specifically tournament theory (Connelly, Tihanyi, Crook, & Gangloff, 2014). Tournament theory was developed to explain situations where differences is wages are not based on productivity or are not proportional to one's skills, abilities, experience or qualifications. If Tiger Woods receives $1,000,000 for winning a golf tournament and the 100th place finisher receives $1,000, is Tiger Woods 1,000 times better than the 100th-place finisher? Probably not. The theory holds that wages from employees at a given rank are withheld and given to employees at higher ranks to motivate lower ranking workers to work hard and get promoted and higher ranking workers to work hard to stay there. Ratings and relative comparisons are central to motivation and performance according to this theory.

Overall, research support for this assumption is mixed. Some studies find relative feedback and rankings improve performance (Blanes i Vidal & Nossol, 2009) while other studies find it negatively affects performance leading employees to behave in counterproductive ways, sabotaging others and artificially inflating their own output (Barankay, 2011; Fehr & Gachter, 2000). Other research suggests these effects depend on the level of performance, that low performers can get demoralized and give up whilst high performers can relax their efforts (Casas-Arce & Martinez-Jerez, 2009). Finally, where there are strong norms of reciprocity, employees may not work as hard under relative performance schemes because they do not want their efforts to negatively affect their peers (Bandiera, Barankay, & Rasul, 2005).

These findings suggest organizations cannot uniformly assume that rating and ranking employees motivates them. There are conditions where these practices hurt motivation and performance, especially in collaborative work environments and when ratings are tied to differential rewards.

***"People are motivated by money and financial rewards."*** There are several research domains that provide evidence critical of this assumption and of classical economic principles in general. The simple fact that millions of people willingly work for no pay as volunteers while others willingly forgo higher paying jobs for lower paying jobs in sectors such as not-for-profit and education would seem to question this assumption. Research on decision biases like loss aversion and the endowment effect also suggests individuals are motivated by more than just money and they do not necessarily maximize their own gains (Kahneman, 2012). Research on the link between money and happiness is also clear (although very complex); money does not necessarily make people happy. Individuals adapt quickly to changes in income and status plays a big role in happiness. Relative income is at least twice as important as actual income in driving happiness and most of the effect of income increases on happiness is due to status effects (see, e.g., Clark, Frijters, & Shields, 2008; Diener, 2000). Organizational research also shows that pay has a very low-level relationship to overall satisfaction (Judge, Piccolo, Podskaoff, Shaw, & Rich, 2010). Other research suggests people have a built-in "extrinsic incentive bias"; they overestimate how much other people care about extrinsic features of a job, such as pay, and underestimate how much people are motivated by intrinsic job features such as challenge and purpose (Heath, 1999). Finally, while 90% of companies report using pay-for-performance programs to retain top talent (Mercer, 2011), research shows a weak connection between pay, pay satisfaction and turnover (Griffeth, Hom, & Gaertner, 2000).

***"Tying individual rewards to individual performance motivates behavior change and performance."*** In 2002 U.S. corporations spent $117 billion on noncash and cash incentives and this number is undoubtedly much bigger today (Stolovitch, Clark, & Condly, 2002). The concepts of pay-for-performance and differentiation of rewards underpin compensation philosophies in most large organizations. This assumption is based on several theories within economics and psychology, including agency theory and expectancy theory. Agency theory comes from labor economics and focuses on the relationship between two parties, a principal and an agent (see, e.g., Eisenhardt, 1989). As it applies to performance management, the principal (a company) delegates work to the agent (an employee). The theory assumes agents are self-interested and their goals will not be aligned with the goals of the principal. As a result, other mechanisms are needed to align agents goals with those of the principal, such as rewards, incentives, or fear of being fired. It also assumes principals have difficulty verifying the agent is performing the work so they need to be monitored. Expectancy theory holds that in order to motivate employees to perform, their efforts should lead to successful performance and successful performance should lead to some outcome they value (Vroom, 1964). It is not surprising given the dominance of economic theories in this area that considerable attention is paid to financial outcomes over other outcomes.

Research across several disciplines (psychology, economics, healthcare, education) casts doubt on the broad applicability of this assumption. Pay-for-performance *can* have positive effects on performance and productivity (see, e.g., Jenkins, Mitra, Gupta, & Shaw, 1998; Stajkovic & Luthans, 1997). Institutional research shows modest performance and productivity advantages (5–10%) for companies with pay-for-performance programs (see, e.g., Gielen & Kerkhofs, 2010). However, when it comes to other outcomes such as turnover, creativity, and innovation, the research is less encouraging. These programs tend not to reduce voluntary turnover controlling for other important factors such as industry, occupation, size of company, and tenure (Batt, Colvin, & Keefe, 2002; Haines, Jalette, & Larose, 2006; O'Halloran, 2009). Similarly, traditional pay-for-performance and incentive systems tend to lead to lower creativity and innovation (Azoulay, Graff-Zivin, & Manso, 2011; Lerner & Wulf, 2007; Manso, 2011). They focus individuals on extrinsic factors and can undermine intrinsic motivation (Deci, Ryan, & Koestner, 1999).

Research also shows that higher levels of pay differentiation (frequently caused by performance-based pay systems) is not always better for individuals and organizations (see, e.g., Mahy, Rycx, & Wang, 2011). While some studies find more differentiation is positively related to performance and productivity, others find it is negatively related to performance and productivity, especially in collaborative environments (Trevor, O'Reilly, & Gerhart, 2012). Other studies suggest the relationship is more complex, finding curvilinear relationships where the relationship depends on the amount of differentiation. With respect to turnover, research is more consistently unsupportive; higher levels of differentiation tends to be associated with higher turnover and lower tenure (Bloom & Michel, 2002).

While research suggests pay-for-performance *can* work, it does so in a relatively narrow range of circumstances: laboratory settings; simple, low-complexity jobs; jobs where the work is boring or noxious; and jobs or tasks where paying attention and working harder can improve performance. In addition, much of this research has been done with piece-rate incentive systems and with jobs where performance is measured quantitatively. There are a large number of jobs in organizations where these conditions simply can't be met. Moreover, the positive effects observed are not always attributable to incentive effects. Institutional research shows that up to 50% of the benefit of pay-for-performance systems is due to "sorting" effects—attracting better people to the organization, versus "incentive" effects—getting employees to work harder (Lazear, 2000). Any positive effects observed also tend to be short term, disappearing after the incentives are removed.

Finally, even when pay-for-performance systems work they can have undesirable "side effects" that can offset any benefits observed. Research suggests these systems can lead to distortion and manipulation of goals and measures, unanticipated (and unwanted) behaviors and outcomes, fraud and illegal behavior, narrow focus on the areas being rewarded, competition (which can undermine collaboration and teamwork), reduced intrinsic motivation, and constant and costly tinkering with the system. There are countless examples of these side effects, some of which have been highly publicized such as the financial crisis of 2008 and the Enron, Tyco, and WorldCom fiascos (see, e.g., Agarwal & Wang, 2009; Denis, Hanouna, & Sarin, 2006; Kerr, 1975; Larkin, 2009).

## SUMMARY OF RESEARCH SUPPORT

It appears many of the assumptions organizations take for granted when designing performance management systems may not hold up under the harsh light of rigorous research. Given how embedded these assumptions are in contemporary business thinking, these findings may be difficult for business leaders and human resources professionals to accept. It may be difficult to accept that feedback is not always be helpful, supervisors cannot rate performance accurately and, employees may be performing despite our performance-based pay systems, not because of them. The research reviewed above suggests organizations need to take a more fundamental look at performance management systems, rethinking their design based on different assumptions and principles. The final section of this chapter explores what it might look like if organizations redesigned their performance management systems to reflect the findings from this research.

## NEXT-GENERATION PERFORMANCE MANAGEMENT

The research reviewed above provides a blueprint for redesigning performance management to achieve better outcomes (performance, productivity, and retention). For the purposes of this chapter, I will refer to this new blueprint as "next generation performance management"—NGPM.

NGPM begins with a clear purpose. Companies ask a lot from their performance management systems. Aguinis (2013) lists 23 objectives in his book on performance management. It can be difficult for a performance management system to effectively accomplish this many objectives. The Conference Board study referenced earlier illustrates the danger of asking too much from a performance management system; it can fail to deliver on any of its objectives. When viewed through an organization architecture lens, performance management should be part of an organization's management, control and governance functions. These functions include strategy/policy deployment, long-range planning, and short-term business planning and budgeting (see, e.g., Judson, 1990). After organizations finalize decisions about strategy, priorities and resources, individual organizations and units make decisions about how best to use available resources to address these priorities. Supervisors establish unit priorities and work with employees on how their work can contribute to these priorities. Finally, supervisors monitor progress, make adjustments and work with employees to help them accomplish their objectives.

Through this lens, performance management should **direct** employee efforts and **align** them with important organizational goals. It should act as a **control** system, ensuring employees stay focused on the right activities. Finally, it should act as a support system, helping employees make **progress** against their goals every day. NGPM is about direction, align-

**Table 9.2. The Path to Next Generation Performance Management**

| *From* | *To* |
|---|---|
| • Use of ratings, rankings, differentiation and money to motivate | • Appeal to other needs to motivate (purpose, autonomy, mastery, and belonging) |
| • Performance evaluation | • Performance support |
| • Employee ownership | • Supervisor ownership |
| • Focus on negative feedback, delivering critical messages | • Focus on positive feedback and supportive messages |
| • Episodic, event driven | • Continuous process |
| • Annual cycle | • Natural work cycle |
| • Documentation—heavy | • Documentation—light |

ment, control and progress, in the service of important organizational goals.

With this purpose in mind NGPM requires a shift from old taken-for-granted principles and assumptions to new research-based principles and assumptions. Table 9.2 summarizes the key changes required to move to NGPM.

First, NGPM makes different assumptions about what motivates employees. NGPM places more emphasis on nonfinancial strategies and less emphasis on financial rewards, performance-based pay and high levels of differentiation of rewards. It also focuses on supporting employees in making progress against their objectives and less on evaluating their performance in order to drive downstream reward decisions (for a useful framework see Amabile & Kramer, 2011). It does this by providing work-related feedback, coaching and other support, and it emphasizes positive and encouraging vs. negative and critical messages. Because performance management is viewed as a management process, supervisors are responsible for the process and any documentation required, not employees. NGPM also aligns with the work cycle, not the annual rewards cycle. Once the connection to the rewards cycle is broken, performance management-related interactions between supervisors and employees can happen regularly and continuously, when they need to happen. Finally, because NGPM is not designed to help defend downstream decisions in the event of litigation, documentation can be kept to a minimum for most employees.

## NGPM PRACTICES

With these principles as a guide, NGPM offers number of practices that are based on the professional research reviewed earlier. These practices are listed in Table 9.3.

**Table 9.3. Next Generation Performance Management Practices**

| *Element* | *Recommended NGPM Practices* |
|---|---|
| Planning | • Employees should have written objectives, both individual and group/unit objectives. Individual objectives should be framed in the context of unit objectives where possible.<br>• Objectives should be specific, clear, and manageable, with some "stretch" built into them. They should be framed positively.<br>• Do not create a formal process for cascading goals throughout the company (at least for performance management purposes).<br>• Supervisors should have regular discussions with employees about their objectives and how their work contributes to higher level organizational and enterprise goals.<br>• Objectives do not need to be quantitative with specific targets, nor should the achievement of objectives be tied to individual incentives or rewards. |
| Feedback and Coaching | • Supervisors should have ongoing discussions with employees, providing feedback about their work tasks and objectives. Feedback should not be personal.<br>• Frame the supervisor's day-to-day performance management role in terms of "progress." Their role goes beyond feedback and coaching to include supporting and enabling progress against objectives.<br>• Employees and supervisors should not be forced to meet on a certain frequency or at fixed points in time. These interactions should follow the natural cadence of the work.<br>• Train supervisors to make feedback and coaching effective and to address factors that get in the way of effective feedback.<br>• Supervisors should focus on positive feedback and use negative/constructive feedback sparingly.<br>• Supplement face-to-face feedback with less personal methods of delivering feedback (e.g., e-mail, social media style tools).<br>• Restrict formal documentation to only that which is necessary, based on the needs of employees and supervisors. |
| Evaluation | • Do not conduct formal performance evaluations (e.g., performance ratings or narrative summaries of performance). If you must have ratings, make them as simple as possible (e.g., 3-point scale), with no complex weighting schemes or algorithms.<br>• Discuss performance throughout the year, not just at predetermined review points in the year.<br>• Develop a special "performance improvement process" for employees not meeting expectations. This process should be separate from the performance management process, with more extensive documentation requirements.<br>• Develop special performance measurement procedures for other processes that require performance input (e.g., talent identification, promotion, succession, staffing).<br>• Instead of final performance management reviews, conduct "after-action" reviews throughout the year as projects finish or when key milestones are reached. |

*(Table continues on next page)*

**Table 9.3. (Continued)**

| *Element* | *Recommended NGPM Practices* |
|---|---|
| Rewards | • Reduce or eliminate reliance on financial rewards and incentives to motivate employees. Tap into other needs to motivate employees (purpose, autonomy, mastery, belonging).<br>• Use individual pay-for-performance programs only where they make sense and only after careful consideration.<br>• Develop a pay-for-performance philosophy that goes beyond individual incentives and rewards to include other elements: aggressive management of poor performance; rewarding performance over time with promotions and internal job movement; use of other "rewards" such as challenging work and special assignments/projects.<br>• If you must have individually based incentives or bonuses, make them a small portion of your rewards mix.<br>• Use market data to make adjustments to base pay.<br>• Pay top talent and employees with critical skills at the top of the market.<br>• Use promotions and internal job movement to increase employee pay over time and to motivate employees. Create more frequent promotion opportunities.<br>• Use team, group, and organization-based reward programs. They are effective, can be used more widely and do not have the side effects of individual pay-for-performance programs.<br>• Use methods other than reward systems to reinforce organizational or cultural changes (and to control behavior). Design recruiting, onboarding/socialization, and training and development processes to get the kind of people desired and to shape the behaviors needed. |

Adopting these practices will require companies to focus attention in other related areas as well. For example, NGPM requires highly skilled supervisors. Companies may need to upgrade their supervisor selection, promotion and training and development processes to ensure they have the requisite skills and are demonstrating critical behaviors. Companies will also need to review the expectations they have for their supervisors. Can supervisors "get ahead" simply by doing their own individual contributor work and not investing the necessary time and attention in supporting their staff? A supervisor's success needs to depend on the success of their employees for these practices to be effective. Companies will also need an effective work-unit planning process where local leaders think about the goals and objectives of their unit and how they align upward to organizational goals. Finally, companies that have invested heavily in technology to support their complex, "rating-centric" performance management systems may need to rethink their technology needs. Adoption of NGPM practices with less emphasis on quantitative ratings and documentation could allow them to simplify their sophisticated technology solutions or abandon them altogether.

## CONCLUSION

Performance management is an important management process for companies. It does not need to be "blown up" or replaced. It needs to be focused and designed around important management functions to enable individual and organizational performance. Implementing NGPM principles and practices will not be easy and it will take time. There are significant gaps between current performance management practices and NGPM practices in most companies. These practices will also require organizations to find new ways to meet other important organizational objectives and to motivate employees in ways other than simply throwing money at them. Organizations moving in this direction will incur transition costs in the short term but they will experience less pain and higher performance in the long term. Abandoning outdated assumptions might also free organizations to develop even more innovative performance management practices. There is good research to guide companies in making the transition to NGPM; they simply need to pay attention to it.

## REFERENCES

Agarwal, S., & Wang, F. H. (2009). Perverse incentives at the banks? Evidence from a natural experiment. *Federal Reserve Bank of Chicago: Working paper.* Retrieved June 27, 2015, from file:C:/Users/z3497979/Downloads/wp2009-08-pdf.pdf

Aguinis, H. (2013). *Performance management.* Upper Saddle River, NJ: Pearson.

Amabile, T., & Kramer, S. (2011). *The progress principle.* Boston, MA: Harvard Business School Press.

Argyris, C. (1990). *Overcoming organizational defenses: Facilitating organizational learning.* Boston, MA: Allyn & Bacon.

Azoulay, P., Graff-Zivin, J. S., & Manso, G. (2011). Incentives and creativity: Evidence from the academic life sciences. *Journal of Economics, 42,* 527–554.

Bandiera, O., Barankay, I., & Rasul, I. (2005). Social preferences and the response to incentives: Evidence from personnel data. *Quarterly Journal of Economics, 120,* 917–962.

Barankay, I. (2011). Rankings and social tournaments: Evidence from a crowdsourcing experiment (Working paper). University of Pennsylvania.

Batt, R., Colvin, A. J. S., & Keefe, J. (2002). Employee voice, human resource practices and quit rates: Evidence from the telecommunications industry. *Industrial and Labor Relations Review, 55,* 573–594.

Baumeister, R. F., Bratslavsky, E., Finkenauer, C., & Vohs, K. D. (2001). Bad is stronger than good. *Review of General Psychology, 5,* 323–370.

Blanes i Vidal, J., & Nossol, M. (2009). Tournaments without prizes: Evidence from personnel records. *Management Science, S7,* 1721–1736.

Bloom, M., & Michel, J. G. (2002). The relationships among organizational context, pay dispersion, and managerial turnover. *Academy of Management Journal, 45*, 33–42.

Carver, C. S., & Scheier, M. F. (1981). *Attention and self-regulation: A control-theory approach to human behavior.* New York, NY: Springer-Verlag.

Casas-Arce, P., & Martinez-Jerez, F. A. (2009). Relative performance compensation, contests, and dynamic incentives. *Management Science, 55*, 1306–1320.

Clark, A. E., Frijters, P., & Shields, M. A. (2008). Relative income, happiness, and utility: An explanation for the Easterlin paradox and other puzzles. *Journal of Economic Literature, 46*, 95–144.

Connelly, B. L., Tihanyi, L., Crook, T. R., & Gangloff, K. A. (2014). Tournament theory: Thirty years of contests and competition. *Journal of Management, 40*, 16–47.

Coens, T., & Jenkins, M. (2002). *Abolishing performance appraisals: Why they backfire and what to do instead.* San Francisco, CA: Berrett-Kohler.

Conway, J., & Huffcutt, A. (1997). Psychometric properties of multi-source performance ratings: A meta-analysis of subordinate, supervisor, peer, and self-ratings. *Human Performance, 10*, 331–360.

Deci, E. L., Ryan, R. M., & Koestner, R. (1999). A meta-analytic review of experiments examining the effects of extrinsic rewards on intrinsic motivation. *Psychological Bulletin, 125*, 627–668.

Denis, D. J., Hanouna, P., & Sarin, A. (2006). Is there a dark side to incentive compensation? *Journal of Corporate Finance, 12*, 467–488.

Diener, E. (2000). Subjective well-being. *American Psychologist, 55*, 34–43.

Dominick, P. G. (2013). Forced rankings: Pros, cons, and practices. In J. W. Smither & M. London *Performance management: Putting research into practice* (pp. 411–443). San Francisco, CA: Jossey-Bass.

Drucker, P. F. (1954). *The practice of management.* New York, NY: Harper and Brothers.

Eisenhardt, K. M. (1989). Agency theory: An assessment and review. *Academy of Management Review, 14*, 57–74.

Fayol, H. (1917). *Administration industrielle et generale: Prevoyance, organisation, commandement, controle.* London, England: Putnam.

Fehr, E., & Gachter, S. (2000). Fairness and retaliation: The economics of reciprocity. *Journal of Economic Perspectives, 14*, 159–181.

Gielen, A. C., Kerkhofs, M. J. M., & van Ours, J. C. (2010). How performance-related pay affects productivity and employment. *Journal of Population Economics, 23*, 291–301.

Goldstein, E. B. (2014). *Sensation and perception.* Belmont, CA: Wadsworth

Gorman, C. A., Ray, J., Nugent, C. S., Thibodeaux, C. N., List, S., Lonkar, S., ... Pokhrel-Willet, S. (2012). *A preliminary survey of performance management practices in the United States.* Paper presented at the annual conference of the Society for Industrial and Organizational Psychologists, San Diego, CA.

Griffeth, R. W., Hom, P. W., & Gaertner, S. (2000). A meta-analysis of antecedents and correlates of employee turnover: Update, moderator tests, and research implications for the next millennium. *Journal of Management, 26*, 463–488.

Haines, V. Y., Jalette, P., & Larose, K. (2006). The influence of human resources management practices on employee voluntary turnover rates in Canadian non-governmental sector. *Industrial and Labor Relations Review, 63*, 228–246.

Hattie, J., & Timperley, H. (2007). The power of feedback. *Review of Educational Research, 77*, 81–112.

Hauenstein, N. M. A. (1999). Training raters to increase the accuracy of appraisals and the usefulness of feedback. In J. W. Smither *Performance management: Putting research into practice* (pp. 404–444). San Francisco, CA: Jossey-Bass.

Heath, C. (1999). On the social psychology of agency relationships: Lay theories of motivation overemphasize extrinsic incentives. *Organizational Behavior and Human Decision Processes, 78*, 25–62.

Hollander, S. (1987). *Classical economics*. Oxford, England: Blackwell.

Institute for Corporate Productivity. (2011). Tying pay to performance. Retrieved from http://www.i4cp.com/news/2011/09/08/companies-tying-employee-pay-to-performance-increases-17-in-last-two-years

Jenkins, D. G., Jr., Mitra, A., Gupta, N., & Shaw, J. D. (1998). Are financial incentives related to performance? A meta-analytic review of empirical research. *Journal of Applied Psychology, 83*, 777–787.

Judson, A. (1990). *Making strategy happen*. Cambridge, MA: Blackwell.

Judge, T. A., Piccolo, R., Podsakoff, N. P., Shaw, J. C., & Rich, B. L. (2010). The relationship between pay and job satisfaction: A meta-analysis of the literature. *Journal of Vocational Behavior, 77*, 157–167.

Kahneman, D. (2012). *Thinking, Fast and Slow.* New York: Farrar, Strauss and Giroux.

Kerr, S. (1975). On the folly of rewarding A, while hoping for B. *Academy of Management Journal, 18*, 769–783.

Klein, H. J. (1989). An integrated control theory model of work motivation. *Academy of Management Review, 14*, 150–172.

Kleingeld, A., van Mierlo, H., & Arends, L. (2011). The effect of goal setting on group performance: A meta-analysis. *Journal of Applied Psychology, 96*, 1289–1304.

Kluger, A. N., & DeNisi, A. (1996). The effects of feedback interventions on performance: A historical review, a meta-analysis, and a preliminary feedback intervention theory. *Psychological Bulletin, 119*, 254–284.

Landy, F., & Farr, J. L. (1980). Performance rating. *Psychological Bulletin, 87*, 72–107.

Larkin, I. (2009). *The cost of high-powered incentives: Employee gaming in enterprise software sales* (Working Paper). Harvard Business School, Boston, MA.

Lazear, E. (2000). Performance pay and productivity. *American Economic Review, 90*, 1346–1361.

Lerner, J., & Wulf, J. (2007). Innovation and incentives: Evidence from corporate R&D. *The Review of Economics and Statistics, 89*, 634–644.

Locke, E. (1968). Toward a theory of task motivation and incentives. *Organizational Behavior and Human Performance, 3*, 157–189.

Locke, E. A., & Latham, G. P. (2013). *New developments in goal setting and task performance*. East Sussex, England: Routledge.

Losada, M., & Heaphy, E. (2004). The role of positivity and connectivity in the performance of business teams: A non-linear dynamics model. *American Behavioral Scientist, 47,* 740–765.

Luthans, F., & Kreitner, R. (1975). *Organizational behavior modification*. Glenview, IL: Scott, Foresman.

Mahy, B., Rycx, F., & Volral, M. (2011). Does wage dispersion make all firms productive? *Scottish Journal of Political Economy, 58,* 455–489.

Manso, G. (2011). Motivating innovation. *The Journal of Finance, 66,* 1823–1860.

Manzoni, J. F. (2008). On the folly of hoping for A, simply because you are trying to pay for A. *Studies in Managerial and Financial Accounting, 18,* 19–41.

McCann, J. (2013). *Performance management 3.0: Building performance management for the emerging workplace* (The Conference Board research report R-1525-13-RR).

Mercer. (2011, May). Next generation of pay-for-performance. Survey report.

Mercer. (2012a, March). Compensation planning in 2012: Today's landscape. Survey report.

Mercer. (2012b). Current trends in performance management. Survey report.

O'Boyle, E., & Aguinis, H. (2012). The best and the rest: Revisiting the norm of normality of individual performance. *Personnel Psychology, 65,* 79–119.

O'Halloran, P. L. (2009). *Do performance pay workers experience less job turnover and longer tenures?* Paper presented at the 9th Global Conference on Business and Economics, Cambridge, England.

O'Neill, T. A., Carswell, J. J., & McLarnon, M. J. W. (2012). *Performance ratings have larger rater and small ratee components, usually.* Paper presented at the annual meeting of the Society for Industrial and Organizational Psychology, San Diego, CA.

Pfeffer, J., & Sutton, R. I. (2006). *Hard facts, dangerous half-truths and total nonsense: Profiting from evidence-based management.* Boston, MA: Harvard Business School Press.

Pink, D. H. (2009). *Drive: The surprising truth about what motivates us.* New York, NY: Riverhead Books.

Pulakos, E. D. (2009). *Performance management: A new approach for driving business results.* New York, NY: Wiley Blackwell.

Pulakos, E. D., & O'Leary, R. S. (2011). Why is performance management broken? *Industrial and Organizational Psychology, 4,* 146–164.

Rynes, S. L., & Gerhart, B. A. (2003). *Compensation: Theory, evidence, and strategic implications.* Thousand Oaks, CA: SAGE.

Spence, J. R., & Keeping, L. (2011). Conscious rating distortion in performance appraisal: A review, commentary, and proposed framework for research. *Human Resource Management Review, 21,* 85–95.

Stajkovic, A. D., & Luthans, F. (1997). A meta-analysis of the effects of organizational behavior modification on task performance, 1975–1995. *Academy of Management Journal, 40,* 1122–1149.

Stolovitch, H. D., Clark, R. E., & Condly, S. J. (2002). Incentives, motivation and workplace performance: Research and best practices. Report published by the International Society for Performance Improvement and the SITE Foundation.

Taylor, F. W. (1911). *The principles of scientific management.* New York, NY: Harper & Brothers.

Thorndike, E. L. (1927). The law of effect. *American Journal of Psychology, 39*, 212–222.

Trevor, C., O'Reilly, G., & Gerhart, B. (2012). Reconsidering pay dispersion's effect on the performance of interdependent work: Reconciling sorting and pay inequality. *Academy of Management Journal, 55*, 585–610.

Van Dijk, D., & Kluger, A. N. (2011). Task type as a moderator of positive/negative feedback effects on motivation and performance: A regulatory focus perspective. *Journal of Organizational Behavior,* 32, 1084–1105.

Vroom, V. H. (1964). *Work and motivation*. New York, NY: McGraw Hill.

Wood, R. E., Mento, A. J., & Locke, E. A. (1987). Task complexity as a moderator of goal effects: A meta-analysis. *Journal of Applied Psychology, 72*, 416–425.

CHAPTER 10

# PERFORMANCE MANAGEMENT AS A STRATEGIC TOOL FOR CHANGE

**Deborah Blackman, Fiona Buick, Michael O'Donnell, Janine O'Flynn, and Damian West**

In this chapter we propose reconfiguring performance management as a framework for change, arguing that performance management provides an integrating mechanism for effectively implementing the human resource (HR) practices necessary to support the development of new initiatives. Enhanced performance is enabled through the adoption of high performance work practices; those considered to have the most impact on achieving high performance are: job design; recruitment and selection; employee development and training; performance management; rewards; and participatory work practices (Blackman, Buick, O'Donnell, O'Flynn, & West, 2012). The argument is made that where such high performance work practices are integrated with each other, organizational benefits will flow (Becker & Huselid, 1998; Boxall & Macky, 2009), including the adoption of new behaviors and ideas required for supporting change. In this chapter we present a new performance management framework which could enable high performance and enhance the possi-

*Human Capital Management Research: Influencing Practice and Process*
pp. 149–162
Copyright © 2016 by Information Age Publishing
All rights of reproduction in any form reserved.

bility of achieving organizational change. First, we explain that performance management is a high performance work characteristic and suggest that it should act as an integrating mechanism for other practices to support change. Next we present the study methodology, demonstrating how it led to the development of a new performance management framework. We argue that this framework provides a new way of configuring existing and/or required performance management. Finally we discuss the implications of our findings and propose the use of the framework as a mechanism for integrating change through performance management.

## PERFORMANCE MANAGEMENT AS A HIGH PERFORMANCE WORK CHARACTERISTIC

In the literature on high performance, performance management is often presented as one of the high performance work practices, but it focuses mainly on the appraisal and measurement aspects (see, e.g., Jensen, Patel & Messersmith, 2013; Kehoe & Wright, 2013). However, if we consider performance management to be the relationships within HR practices (Jiang, Lepak, Han, Kim, & Winkler, 2012) or as something that is a broader management function and not exclusively an HR practice (Aguinis, Joo, & Gottfredson, 2011), it is seen as a mechanism for individuals to understand "how their work ties to the broader organizational goals and activities, they should set out clear expectations of behavior and then bestow rewards for achieving this" (Alford & O'Flynn, 2012, pp. 244–245). Here the emphasis is on performance management as an integrating mechanism that manages the expectations of employees and managers and aligns individuals to high-level goals. In this sense, performance management is the "use of interrelated strategies and activities to improve the performance of individuals, teams and organizations" (Management Advisory Committee, 2001, p. 14). The strategies and activities are likely to involve more than performance appraisal activities; they encompass *any* management practice aimed at enhancing the performance of individuals, groups and organizations. Therefore, we posit that performance management should be an interconnected mechanism which underpins and integrates other management practices, thereby providing a strategic tool for implementing change.

## METHODOLOGY

The research was designed to explore how performance management could support the achievement of high performance; in this case in the

Australian Public Service (APS). A predominantly qualitative case study approach was used to facilitate understanding and provide a boundary around the subject of investigation (Yin, 2014). In particular, a collective case study approach was adopted as it allowed cross-case analysis and comparison, and the investigation of a particular phenomenon in diverse settings (Darke, Shanks, & Broadbent, 1998). Case studies were selected using a combination of purposive and convenience sampling techniques. The sampling frame was designed to ensure that, collectively, the cases represented a spectrum comprising low, medium, and high levels of performance management effectiveness which was determined from the annual State of the Service Report (Australian Public Service Commission, 2012). The purposive sampling involved targeting specific organizations that provided a range of effectiveness types, covering low, medium and high effectiveness. The convenience sampling involved public service organizations that volunteered to participate as a case in the study. In combination seven case study organizations participated (see Table 10.1 for details).

In case study research, multiple sources of evidence are collected and data created (Yin, 2014) to gain a deeper understanding of the studied phenomenon. This study utilized the qualitative methods of semistructured individual and group interviews. The primary qualitative data was complemented by: (a) documentary analysis of official internal (organizational) and public documentation; and (b) analysis of secondary data from the annual State of the Service Report (Australian Public Service Commission, 2012) data. In this study, individual interviews were conducted with 90 participants who were asked a series of questions designed to identify the factors that enabled or impeded the implementation of performance management and what impact this had upon high performance. Twenty-two group interviews were conducted with 136 participants. A recruitment strategy aimed at having 10 participants per group, allowing for nonattendance, meant that each group had six to eight participants.

**Table 10.1. Case Studies Used in This Study**

| *Organization Code* | *Organization Size* | *Organization Type* | *Number of Employees* |
|---|---|---|---|
| A | Large | Policy | 3,000–5,000 employees |
| B | Large | Policy | 3,000–5,000 employees |
| C | Large | Operational | 5,000–7,000 employees |
| D | Large | Operational | 8,000–10,000 employees |
| E | Medium | Policy | 500–1,000 employees |
| F | Medium | Operational | 500–1,000 employees |
| G | Small | Regulatory | < 100 employees |

**Table 10.2. Overall Participant Sample**

| *Phase/Level* | *Operational* | *Middle Manager* | *Senior Manager* | *Total* |
|---|---|---|---|---|
| Individual interviews | 0 | 48 | 42 | 90 |
| Group interviews | 71 | 65 | 0 | 136 |
| Total participants | 71 | 113 | 42 | 226 |

Participants were selected through a stratified purposive sampling technique which involved the selection of participants from particular subgroups of interest. Invitations were sent to public servants within each case study based on their hierarchical level (senior manager, middle manager, operational staff) and geographical location (National Office, selected state and regional offices). This led to an overall sample of 226 participants (see Table 10.2).

The researchers undertook inductive analysis in NVivo using a combination of open, axial and selective coding; they immersed themselves in the data to identify patterns, themes and interrelationships that emerged from the data (Ezzy, 2002; Patton, 1990).

## DEVELOPING A NEW PERFORMANCE MANAGEMENT FRAMEWORK

Despite widespread agreement that performance management should be used to develop high performance, it was recognized that, in many instances, performance management was poorly implemented and was often seen as a compliance exercise or as shorthand for managing underperformance. Selective core themes became apparent, both within and across the case studies, as indicated by the frequency and specificity with which they were mentioned. Eleven recurring themes were evident (see Table 10.3).

Analysis revealed commonalities and complementarities between these themes, leading to the 11 themes being clustered into four core principles and three foundation elements that form the basis of a performance management framework for high performance. Some themes, depicted as principles, were critical to the design of any performance management system; they influence application and implementation of a system in terms of how the content of performance management agreements are developed. Other themes, depicted as foundation elements, form the necessary support structure underpinning the implementation process (see Figure 10.1).

**Table 10.3. Illustrative Quotes Developing the Themes**

| *Theme* | | *Illustrative Quotes* |
|---|---|---|
| Clarity | 1. | "When you talk about high performance, it's everyone being on the same page driving toward common goals [and] driving toward common outcomes" (Middle manager, D). |
| | 2. | Lack of clarity regarding what high performance affects change outcomes as: "Change doesn't seem to be managed that well in terms of people communicating what the objectives are and having that filtered down to staff so that they know what's expected of them" (Middle manager, G). |
| Purpose | 1. | "For me, what contributes to that high-performing team is very much having a clear vision of where you're going, what you're trying to achieve, you have people understanding what their role is and getting that feedback along the way" (Middle manager, B). |
| | 2. | "In 20 years, every performance management issue I've dealt with, with the exclusion of one or two ... have been about complete lack of clarity of what they were supposed to be doing" (Senior manager, F). |
| Alignment | 1. | 'So there's got to be a clear ... high level plan for the team that everybody understands and can see how their work relates to. There has to be clear priorities and the priorities have to be matched to the resources that are available' (Middle manager, D) |
| | 2. | "I've had the benefit of working for a really strong [senior executive service] hierarchy, so in developing [performance agreements] we've always got the departmental plan and synthesized that down into a cluster plan, synthesized that down into a group plan, synthesized that down to a branch, and then that flows into your [performance agreement] ... it gives people purpose" (Middle manager, A). |
| Integration | 1. | "Well, there's no link to recruitment. There's no link to a career path with the performance system. It's conditional selection by merit and your performance is irrelevant to that process. So, again, there's that disconnect" (Middle manager, C). |
| | 2. | "[I've] just been doing that this morning; banging my head, just going 'we can't just recruit people.' First of all we've got to work out ... are they the right people working ... but then, having brought them in ... we'd just need to make sure that they're equipped with the right support and learning and development and it's not rocket science" (Middle manager, F). |
| Mutuality | 1. | "I think that it's every individual's responsibility to understand where they work, what they do, how it fits in, know the strategic framework, know the business plans, know how your work fits in ... We have the tools ... there's enough information out there that if you want to know you can find it." (Middle manager, B). |
| | 2. | Mutuality enables employees to adapt to change through maintaining awareness of changing priorities: 'the hypothesis [that] "OK 1 July 2012, 20% cut in resources' ... 'What are we going to stop doing? What are we going to do differently?" ... So staff were fully engaged in that process about well, how are we going to do that differently?" (Senior manager, A). |

*(Table continues on next page)*

**Table 10.3. (Continued)**

| *Theme* | *Illustrative Quotes* |
|---|---|
| Motivation | 1. "I think alignment is really critical for ... engaging the hearts and minds of the people who do the work. I mean, that's why they need to see a connection between what they come to work to do every day, and what the purpose of the agency is ... people will usually describe what is their value for being here is to make a difference, and it is that delivering to the Australian community" (Senior manager, F).<br>2. Lack of consultation often meant that many employees felt unprepared for the change and as though it was thrust upon them: "What I believe we don't tend to do is communicate what we know to be indicators of change until the change is almost inevitable ... [meaning that] change has come out of the blue" (Middle manager, C). |
| Adaptability | 1. "Adaptability and flexibility, responsiveness ... that's the key [to high performance] ... you've got to be flexible and you've got to accept that things are going to change, it's never going to be the way you want it to be and you've got to sort of be flexible around that" (Senior manager, D).<br>2. "We have to have staff who are agile, who are flexible, who can respond to changed circumstances, particularly novel changed circumstances, in a way that ... enables us ... to meet the needs of the minister and to meet the needs of the department" (Senior manager, B). |
| Progress | 1. "I think that's critical to ... revisit [our goals] as well because it's not going to be the same, what we started with six months ago changes very quickly, so it's about having that ongoing "how are we tracking?'" (Middle manager, B).<br>2. "So, I think we identify the ... resting points along the way ... you know when you're hiking up a mountain or something, you stop at a couple of different places and look back to where you've come from and you look forward to where you go. We're not very good at creating those places, so it's, kind of, "We must do something; this is something, let us do this" rather than "Where do I want to get to in the long run?" ... we're responsible for what it looks like in 10 or 20, or 30 years' time and if we keep doing what we've always done, we get what we've always got" (Senior manager, B). |
| Evidence and data | 1. 'It's that old adage of what gets measured gets done ... And making sure that there's focus on things ... [It requires a clear idea of what the mission goal is] and what we're trying to achieve' (Senior manager, E).<br>2. "We sometimes here fall into the trap of too much process to measure what you're doing, and lose sight of the outcome. So personally I think our current business plan process has set up all these activity plans, and everyone's got to do a monthly report, and so ... we're doing a lot of reporting against process, and less against the deliverable, and getting that deliverable and outcome right" (Senior manager, F). |

*(Table continues on next page)*

**Table 10.3. (Continued)**

| *Theme* | | *Illustrative Quotes* |
|---|---|---|
| Capabilities | 1. | "We have to have staff who are agile, who are flexible, who can respond to changed circumstances, particularly novel changed circumstances, in a way that enables us to meet the needs of the Minister and to meet the needs of the Department" (Senior manager, B). |
| | 2. | "I've had several supervisors who are in their 30s maybe, and they just have no ... managerial experience. It's just so obvious to me what they're lacking. There's not a system in place to make sure that if someone is in charge of someone else that they actually have the skills to do that ... In the climate of the APS missing out on those higher echelons, a lot of the older more senior staff retiring, I think it's just going to be a bigger problem over the next ten years ... it's not just to do with performance management that it's actually recognized as a skill set that is important to productivity and the outcomes of the APS" (Middle manager, E). |
| Pragmatism | 1. | "I think it's good if you can tailor it to the individual organization" (Senior manager, F). |
| | 2. | "Accepting that that's the fact that we can't do all of those things to the extent that we would like ... acknowledge the constraints in which we work, and that if we are to be high performing that we are going to need to reprioritize our focus" (Senior manager, G). |

The distinction between principles and foundation elements was made because it was apparent that clusters of themes played different roles in the framework (see Table 10.4).

In order to achieve high performance we propose that the principles operate as an ongoing feedback loop, starting with clarity and purpose, where a clear and shared understanding of what high performance represents and the purpose of an organization, group and role provide the basis for establishing alignment and integration. All implementation initiatives, which by their very nature will imply some form of change, then need to reflect mutuality and motivation to ensure that those involved are, and remain, committed to the achievement of high performance at all levels of the organization. Then progress and adaptability need to be interwoven into the process to ensure that processes, measurements and reviews support the intended outcomes and enable adjustments to performance if necessary. This will only be possible if the purpose is clear, requiring ongoing feedback loops.

## USING THE PERFORMANCE MANAGEMENT FRAMEWORK

The findings demonstrated that both poor and exemplary performance management practices were evident across APS organizations, irrespective

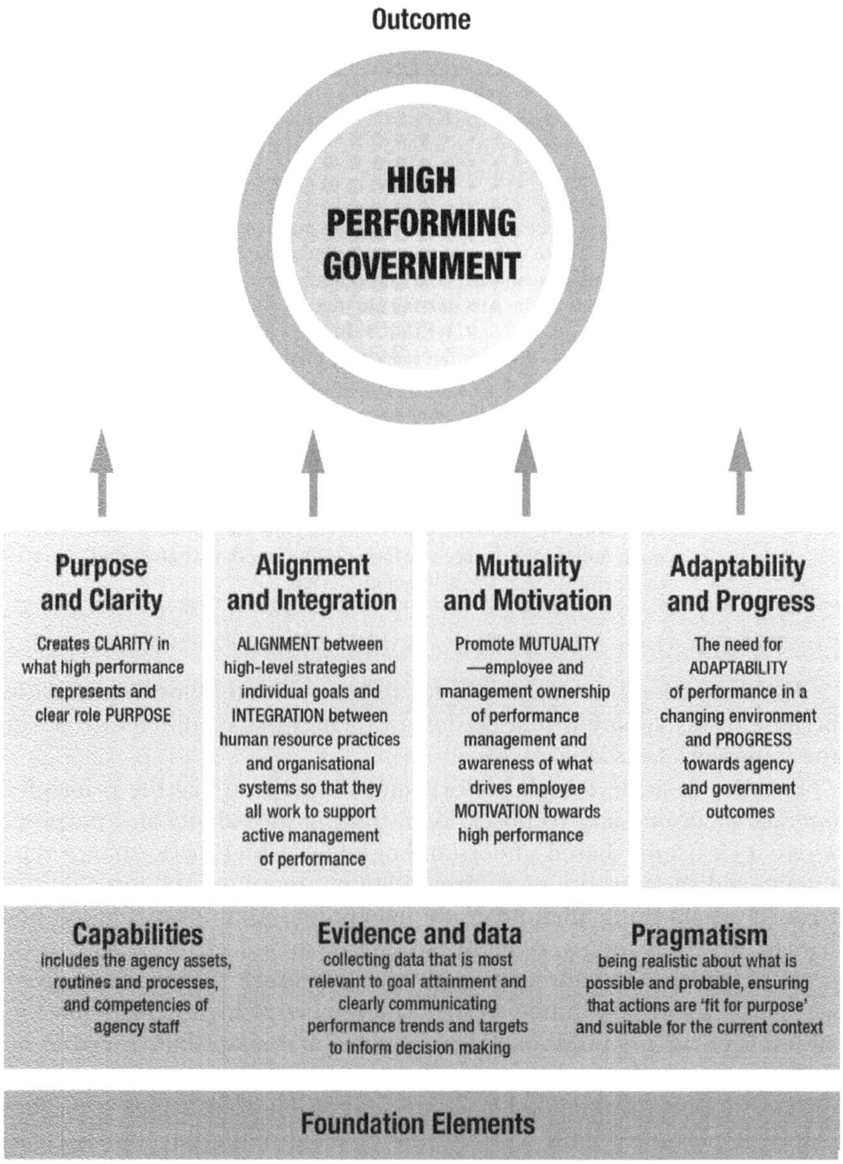


*Source:* Blackman, Buick, O'Donnell, O'Flynn, and West (2013, p. 6).

Figure 10.1. A framework for performance management.

**Table 10.4. Explanation of the Principles and Foundations**

| *Principle* | |
|---|---|
| CLARITY in what high performance represents and clear role PURPOSE | Participants highlighted that a high-performing organization needed clear definitions of high performance that could be cascaded through the hierarchical levels. However, findings demonstrated no consistent, or shared, understanding regarding what constituted high performance in *any* of the case study organizations. This meant that many employees did not know what was expected of them in terms of their performance, or the standard that was considered to be high performance in their organization or group.<br>Where people identified as working in a high-performing area, they placed role and goal clarity of the organization, group and individual employees at the center of their performance. |
| ALIGNMENT between high-level strategies and individual goals and INTEGRATION between HR practices and organizational systems | Employees need to understand the interdependencies that exist within and across organizations and why they need to perform to a high standard. Participants described that where alignment was successful, groups engaged in open and frequent communication and employees had exposure to strategic conversations. This created a clearer understanding of why a particular direction or focus had been adopted. However, our research revealed that the ability to obtain a clear line of sight was rare. |
| MUTUALITY of employee and management participation in performance management and awareness of what drives employee MOTIVATION toward high performance | Effective performance management involves both managers and employees being accountable and accepting mutual ownership of performance. This involves employees performing at an agreed level and the manager providing support to employees. Where mutuality was evident, both parties were more willing to give and receive feedback in a constructive manner and to actively engage in ongoing performance discussions. |
| Principle 4: ADAPTABILITY of performance in a changing environment and PROGRESS toward organizational and government outcomes | The ability of organizations to address environmental demands within short time frames relies on the ability of groups to reconfigure, adjust and adapt to change. We found that adaptability to change relied on employees being multi-skilled and flexible, adjusting their own priorities, responsibilities and workloads. In many organizations performance management systems were widely considered to be overly static in nature with a tendency to focus on short-term goals. It was recognized that setting realistic stretch and ambitious goals and targets would aid the achievement of continuous performance improvement toward a long-term vision. |

*(Table continues on next page)*

**Table 10.4. Explanation of the Principles and Foundations**

| *Foundation* | |
|---|---|
| Capabilities | In our research, participants stressed that one of the biggest challenges was the lack of capacity of those involved in implementing performance management, coupled with a lack of development opportunities to nurture this capacity. However, the emergence of high performance requires the identification of organizational competences which will enable strategic outcomes to be achieved, for example leadership, innovation and the capacity to manage change. The identification of these competences will then enable the determination and development of the requisite individual competencies (individual skills, attributes and knowledge). |
| Evidence and Data | Participants advocated a strategic approach to collecting data relevant to both goal attainment as well as strategic and operational decision-making. There was a strong emphasis on evidence, but the focus was on measuring targets rather than using evidence and data to inform decision-making, to establish goals in performance agreements and to monitor progress. Available data should be used to enable performance improvement through the effective communication of performance trends, targets and attainments. |
| Pragmatism | Participants emphasized the importance of being realistic about what was possible and probable, including the prioritization of effort within available resources. The findings demonstrate the need for organizations to adopt practices that are 'fit for purpose.' These practices need to fit the organization's context and capacities (including people and financial resources). |

of the performance management system in place, leading us to view implementation as the key to high performance. Where performance management was seen to be effective in developing high performance, it was used as a tool for gathering information and feedback on progress, providing the ability for managers and employees to learn from what was working and to make adjustments to performance goals where necessary. This leads us to consider the potential use of performance management as a tool for the strategic implementation of change.

Strategic change is when an organization plans to create differences in its outcomes as a result of alterations that it makes in its outputs, structures, processes et cetera (Rajagopalan & Spreitzer, 1997). It has a long-term, proactive outlook and, once the desired differences have been identified, a range of tools will be adopted to enable the alterations to take place. The capacity of the organization to reassemble its resources in a way to effect change is sometimes considered to be a dynamic capability (Helfat et al., 2007), involving the integration of internal and external competences. Often, as a part of such alterations, the employees will need to change what they do and/or how they do it so that the individual and organizational effort becomes aligned. This is where performance management can become a strategic tool if the way it is implemented is designed with the change at the center of the desired outcomes. Once we had accepted that change could be supported by the planned implementation of employee performance management (Buick, Blackman, O'Donnell, O'Flynn, & West, 2015), we considered how to implement the framework in a way that would enable this to occur.

Figure 10.2 shows how each of the elements in the framework is applied to change. The first, potentially most critical, step is a clear definition of the altered organizational state that is required. In order to make this possible we found there were two aspects that need to be overcome and thought through. First, a lack of a shared understanding about the purpose of performance management was a key issue in many case study

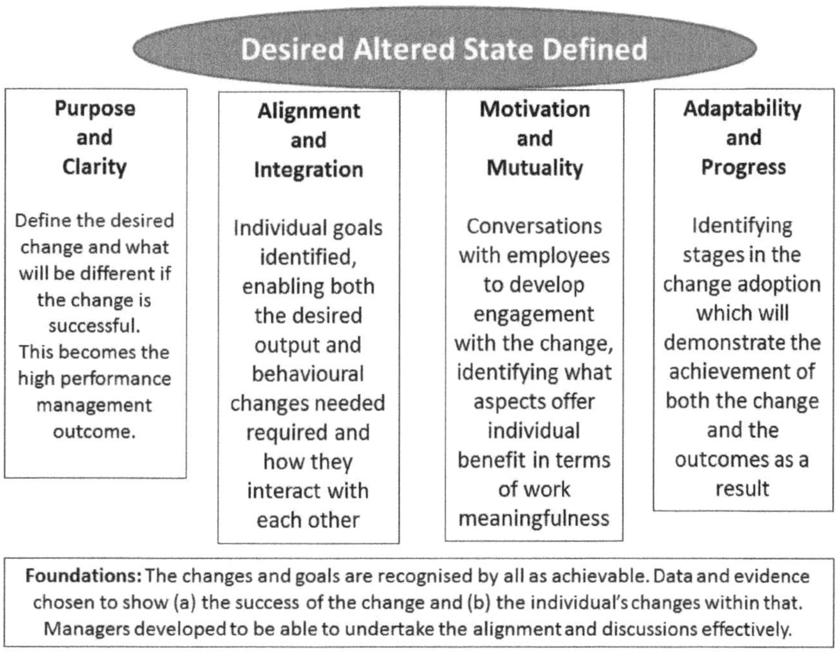


Figure 10.2. Using the performance management framework as a strategic tool for change.

organizations. Many saw the process as merely a compliance exercise; it was not seen as being core business or as a priority. Consequently, it was not considered to offer any real value to the organization; it certainly was not seen as a mechanism for achieving high performance or supporting change. Where there was success it was because an individual manager had managed to create understandings that had led to changes in performance, rather than a systemic approach to doing so. Consequently, to be a tool for change what the organizational requirement is from the change needs to be clearly outlined and shared across the organization.

This links to the second important issue, which is that of management preparation. In each case study, the performance management process was initiated by the HR department sending out guidelines on the process, deadlines and the latest sets of policies and rating definitions. Consequently, the dominant focus was on performance management as a compliance process. The majority of performance conversations occur between middle managers and their subordinates, with the effectiveness of these conversations relying on the capacity of managers to hold them. However, in our data managers received very little training in the long-term purpose of performance management or how to undertake effective performance conversations aimed at performance improvement. Most training offered was about undertaking the process (that is, filling out the performance agreement or navigating the information technology system), or how to have a "difficult" conversation, thus perpetuating the negative and compliance perceptions. This has serious implications for the ability of performance management to support change. The performance conversation needs to have a clear focus on what is needed to effectively implement the change. If managers are not being trained and developed effectively, performance conversations might be nonexistent, fragmented and/or not supportive of the overall change objectives. The objective of performance management becomes about developing readiness for change, accepted as a critical part of change management (Amis & Aïssaoui, 2013; Jones, Jimmieson, & Griffiths, 2005), through conversations which explain and sensitize the change. Another objective is to define and support the actual tasks and behaviors that are necessary to create the differences. We suggest that if leaders and managers are developed to see performance management conversations as triggers for change, they could be undertaken in different ways, leading to the development of new knowledge and perceptions, employee buy-in and commitment to the change process.

## CONCLUSION

This chapter has outlined a high performance framework for performance management that highlights its potential to provide a strategic tool to managers in the implementation of change. We suggest that performance management should begin with a focus on clearly defining what high performance means in a particular organizational context to ensure that all organizational members are aware of what is expected of them. This then allows for the possibility of alignment between high-level strategies and the goals of individual employees; it also offers the potential for the integration of other HR practices and other organizational systems. This requires enhanced communications between all levels of the organization and leadership from senior management to reiterate the importance of these conversations. This has the potential to increase the likelihood of joint ownership and accountability for performance management goals and outcomes, and also requires managers to ensure that appropriate supports are provided to employees to assist them to achieve agreed goals.

This approach to performance management also aims to enhance the adaptability of the organization to change and promotes a focus on goal attainment over a longer time frame based on continuous improvement and organizational learning. These principles of performance management are underpinned by three foundational elements: enhancing the capabilities of managers with responsibility for performance management; enhancing the ability of the organization to capture relevant information and data to assess progress in achieving performance goals; and the adoption of a pragmatic approach that aims to ensure that performance management practices are "fit for purpose" and adequately take account of the organization's context and capabilities.

## REFERENCES


Aguinis, H., Joo, H., & Gottfredson, R. K. (2011). Why we hate performance management—And why we should love it. *Business Horizons, 54*(6), 203–507.

Alford, J., & O'Flynn, J. (2012). *Rethinking public service delivery: Managing with external parties*. Basingstoke, England: Palgrave Macmillian.

Amis, J. M., & Aïssaoui, R. (2013). Readiness for change: An institutional perspective. *Journal of Change Management, 13*(1), 69–95.

Australian Public Service Commission. (2012). *State of the service report 2011-2012*. Canberra, Australia: Commonwealth of Australia.

Becker, B. E., & Huselid, M. A. (1998). High performance work systems and firm performance: A synthesis of research and managerial implications. *Research in Personnel and Human Resources Management, 16*, 53–101.

Blackman, D., Buick, F., O'Donnell, M., O'Flynn, J., & West, D. (2012). *Developing high performance: Performance management in the Australian Public Service*. Retrieved May 30, 2015, from http://www.apsc.gov.au/projects/performance-framework/related-research/conceptual-performance-framework

Blackman, D., Buick, F., O'Donnell, M., O'Flynn, J., & West, D. (2013). Strengthening the performance framework: Towards a high performance APS. *Commonwealth of Australia.* Retrieved May 30, 2015, from http://www.apsc.gov.au/__data/assets/pdf_file/0005/18536/Performance_accessible.pdf

Boxall, P., & Macky, K. (2009). Research and theory on high-performance work systems: Progressing the high-involvement stream. *Human Resource Management Journal, 19*(1), 3–23.

Buick, F., Blackman, D., O'Donnell, M., O'Flynn, J., & West, D. (2015). Can enhanced performance management support public sector change? *Journal of Change Management, 28*(2), 271–289.

Darke, P., Shanks, G., & Broadbent, M. (1998). Successfully completing case study research: Combining rigour, relevance and pragmatism. *Information Systems Journal 8*, 273–289.

Ezzy, D. (2002). *Qualitative analysis: Practice and innovation*. Crows Nest, NSW, Australia: Allen & Unwin.

Helfat, C. E., Finkelstein, W., Peteraf, M. A., Sigh, H., Teece, D. J., & Winter, S. G. (2007). *Dynamic capabilities: Understanding strategic change in organizations.* Oxford, England: Blackwell.

Jensen, J. M., Patel, P. C., & Messersmith, J. G. (2013). High-performance work systems and job control: Consequences for anxiety, role overload, and turnover intentions. *Journal of Management, 39*(6), 1699–1724.

Jiang, K., Lepak, D. P., Han, K., Kim, A., & Winkler, A. K. (2012). Clarifying the construct of human resource systems: Relating human resource management to employee performance. *Human Resource Management Review, 22,* 73–85.

Jones, R. A., Jimmieson, N. L., & Griffiths, A. (2005). The impact of organizational culture and reshaping capabilities on change implementation success: The mediating role of readiness for change. *Journal of Management Studies, 42*(2), 361–386.

Kehoe, R. R., & Wright, P. M. (2013). The impact of high-performance human resource practices on employees' attitudes and behaviors. *Journal of Management, 39*(2), 366–391.

Management Advisory Committee. (2001). *Performance management in the Australian Public Service: A strategic framework*. Canberra, Australia: Commonwealth of Australia.

Patton, M. Q. (1990). *Qualitative evaluation and research methods*. Newbury Park, CA: SAGE.

Rajagopalan, N., & Spreitzer, G. M. (1997). Toward a theory of strategic change: A multi-lens perspective and integrative framework. *Academy of Management Review, 22*(1), 48–79.

Yin, R. K. (2014). *Case study research: Design and methods* (5th ed.) Thousand Oaks, CA: SAGE.

CHAPTER 11

# CONCLUSION

## Where to From Here?

**Deborah Blackman, Michael O'Donnell, and Stephen Teo**

The title of this book is *Human Capital Management Research: Influencing Practice and Process,* and in this conclusion we ask, what has been presented that will enhance current human capital management practice, and what needs to happen in the future to increase the potential for continuous improvement based on current, ongoing research? Human capital management emerges from an acknowledgment that "individuals possess a stock of skills, knowledge, and experiences that can be leveraged for organizational and/or personal benefit" (Ployhart & Moliterno, 2011, p. 127; see also Collings & Mellahi, 2009). The classic areas of human capital management are those involved in the talent pipeline, where such a pipeline ensures there is a pool of talent (recruitment) to be able to choose from (selection), then support to be high performers (probation and performance management) developing as necessary (learning and development) (Cappelli, 2009). The argument for the need for research in this area is that for human capital to be appropriate to support the organizational strategy, it will need to be flexible, adaptable, evolving and, by implication, reflect new research to enable progress to emerge. Yet there is ongoing evidence that as few as one third of HR

*Human Capital Management Research: Influencing Practice and Process*
pp. 163–169
Copyright © 2016 by Information Age Publishing
All rights of reproduction in any form reserved.

directors really understand the true cost of developing and maintaining effective human capital (Hagel, 2012).

In the book's introduction, we explained that this book was developed on the premise that although there was research into human capital development, it was often not taken up by practice and, therefore, few evidence-based actions had been adopted (Rynes, Bartunek, & Daft, 2001). In particular, the level of complexity and the nuances found in the extant research had not been adequately integrated into practitioner implementation. Reflecting Rynes, Colbert, and Brown (2002), we suggest there is a need for more evidence-based work in the research–practice realm if there is to be significant progress.

Reflecting on the research presented within the chapters, there are several areas where differences between scholars and practitioners have been suggested as affecting the potential for either developing effective human capital management or for creating potential schisms between research and practice. These include: the types of data used, where the research is presented, the level of complexity presented around a topic, the context/prediction divide, and who the researchers are.

## TYPES OF DATA USED

Cotton, Warren, and Blackman opened this discussion in Chapter 2 suggesting that one way to bridge the divide is for academics to use the practitioner data, but that such data needs to be much more carefully designed and collected. Implicit in their chapter is the suggestion that much current organizational data is not robust. Jones and Sambrook (Chapter 3) also highlight data problems when discussing the particular issues faced when trying to develop engagement within the public sector. First, they note that there is a strong dependence on evidence from the private sector, so the data is not contextually appropriate. This problem is also noted by Johnson, when discussing commitment in Chapter 6. Jones and Sambrook go on to suggest that one of the issues is the type of research data being used to shape practice; they argue for more qualitative, less formulaic data sets as they suggest that context and complexity are more likely to be reflected in such data. *Our first suggestion for change is that by working together scholars and practitioners can develop a wider range of data sources, use a more extensive suite of collection methods and develop hitherto inaccessible research questions and solutions.*

## HOW THE RESEARCH IS PRESENTED

The first, apparently simple, difference is that academic research is usually published in academic journals, many of which have been referenced within the chapters of this book. Sometimes described as arcane (Johnson, 2015), they have not evolved much despite technological developments or disciplinary changes. Their primary function is not to create practice change; rather it is to offer the opportunity to a researcher to publish their research and to gain credibility within their university and the wider academic community. Although there are a few journals that do try to bridge the gap,[1] for the most part practitioner application would be a by fortuitous by-product rather than a plan.

Practitioners, always pressed for time and needing to learn new ideas as fast as possible, are looking for accessible articles that can be read quickly and offer a clear plan for the future. Many professional papers feature articles with case study examples or a checklist for implementation. However, unlike their academic counterparts, the data sources and the evidence are rarely included (as implied by Cotton et al. in Chapter 2).

The need for different styles of papers has been widely noted in the research–practice gap literature (Buick, Blackman, West, O'Donnell, & O'Flynn, 2016), but there has been less discussion of the divide being not just about style but also about the credibility of the sources and ideas. This book is an example of the developments we would like to see emerge—more joint research presented with both the research and the implications clearly laid out. Kanar, Montgomery, Fraser, and Behrend in Chapter 7 give an excellent example of this when they discuss the Office of Personnel Management case; there is more detail regarding how the case was done as well as the results and the findings. This gives important context and enables the problems as well as the highlights to be considered. Moreover, the sole authored chapters are by pracademics, reflecting a specific decision taken when developing the book not to focus on purely academic research. All involved are actively seeking to support and encourage evidence-based research–practice developments.

## LEVEL OF COMPLEXITY PRESENTED AROUND A TOPIC

The next issue, as is seen in several of the chapters, is the importance in ensuring that an aim of clarity does not lead to an oversimplification of ideas or the replacement of complexity; too often there is an apparent focus on finding the silver bullet or perfect answer (Davis, 2007; National Commission on the Public Service, 2005). The importance of framing practices within effective processes is raised by several authors, including both authors who discuss commitment. West (Chapter 4) suggests that the dynamics between employees and their supervisors is more complex than current practitioner literature would suggest. Although it is widely accepted that employees join organizations and leave managers, the research presented helps to explain the nuances and complexity of the way such a relationship actually grows. A key theme of the chapters on performance management is that it is not about the details of the practice definition, but instead the processes that surrounds it. This suggestion that there are unexpected consequences when not looking at the full implications of research is found again in the chapter by Johnson, who explains that by developing an apparently fair, equitable and merit-based system, the outcome may be a "good practice" system which actually undermines organizational progress. The problem is that significant differences in the forms of commitment are ignored because commitment is a "good thing" and to discuss all its possible forms would both potentially confuse, but also make commitment less "sexy."

Here is one of the apparent differences that emerge: scholars are interested in learning more about the phenomenon. The majority of journal articles open with claims that the current literature has inconsistent definitions, lacks clear conceptual boundaries or is full of, as yet untested, assumptions (Collings & Mellahi, 2009; Wright, Coff, & Moliterno, 2014). However, as Schmidtchen so clearly explains in Chapter 1, practitioners also want a clear answer and, preferably, a predictable process. The "it depends," contextually specific model apparently favored by academics will be less popular, as it is not seen to be predictable enough. Nevertheless, Trueren and Goods challenge this conception of overly esoteric research in Chapter 5. Instead, they demonstrate that it is the interplay between different parts of quite specific data emerging from disparate strands of the research literature that offers the most added value. So often the latest fad overtakes the last (Gibson & Tesone, 2001), rather than the whole being, seen to have been redefined, leading to more appropriate forms of practice. *We suggest, therefore, that by working together in ways seen within this book there will be less seeking one best way and more research-based development of human capital practices.*

## THE CONTEXTUAL/PREDICTION DIVIDE

Several chapters stress the importance of context for effective practice implementation. Simola (Chapter 8) focuses on the importance of context in terms of choices and applications. She argues that oversimplification leads to inappropriate forms of training which may be suitable in a few cases, but will not address note systemic organizational weaknesses. The desire to turn ethical or moral decision making into a tick-box list fails to recognize the complexity of each judgment to be made.

This lack of predictability, and an acceptance of it, is found elsewhere in the book. Colquitt in Chapter 9 suggests that the expected responses of an employee to incentives can be problematic and that many performance management problems emerge because "many of the assumptions and beliefs we take for granted when designing performance management systems may not hold up under the harsh light of rigorous academic and applied research." He further advocates that there needs to be a major rethink about performance management but not to "blow it up." He intimates that each time there is a problem with a process, such as performance management, a new solution is sought by practice, which is brought in to replace the broken item. Blackman, Buick, O'Donnell O'Flynn, and West (Chapter 10) support this view and note that where there is an apparent system failure it is often the process that is replaced rather than considering the contextually specific issues of implementation that may be undermining a performance management process. In other words failure is attributed to the process, rather than asking if the context provides more insights to the system breakdown. Blackman (2013) argues that context is an often discussed, but rarely analyzed as an element of both academic research and actual practice. *These chapters provide evidence that all those researching into aspects of human capital will need to be much more contextually aware and that working together on this will lead to more nuanced insights in terms of contextual impacts.*

## WHO ARE THE RESEARCHERS

We hope you will agree that the chapters in this book make both an interesting read and a compelling argument for the advantages of academics and practitioners working together. In the Introduction we alluded to the fact that there is much discussion of the research–practice gap and the seemingly insurmountable problems in overcoming it, and Schmidtchen in Chapter 1 developed this theme more fully, implying there is a real problem when we have one without the other.

Faced with such high quality chapters outlining excellent research that has strong implications for practice and is clearly translated into practice recommendations as well as ideas for future research, we asked ourselves why there seems to be such a problem. We were particularly struck by this question when reflecting that, where there are any single-authored chapters in this book, it is because there is a practitioner who has become, at some stage, a researcher who is applying their own research in some way.

One possibility is the implicit assumption in so much of the literature that the academics are the researchers and the practitioners only practice (Buick et al., 2014). From the content of this book this is patently not true.

Here are examples of complex research undertaken in an academically rigorous way. However, building on the work of Cotton et al. in Chapter 2, the important lesson may be that it is not that practitioners do not research, rather that it is often rejected by academics who regard it as methodologically suspect or not useful for them. If the practitioners are not perceived as researchers, then potential partnerships will fall down.

## WHERE NEXT?

We thank all the contributors in this book for their thoughtful reflections on current human capital research. We call for two major areas for development: first, an increase in working together to develop new practice that is contextually sensitive and based on a range of integrated ideas. As Davis asks: "who are the modern-day gurus—Tom Peters, Bill Gates, Maya Angelou, Hillary Clinton, Al Gore, Margaret Wheatley, the Dalai Lama?" The answer is: all of them and none of them. It depends on one's point of view, the context, and situational factors. Not one, however, possesses a "silver bullet" (2007, p. 575). We ask that scholars and practitioners develop research agendas together, create shared data sets and plan to learn and develop new ideas rather than "fix" human capital practice. Our second area relates to the first. We ask scholars and practitioners to think of each other as researchers that have complementary skills. We know it will not be easy to overcome well-documented research–practice divides, but we hope we have presented compelling evidence for why we need to in order to progress human capital research.

## NOTE

1. See for example the *Harvard Business Review*.

## REFERENCES

Blackman, D. (2013). Contextualizing the learning organization: How will it help us learn in the future? In A. Örtenblad (Ed.), *Handbook of research on the learning organization* (pp. 372–383). London, England: Edward Elgar.

Buick, F., Blackman, D., O'Flynn, J., O'Donnell, M., & West, D. (2016). Effective practitioner–scholar relationships: Lessons from a coproduction partnership. *Public Administration Review, 76*(1), 35–47.

Cappelli, P. (2009). *Talent on demand—Managing talent in an age of uncertainty*. Boston, MA: Harvard Business Press.

Collings, D. G., & Mellahi, K. (2009). Strategic talent management: A review and research agenda. *Human Resource Management Review, 19*(4), 304–313.

Davis, S. H. (2007). What's good, what's bad, and how can one be sure? *Phi Delta Kappan, 88*(8), 568–578.

Gibson, J. W., & Tesone, D. V. (2001). Management fads: Emergence, evolution, and implications for managers. *Academy of Management Executive, 15*(4), 122–133.

Hagel, J. (2012). Developing the talent pipeline. *Journal of Accountancy, 214*(5), 24–25.

Johnson, M. E. (2015). *Publish or perish: Finding new models to sustain academic research journals.* Retrieved May 19, 2015, from http://blogs.owen.vanderbilt.edu/deanjohnson/publish-or-perish-finding-new-models-to-sustain-academic-research-journals/

National Commission on the Public Service. (2005). Urgent business for America: Revitalizing the federal government for the 21st century. In R. Klitgaard & P. C. Light (Eds.), *High-performance government: Structure, leadership, incentives* (pp. 9–88). Santa Monica, CA: RAND Corporation.

Rynes, S. L., Bartunek, J. M., & Daft, R. L. (2001). Across the great divide: Knowledge creation and transfer between practitioners and academics. *Academy of Management Journal, 44*(2), 340–355.

Rynes, S. L., Colbert, A. E., & Brown, K. G. (2002). HR professionals' beliefs about effective human resource practices: Correspondence between research and practice. *Human Resource Management, 41*(2), 149–174.

Ployhart, R. E., & Moliterno, T. P. (2011). Emergence of the human capital resource: A multilevel model. *Academy of Management Review, 36*(1), 127–150.

Wright, P. M., Coff, R., & Moliterno, T. P. (2014). Strategic human capital: Crossing the great divide. *Journal of Management, 40*(2), 353–370.

# ABOUT THE CONTRIBUTORS

## EDITORS

**Deborah Blackman** is a professor of public sector management strategy in the School of Business, UNSW Canberra, Australia. She researches knowledge transfer in a range of applied, real world contexts. The common theme of her work is developing effective knowledge acquisition and transfer in order to improve organizational effectiveness through improved leadership, management and implementation. Recent projects include: leading a team that developed a new performance management framework and diagnostic with the Australian Public Service Commission which focuses on supporting the achievement of high performance organizations; applying the framework to support cultural change; and working on determining the real challenges facing public sector middle managers. The strengthening the performance management framework research received both the Charles Levine and the Carlo Mancini awards from the Academy of Management conference in 2013. Deborah's research interests include strategic human resources management; organizational learning; soft knowledge management, and organizational effectiveness. She has published extensively in a range of international journals including the *Australian Journal of Public Administration*, *Management Decision,* and *Management Learning*. She has recently co-edited a book, *Crossing Boundaries in Public Management and Policy: The International Experience,* with Professor Janine O'Flynn and Professor John Halligan.

**Michael O'Donnell** is a professor of human resource management in the School of Business, University of New South Wales, Canberra, Australia. Michael's principal areas of research include performance management and collective bargaining in the public sector and international employment relations. Michael participated in a team that developed a performance management framework with the Australian Public Service

Commission. This framework provides a diagnostic tool to assist public sector organizations to develop their managers' capabilities to manage staff performance. The strengthening the performance management framework research received both the Charles Levine and the Carlo Mancini awards from the Academy of Management conference in 2013. Michael has published in a range of international journals that include the *Strategic Management Journal, the International Journal of Human Resource Management,* the *Journal of Industrial Relations,* and the *Australian Journal of Public Administration*. In 2012, Michael coauthored the book, *Unions and Globalisation: Governments, Management, and the State at Work* (Routledge) with Peter Fairbrother, John O'Brien, Anne Junor, and Glynne Williams.

**Stephen T. T. Teo** is a professor of HRM at RMIT University, Australia. Prior to joining RMIT University, he was the head of Department of Management in AUT Business School, Auckland University of Technology, New Zealand. Stephen has a PhD from the Australian Centre in strategic management at the Queensland University of Technology (Australia). Prior to joining academe, he has 10 years professional experience in the banking and public sectors in Malaysia and Australia. Professor Teo has published more than 120 refereed journal articles and conference publications in the areas of strategic human resource management and international human resource management in top ranking international journals such as *Human Resource Management* (USA, Wiley), *Human Resource Management Journal, Journal of Vocational Behavior, International Journal of Human Resource Management, International Business Review, Public Management Review,* and the *Asia Pacific Journal of Management*. Professor Teo is on the editorial boards of *Public Management Review, Journal of Small Business Management, Career Development International,* the *International Journal of Human Resource Management*, and the *Journal of Management & Organization* (associate editor). He has just been appointed as a research fellow (2015–2017) by the Australia and New Zealand Academy of Management to mentor early career researchers and research students in Australasia.

## CONTRIBUTORS

**Tara Behrend** is an associate professor of industrial-organizational psychology in the Department of Organizational Sciences at the George Washington University. She is the director of the WAVE Lab, where she and her team conduct research on technology use in the contexts of training, recruitment/selection, and science, technology, engineering, and mathematics education. Her work has been funded by the National Science Foundation and has been published in the *Journal of Applied Psychology, Journal of Business and Psychology,* and *Computers in Human Behavior.* She is an active member of the Society for Industrial-Organizational Psychology. She has provided consulting for a wide range of public and private organizations internationally, and teaches courses in training, performance management, and psychometrics. She holds a PhD in psychology from North Carolina State University.

**Fiona Buick** is an assistant professor in management at the University of Canberra. She completed her PhD in management entitled "Organizational Culture as the Panacea for Joined-up Working: The Rhetoric and Reality Gap" at the University of Canberra in 2012. Fiona's particular research focus is on the role of human capital in developing organizational effectiveness within the public sector. Previously she has worked on the "strengthening the performance framework" project, a coproduction research project that involves collaboration between two Australian universities and the Australian Public Service Commission. Fiona also worked on an Australian Research Council project titled "Whole of Government: Evaluating Frameworks for Integrating Policy Development, Implementation and Delivery of Public Services." Prior to commencing her PhD, Fiona worked as a human resource practitioner in the Australian Public Service and Commonwealth Scientific and Industrial Research Organisation, gaining experience in learning and development, strategic human resource management and generalist human resources. Her previous qualifications include a masters of human resource Management, graduate diploma in employment relations and a bachelor of applied psychology, all from the University of Canberra.

**Alan Colquitt** is the director of global assessment, organization effectiveness and workforce research at Eli Lilly and Company in Indianapolis, IN. His group is responsible for all testing and assessment efforts related to recruiting, selection, development, talent identification and promotion. Alan is the architect of Lilly's employee survey strategy including employment life cycle, customer satisfaction, 360 feedback, team health, and alliance surveys. His group also conducts workforce research projects in the areas of attraction, hiring, on-boarding, engagement, performance, retention, diversity, innovation, and customer satisfaction. Alan's group also has responsibility for Lilly's global performance management system. He has worked on many different performance management projects over his career and has written and presented about effective performance management systems in many forums inside and outside of the company. Alan has been a member of i4cp's performance management exchange group and he leads a performance management subgroup within the Mayflower group survey consortium. Alan joined Lilly in 1990 after spending 5 years at Procter & Gamble in Cincinnati, Ohio. Alan received his BA from Indiana University in 1982 and his PhD in industrial and organizational psychology from Wayne State University in 1986. Alan is a member of Society of Industrial and Organizational Psychologists, the American Psychological Association, and the Academy of Management.

**Tony Cotton** is a registered psychologist with more than 30 years of experience delivering organizational psychology and mental health services in large and complex workplaces. He is currently the director of human capital research and analysis at the Australian Public Service Commission where he is responsible for a wide range of workforce research across the APS. Immediately prior to this he spent 5 years as the senior psychologist for the Australian Federal Police and before that held the dual role of director of psychology and director of mental health for the Australian Defence Force (ADF) where he was responsible for developing and implementing the ADF Mental Health Strategy and sat on a number of international collaborative research panels. He is a member of the Beyondblue Expert Advisory Group on workplace mental health and the Australian Defence Human Research Ethics Committee.

**Rebecca Fraser** is a personnel research psychologist in the Human Resources Solutions division of the U.S. Office of Personnel Management. In her role, Rebecca conducts job analysis studies and develops assessment tools such as structured interviews, work simulations, job knowledge tests, and situational judgment tests, for selection, promotion, and certification. In addition, Rebecca leads competency gap analysis studies to assist organizations with identifying proficiency gaps and prioritizing training and development needs. She also leads an open enrollment HR training program and delivers training on best practices in job analysis and assessment development. Rebecca has a BA in psychology from The College of New Jersey and a PhD in industrial/organizational psychology from the George Washington University.

**Julie Goods** is currently the director workforce with Helping Hand Aged Care and previously held the role of manager corporate services. Julie has a strong background in organizational development in both education and health and has a human resources career spanning more than 20 years that has included key senior roles within the university sector. Julie's current role as director workforce leads the development of workforce capability and culture aligned to the vision, values, and long-term strategic objectives of Helping Hand. The role encompasses the development and implementation of a contemporary, business driven human resources function to deliver strategic business success. Her current focus includes exploring innovative methods to create and sustain a learning culture, staff retention, peer support learning models, and workforce engagement. Research collaboration and partnerships continue to play a significant role in influencing future directions for Helping Hand's organizational and workforce development.

**Samantha Johnson** is a behavioral scientist who specializes in public sector performance and capability development. As a consultant to the Australian Federal Government, she works with middle, senior, and executive managers in management and leadership capability development. Samantha holds a principal consulting role with the Centre for Public Management at the Australian Institute of Management. Samantha is a visiting fellow at the University of New South Wales (Canberra) and a professional associate of the University of Canberra. In this capacity she has presented her research in Australia and the United States and supervises doctoral candidates. She is a certified professional with the Australian Human Resources Institute; an associate fellow of the Australian Institute of Management; a member of the Academy of Management and a member of the American Psychological Society. She is also an accredited executive coach with the Australian Institute of Executive Coaching and Leadership. Samantha holds a PhD in management (organizational behavior), a graduate diploma in human resource management and a BA in psychology and political science.

**Natalie Jones** is deputy head of knowledge exchange at the Economic and Social Research Council (ESRC), the United Kingdom's largest organization for funding research on economic and social issues. ESRC funds researchers at all stages in their careers to conduct excellent research with impact. She is responsible for building relationships with nonacademic organizations to increase engagement in and with academic research. Her research interests include innovation in research methodologies and workforce and management wellbeing in the public services. Following a career in local government focused on local economic development and research management, in 2012 she completed a doctorate in management studies at Bangor University North Wales, United Kingdom.

**Adam M. Kanar** is an associate professor of human resource management in the Department of Organizational Behavior, Human Resources, Entrepreneurship, and Ethics at Brock University. He holds PhD and MS degrees in human resources management from Cornell University in Ithaca, New York. He earned his bachelor of science degree in economics and industrial psychology from Bowling Green State University in Bowling Green, Ohio. Dr. Kanar's research focuses on learner-control in the context of technology-based training and employment branding in the context of employee recruitment. His work has been published in respected scientific journals including *Human Performance, Personnel Psychology,* the *Journal of Educational Psychology,* the *International Journal of Human Resource Management,* and the *Journal of Applied Social Psychology.* In addition, Dr. Kanar has published chapters that have appeared in edited research volumes and he presents regularly at major conferences, including the Society for Industrial and Organizational Psychology, the Academy of Management, and the Administrative Sciences Association of Canada. Dr. Kanar currently teaches courses in human resource management and staffing to MBA and undergraduate students. He has worked in the management and organization development departments at Goodrich Corporation and JP Morgan Chase and has worked as an human resource consultant for multiple private and public firms.

**Matisha Montgomery** is a senior personnel research psychologist at the U.S. Office of Personnel Management. Matisha was selected as a President's Management Council Fellow to the Department of Homeland Security's Immigration and Customs Enforcement Agency. Throughout her career she has worked to develop and implement selection tools, training programs, executive assessments, and organizational development and survey programs across the federal government. Working with large and small agencies alike, she has consistently provided products and services to meet agency needs and accomplish missions. Matisha has helped improve the performance of organizations through evaluations and assessments, and designing and implementing interventions to address performance gaps. Matisha has been an invited guest speaker, delivered presentations at the national meetings of numerous professional organizations, and maintains an active affiliation with the Society for Industrial and Organizational Psychology, the Personnel Testing Council of Metropolitan Washington, the International Congress on Assessment Center Methods, and has held leadership positions with the International Personnel Assessment Council. She earned her master's in industrial/organizational psychology from Missouri State University and her bachelor's in psychology from the University of Central Oklahoma.

**Janine O'Flynn** is a professor of public management at The University of Melbourne. Her expertise is in public management, particularly in the areas of public sector reform and relationships. Janine is an editor of the *Australian Journal of Public Administration,* and sits on the editorial boards of *Public Administration, Journal of Management & Organization,* and *Cana-*

*dian Public Administration*. She has received several awards for academic achievements including the 2013 Best Book Award (Public and Non-Profit) from the Academy of Management for *Rethinking Public Service Delivery: Managing with External Providers* (with John Alford). And, as part of the strengthening the performance management framework team, both the Charles Levine and the Carlo Mancini awards from the Academy of Management in 2013. She is a Fellow of the Institute of Public Administration Australian (Victoria) and sits on the executive board of the International Research Society for Public Management.

**David Schmidtchen** has had a varied career as a senior executive in the public and private sector, and serving 17 years in the Australian Army. David has been employed in a wide variety of roles. He has led innovation in the private sector and implemented workforce reform in public sector. He has been a strategic researcher developing concepts of future warfare and an academic teaching postgraduate leadership and organizational behavior. David is a published author, a registered psychologist, and a visiting fellow at the University of the New South Wales. He has written three books on the need for organizations to adapt to changes in the nature of work and organization. He has also written on organizational change, leadership, and other workforce management topics.

**Sally Sambrook** is a professor of human resource development, director of the Centre for Business Research and former deputy head of school and director of postgraduate studies at Bangor Business School. Sally is a founding member of the University Forum for human resource development (HRD) and served as an elected member of the American Academy of HRD. Before entering academia, she was a nurse and became involved in nurse education, training and personnel management. Sally employs a critical and autoethnographic approach to HRD research, particularly management learning and development, and in the healthcare context. Her research links to other areas of human resource management, including the psychological contract and employee engagement. She recently led the Bangor contribution to a £5m European funded LEAD Wales project, delivering and evaluating a leadership development intervention for small and medium enterprise owner-managers. Sally has published widely on HRD in large and small organizations, health management, research methods, and doctoral supervision, and holds various editorial roles on leading HRD, management education and ethnography journals.

**Sheldene Simola** is an associate professor of business administration at Trent University, Peterborough, Ontario, Canada. She teaches primarily in the area of business ethics, including individual ethical decision making in business and organizations and ethics of corporate governance. Her primary research areas are relational and care ethics perspectives in business and organizations, moral courage, diversity, crisis prevention and management, and the social or human aspects of sustainability. She also conducts research on teaching and learning, and provides workshops nationally and internationally on various related topics, including experiential learning. Her research has been published in *The Leadership Quarterly*, *Journal of Business Ethics*, *Consulting Psychology: Practice and Research*, *Canadian Journal of Administrative Sciences*, *Society and Business Review*, *European Journal of Training and Development*, *Journal of Applied Research in Higher Education*, *Education + Training* and others. She has also published numerous book chapters, including forthcoming chapters on "Realizing the Promise of Experiential Learning in Poverty-Related Management Education" and "Fostering High Quality Relationships Across Difference: Exploring a Care Ethics Approach to Life Story-Telling and Life Story-Receiving."

**Gerrit J. M. Treuren** is a senior lecturer in the School of Management in the University of South Australian Business School, and a researcher in the Centre for Human Resource Management. Dr. Treuren is currently program director of the postgraduate human resource management program, and teaches strategic human resource management, recruitment, and selection. His main research interests are turnover and retention (Why do some people stay and others leave an organization?), job search (How important are individual personality characteristics and social networks in finding employment?), and volunteering (Why do people decide to volunteer and why do people continue to volunteering?).

**Alastair Warren** graduated with a bachelor of arts with honors in psychology from the University of Tasmania in 2004. After working as a research assistant on several projects including looking at the potential effects of manganese exposure on an industrial workforce, he moved to the Department of Defense. Here work focused primarily on examining the psychometric properties of military selection tests to ensure their robustness and defensibility. Other work focused on identifying predictors of language learning aptitude, as well as the effect of computer usage and gaming on performance in computerized selection testing. Alastair has since moved to the Australian Public Service Commission, a central agency within the broader Australian Public Service which supports individual agencies to meet the human capital challenges they share with others. Here work focuses on workforce survey research as well as designing and evaluating the tools and interventions used by agencies. This includes contributing to the annual State of the Service Report and developing the APS performance culture model. Alastair is currently completing a PhD through the University of New South Wales.

**Damian West** has extensive policy and program delivery experience in the public sector. He has led the implementation of significant policy programs, and has a deep understanding of public sector governance, administration, and human resource development. He had a lead role in the project team which completed work on the Blueprint for Reform of Australian Government Administration. This work supported broad range reform across the APS. He currently manages an international public sector development program which includes major projects in Indonesia, PNG, the Pacific (Kiribati, Samoa, Marshall Islands), the Solomon Islands, and Africa (Ghana, Nigeria). Current projects include work to improve public sector governance, agency capability and various human resource development activities. He also has oversight of the APS recruitment processes, APSC communications and APS wide learning and development procurement. Damian's PhD explored the impact of organizational size on employee commitment. He has also has written articles on organizational development, performance management, collaboration, mentoring, and group mentoring programs.

Printed and bound by CPI Group (UK) Ltd, Croydon, CR0 4YY

15/09/2026

14962340-0001